MW01131026

Enduring Your Season of Suffering

By John C. Thomas, Ph.D., & Gary Habermas, Ph.D.

ISBN 13: 978-1-935986-23-2

Dr. John C. Thomas
www.source1strategies.com
Dr. Gary R. Habermas
www.garyhabermas.com

LIBERTY

UNIVERSITY™

Press

Lynchburg, VA

JOHN'S DEDICATION

To my beautiful and amazing wife, without whose support, love, and
grace I would not be able to fulfill my God-given call in life.
Katie and Stephen, thanks for bringing joy and excitement into my life.
To the glory of God!

In loving memory of
Nathaniel David Sours
December 2, 1991, to June 7, 1998

GARY'S DEDICATION

With much love to my nine grandchildren: Austin, Madelynn, Ethan,
Kaitlin, Jackson, Hannah, Tyler, Lilly, and Elam.

PUBLISHER'S ACKNOWLEDGEMENTS

A special thank you to all the individuals who assisted in the creation of this publication:
Proofreader: Kirstin Cornfield
Editorial Assistant: Alicia Whitecavage
Project Editor: Mark Lamport
Editorial Manager: Sarah Funderburke
Layout and Graphics: Caleb Atkins
Special Help: Timothy John MacLeod

Enduring Your Season of
SUFFERING

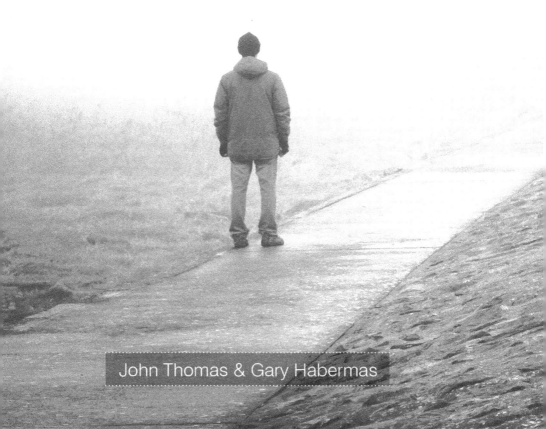

John Thomas & Gary Habermas

CONTENTS

INTRODUCTION

"…My God, my God, why hast thou forsaken me?" (Matthew 27:46).

While hanging on the cross, our Lord spoke very little. What He did say during those seemingly unending hours of suffering, however, is certainly worthy of close scrutiny and consideration.

Before we can even try to make sense of Matthew 27:46, we must envision the situation and the setting. The baby that at one time was nestled in Bethlehem's wooden manager is now nailed to wooden beams. The promise of life had eroded to the apparent finality of death. The heralded Messiah was now suffering the demise of criminals. In the shadow and coldness of those interminable hours, an innocent man suffered the unimaginable horror of crucifixion at the hands of evil personified in human form. The oppressive weight of human sin, even the actions of those involved in the crucifixion lay heavily upon His battered back. Disfigured by the hate of human hands, stripped of all clothing and dignity, the Creator God subjected Himself to inconceivable suffering.

Not only was the scene of the crucifixion appalling, but the words uttered by our Lord are perhaps the most unnerving and perplexing ever to be spoken. "My God, my God, why hast thou forsaken me?" Christ was not only compelled to go to the Cross, He did so with full knowledge of what the mission required. So how could God turn His back on His only Son? Jesus Christ always sought to love and honor His Father. He wasn't a good son; He was a perfect Son. The perfect intimacy that Christ and God have shared through eternity is abruptly ruptured. It is beyond our imagination to understand how our Savior Jesus Christ could feel forsaken, especially while suffering the most unimaginable experiences conceived. Even an ordinary and fallible human father could not be wrestled away from his son or daughter during such suffering. The Scriptures clearly reveal that Jesus felt abandoned. He who knew only perfect harmony was now profoundly alone. At that moment the soul of Christ must have reached the bottom of misery. As one pastor said, "At that moment eternity was compressed upon him."

The crucifixion of the Son of God was the most extraordinary event to ever happen on earth. We have never begun, even in moments of keenest insight, to fathom its depths. Even attempting to describe it is not our purpose in this book. Our intent is to bring you face to face with the reality of human existence, suffering. No one is exempt; not even the United States Congress can mandate immunity from suffering. But further to the point, God Himself also suffered. God entered into our tragically fallen story to identify with us. He experienced the stigma of being born out of wedlock, He endured temptation and the taunting of Satan, felt the sting of rejection, knew the confusing reality of betrayal, tolerated mocking humiliation, endured scarring and disfiguring physical abuse, experienced the hollowness of abandonment, and even walked the lonely path of death. Our High Priest sought to identify with every aspect of our broken reality.

The cry of Christ's question forces us to ask questions that should not have to be asked. Can God forsake anyone? Is it possible that God literally abandoned His only begotten Son? Does God really forsake those who wear the cloak of sin?

Like Christ, we, too, wrestle with the notion of being forsaken. The word "forsaken" is a troubling word. It brings up images of uninhabitable places, inhumane acts, and the insincerity of friends who failed to live up to the ideals of friendship. Simply put, being forsaken is an awful experience, especially when you are hurting. During the aftermath of losses, Job's friends came to see him. Though they were physically present, their counsel left Job feeling forsaken. Totally alone; yet in the company of others. Perhaps you have been there.

If you are like most people you have experienced, at least once, the sense that God has abandoned you. Whether the feeling was a result of habitual sin or the accumulation of suffering, the impression that God has walked way leaves one beleaguered and demoralized. Such was the case of Carl, a twenty-one year old college student. Though he grew up in a Christian home and was taught the truths of God, he struggled to possess those truths for himself when faced with adversity. Carl had entered the military following high school and soon found himself fighting in the Middle East. Not only did he lose friends in combat, several of his friends with whom he went through boot camp were killed in the base shooting in Texas. During one mission, Carl was injured by shrapnel and soon thereafter discharged.

Long before Carl experienced the horrors of war, another war had been raging in his life for nearly ten years—internet pornography. The thrill of viewing naked women continually brought Carl to pornography sites. Virtual reality was one thing, but seeing a girl in the flesh was another. Over the course of middle school and high school he chased after girls to see how far he could go. Soon his reputation as a sexually aggressive teen preceded him. The battle inside his soul continued to create problems in his life. While in college, Carl struggled academically. He saw himself as a misfit and incapable of doing academic work. Although his parents tried to reach him and help him, Carl distanced himself. In counseling sessions, Carl spoke of repeatedly pleading with God to deliver him from his strongholds. He asked God for peace in His heart, yet he received no reprise from the internal war. The sum total of his experiences was that he became disillusioned with his Heavenly Father. God could not be trusted, nor was He good. Carl reasoned that God was simply not there for him. That the things he had heard throughout his life about God and walking with Christ were a farce. Even with loving parents, good Christian friends, and training in Christian living Carl believed he was alone.

Indeed, Carl was alone. There is perhaps no greater loneliness in the world than to feel forsaken by God. Centuries before Jesus hung on the cross, the Psalmist penned prophetic words, yet words that likely captured his present experience, "My God, my God, why hast thou forsaken me?" (22:1). He too felt abandoned by God.

Loneliness can come from being alone or the psychological experience of being ignored, not understood, rejected, or abandoned. You may believe that no one hears you; that your voice really doesn't matter. It might be that no one understands what you are going through; your suffering is exacerbated by being discounted. Perhaps you have been told that your suffering is your own fault; not only are you the wounded victim but the malicious perpetuator. It may be that your best friend has abandoned you and your other friends seem indifferent to your pain; you suffer in ways no one knows or seemingly cares to know. Most of all, you suffer alone. The dreams that kept you moving forward may be shattered leaving you directionless. Hope has been obliterated. No matter what you do, you cannot free yourself from the solitary confinement of pain; every possible choice comes packaged with more problems and suffering. If matters could not be worse, God seems silent. Has He left you too? Bewildered, trapped, and lost you live forsaken of all that is desirable.

Though Jesus has journeyed the road of suffering, it is hard for many of us to believe He could understand our experience. After all, we assume that if He did He would deliver us from it or at least lessen its intensity. When in pain isn't God the only one we have? Doesn't the writer of Hebrews say "For He hath said, I will never leave thee, nor forsake thee" (13:5). Where is He?

"For He hath said, I will never leave thee, nor forsake thee"

Interestingly, while we complain and lament the fact that we feel God has abandoned us, He never does. The Bible is crystal clear on that matter. King David said that he has never seen the righteousness forsaken, yet here we consider the only Righteous One forsaken. Paul tells us that we have the seal of God on us (2 Corinthians 1:22) and in 2 Corinthians 4:7-11 Paul writes that we can be persecuted yet never forsaken. Perhaps one of the best verses on God's omnipresence in our lives is found in Hebrews 13:5-6 where God assures us that He will never give up or turn His back on us. Though God has promised never to abandon us, Christ was literally abandoned by God. We only whine that we have been abandoned by God when in reality it has not occurred, whereas Christ was abandoned, yet without complaint. However, He did question.

The bottom line is that we do not want to suffer. As a result of our commitment to comfort, we want answers when we hurt. The suffering had better be justified—and of course, in our minds it rarely ever is—so we continue suffering over the fact that we struggle. If we have physical pain that has escaped diagnosis we hunt until we can find a physician who can identify the cause. When the pain is psychological, we want to understand how we ended up in the pit of heartache. Our human condition drives us to solve the riddle.

Such was the case with Dave and Nia Sours, high school sweethearts who married shortly after graduation. Soon thereafter they brought their first child, Ashley, into the world. She was a blessing to her parents, and today Ashley is a young married blonde with a big smile and an even bigger heart.

Like most parents, Dave and Nia looked forward with energetic anticipation to the birth of their second child. In the twentieth week of pregnancy, however, they were told that their unborn baby boy had a very serious medical condition. Three choices were offered to them: do nothing, which would result in the inevitable death of their baby; abort the child; or allow a potentially dangerous and experimental surgery to be performed on the unborn child. Even if the surgery was successful, there was no way to assess the extent of damage already done to the baby's tiny lungs and whether or not they would be able to support life. Further testing revealed that their baby had only a one in four chance of survival. And if he did survive, he would probably suffer significant brain damage and deformities. With the odds against them, Dave and Nia decided to do everything humanly possible to give their child a chance to survive. They would risk the experimental surgery and leave the results in God's hands.

The operation was performed, but the results were inconclusive. Over the next few months, doctors closely monitored Nia's pregnancy. Then on December 2, 1991, complications dictated an emergency C-section, and the delivery room was filled with medical professionals ready to respond to the needs of a dangerously unhealthy newborn. There was complete silence—a combination of anxiety and fear—as the tiny infant was lifted from the open womb. Then the world's most beautiful sound filled the room as the tiny miracle child let out his first cry. Dave and Nia gave him the name Nathaniel, which means "gift of God." During the course of the following weeks, the doctors discovered that Nathan's brain was not damaged, nor were any deformities detected in his lungs. He had, however, sustained significant damage to his entire urinary system.

Nathan's care demanded much of her time, and it didn't take long before experience and research made Nia a very medically astute caregiver. The next few years were spent dealing with frequent hospital stays, numerous infections, a number of surgeries and medical procedures, much blood work, and countless visits to the doctor. These were indeed trying times for the whole family. Their faith was shaken and hopes were dashed time and time again. And yet they repeatedly found the love of God and the common grace they needed to make it through the trials.

Over time, Nathan became more stable and was finally able to attend school to address his developmental delays. At two-and-a-half years of age, he began attending an early childhood class, where he blossomed into a promising student.

Unfortunately, over the next several years, Nathan's already limited renal functions began to fail. It became evident that a kidney transplant was necessary. The Sours family became local celebrities as the community organized a "Nickels for Nathan" campaign to offset the expenses of the pending transplant surgery.

A persistent pattern of complications delayed the surgery, and in August 1997, peritoneal dialysis was begun. As the dialysis temporarily managed the kidney failure, preparations for a transplant continued. Dave was found to be the perfect match for Nathan, and as soon as Nathan was infection free, doctors planned to do the transplant.

The church organized daily prayer vigils to intercede for the family and physicians and to pray that God's will would be done. Church members and friends prepared to help the family through Dave's one-month recuperation and Nathan's equally long hospital stay.

After years of anticipation, the day for the transplant finally arrived. The waiting room and hallway were filled with family and friends who gathered to await the outcome. After eight hours, word came that the surgery had finally been completed. Father and son were fine, and Nathan's new kidney was functioning perfectly. While Dave had a difficult postsurgical experience, Nathan amazed everyone with his smooth recovery.

Two days after the transplant at the University of Virginia Medical Center, Dave was in a wheelchair by his son's side and Nathan was using a remote control to find the Cartoon Network. I (John) went to visit them and was delighted to find them well. We laughed at sleepy Nathan's struggle to keep his eyes open and his treasured attempts to cuddle with his mother. After long hugs and encouraging words, I left with the promise to return soon. News quickly spread that Nathan and Dave were doing well, and we all gave thanks to God for His continued blessings in the life of this family.

When the telephone rang at four o'clock the next morning, I knew something must be wrong. Nia's shaky voice confirmed my notion, and in the space of mere seconds, the joy we had all felt evaporated into fear.

"Nathan has taken a turn for the worse," she said. "The doctors are working on him, but they don't expect him to make it. We need you to pray."

"Oh, Nia," I muttered. Years of psychological and theological training had provided me with no words of wisdom or comfort. "We will pray, and we will be there," I said. As I hung up the phone, I was still in a state of disbelief. Everything had been going so well. Only hours before we had praised God for what He was doing in and through Nathan, and now this!

That day at the hospital was a long one. At least thirty people sat on the floor or stood against the walls outside the pediatric intensive care unit. Apparently, Nathan had had a serious reaction to one of the antirejection medications, which led to breathing difficulties. He was placed back on the respirator. Shortly after that, he had had a massive heart attack. The doctors worked passionately for over four hours to revive him. Unwilling to let him go, they put him on life support. Because artificial resuscitation does not efficiently provide oxygen to the brain, a neurological consultation was ordered. Unfortunately, the neurologist was unable to find any response. Hoping that medication might be hindering his ability to respond, the doctors decided to discontinue the medication and wait for four hours to see if Nathan would show any signs of neurological functioning. And so we waited, only in the end to be convinced of the worst. Late Sunday evening, on June 7, 1998, Nathan was pronounced dead.

Dave and Nia's initial response was like that of almost anyone who has helplessly watched as their world unfurled around them: Why? Why had God allowed Nathan to die? It was as if a priceless string of pearls had suddenly broken and scattered across the ground, lost forever. The miracles that had caused Nathan to survive—and even thrive—during his short life brought glory to God and hope to His people. Certainly, God had many opportunities during the pregnancy to keep Nathan from being born and thereby absolve the family of such pain. What purpose could He have had in Nathan's death? Is such a purpose important enough to justify the agony that Dave and Nia were experiencing or the loss that we all felt?

As a counselor and philosopher, we are captivated by the questions that sufferers ask. Indeed, we even ask questions that have not been asked by others, but believe that they should have been. Questions that are easy to answer rarely intrigue us enough to consider them. It is the questions that have no apparent answers with which wrestle. As part of our clinical, academic, and scholarly work we have heard many questions that pertain to the reality of evil and suffering in this world. For our purposes in this book, we have collapsed them into four questions:

1. How could this happen to me?
2. Can anything good come out of this?
3. Are you there, God?
4. Will I ever get over this?

Philosophically the approach we are taking to this topic is known as "soul making," which we will address in more detail later. Soul making is a philosophical term for the way in which suffering is a means to personal growth. As we begin our study of soul-making, our hope is that you will begin to understand the amazing way God uses suffering to give His children a higher quality of life. Through soul-making, new characteristics and abilities develop within the sufferer. These may include Christlikeness, humility, an ability to minister to others, a stronger and more personalized faith, and even heavenly rewards. Together, we will explore the many ways in which trials and difficulty can actually make believers more mature, even increasing our appreciation for life.

The famed and fabled story of Chicken Little captures the essence of this section. We all recall reading about that fateful day when Chicken Little was hit on the head by an acorn while walking through the woods. Concluding that the sky was falling and terrified at the consequences, Chicken Little hurriedly headed off to the palace to inform the king. On his journey, he met up with other animals along the way and warned them of the impending danger. Concerned by the news, they joined Chicken Little on his quest to the palace. Although various versions of the story exist, the fable's main message is that jumping to the wrong conclusion is disastrous.

Before we proceed with our exploration of the questions sufferers ask, we have a few cautions. First, knowing "why" does not eliminate the pain. Many years ago, I (John) developed plantar fasciitis, which is a chronic inflammation of the tissue along the bottom of the foot that connects the heel bone to the

Soul making is a philosophical term for the way in which suffering is a means to personal growth.

toes. It is a common yet painful problem in people who exercise a lot or who are overweight. When I tried to walk on my foot in the morning, the pain was unbearable. Since I'm both overweight and a regular exerciser, I knew why my foot hurt, but that didn't change the fact that I still had to cope with the recurring pain. We may know why we are going through a particular crisis, but that does not in and of itself get rid of the sting of pain.

Second, the Bible speaks comparatively little about the "why" of our suffering. Philosophers and theologians read between the lines, and while there are some broad areas of agreement, some differences also emerge. But God chooses to deal deeply with the "how" of suffering. As in the story of Job, many would say that the way we respond to difficulty is more important than why it is occurring. God's direction tends to be future oriented, moving us forward and upward through our pain.

Finally, even after reading about the questions sufferers ask, you might never know why you are going through your trial. Therefore, do not become consumed with searching for the specific reason. Rather, our prayer is that you will become consumed with knowing and being with God, because when that is your passion, knowing the reasons for your pain are unimportant.

SECTION 1

HOW COULD THIS HAPPEN TO ME?

Candice was completely lost. In her worst nightmares, she had never felt so helpless and alone. What had caused her 33 year-old husband to die in his sleep? Had he struggled or called out? Had she, though lying next to him, failed to be aware of and help him in his distress? How could this be happening to her?

Four months ago, Jason's sudden death had shaken every aspect of her life. In the days following the funeral, her parents had helped her pack up their belongings and move Candice and her two young children to their home in a neighboring state. She left behind Jason's parents and her sister, the school where she had taught for four years, their church family and her friends. Now, on the eve of her birthday, Candice's grief was overwhelming her, threatening to take her down for the count.

The questions that arise in the face of unexpected and unexplained suffering can threaten not only our emotional and physical well-being but can also shake our spiritual foundations. Are there answers for these questions? What do these questions tell us about ourselves? Our world? Our God?

Chapter 1

Once on a vacation, I (John) learned of a cornfield maze the size of three football fields that had just opened to the public. Since it was patterned after Noah's ark, I joked with my family that going through it would be a "spiritual experience." So after being given a clue to help us navigate the maze, we excitedly entered the cornfield and began our quest.

As we wandered around the heavily trampled paths, I couldn't help but think of Stephen King's story "Children of the Corn." Hopelessly lost in the maze of maize, we quickly found that heat and fatigue were giving way to frustration. At times, we thought we were heading in the right direction, only to find ourselves face-to-face with people we had just passed. After taking time to regroup, we set out with a new strategy. But before we had traveled far, we met the same group of people again! My children began to wonder if they would ever get out, let alone find the next water cooler.

Suffering is much like being in a disorienting maze; it produces the confused and desperate feelings of being trapped. And we don't have to look far to see that suffering is a disturbing and inescapable reality that we all must face. At any time, tragedy can zero in on us and turn our world upside down. Other times, suffering develops slowly over seasons, eroding away our resources until there is nothing left of us and the happiness we seek. Suffering comes in a variety of shapes and sizes. Regardless of how we experience it and what wrapping it comes in, suffering always redefines our reality. As a result of such disorientation our human inclination is to question. The problem is that we have more questions than answers.

Why me? Why this? Why now? We have all asked those questions when in the crucible of suffering. When Christ was suffering, He questioned God. Just as we do, He asked "why?" Though He had the heart of God, in His agony He turned to His Father with that very human question. Our why questions seem to come not from the heart of God but from our own commitment to living in a perfect world, despite abundant evidence to the contrary. While we long for the peace of the Garden of Eden, we often find our experience closer to the Garden of Gethsemane. In our turmoil, our hearts ask questions such as: Why God would allow suffering in the first place? Why would He allow suffering to continue? Why doesn't He do something?

As a toddler, my daughter was very inquisitive. She asked questions about almost everything. All of her questions seemed to begin with "Why . . . ?" Unfortunately, the answers seldom satisfied her curiosity. Each answer led to another question. Eventually, we would end up on God's doorstep, saying, "Because God made it so!"

Within each of us is a desire for answers, a desire to understand this world and make sense of it. When we suffer, asking "why" is more of a reflex than a conscious choice. The problem is that our questions often have no answers, or, at least no apparent answers. They include:

> *"What did I do to deserve this?"*
> *"How long will this pain continue?"*
> *"Why didn't God stop this from happening to me?"*
> *"Where do I go from here?"*
> *"How can I make it through this?"*
> *"What possible good can come from this mess?"*

As natural as these questions may be, they breed only deeper confusion. And yet we continue to ask. In fact, these questions are really a demand for an explanation. We require that God explain Himself in order to relieve our puzzlement. But God is not obligated to answer our questions. And even if

God did provide answers, we probably would not accept them as justification for our suffering. Confusion abounds when we are suffering.

The questions that sufferers ask arise from the recognition that their circumstances do not fit with their worldview. Subsequently, sufferers are shocked and bewildered when nothing seems to be as they thought. Suddenly, the beliefs that they have never questioned are unmasked as unreliable.

When confronted with our own fragility, we naturally pose questions. Such questions tend to fall into one of three categories – why me, why this or why now (though sometimes we might pose all three at the same time).

Why Me?

Because we are self-centered people, to us the worst kind of suffering is usually our own. It is one thing to learn about earthquakes, hurricanes, and tornadoes destroying the lives of other people. In fact, the more removed the tragedy is from us the easier it is to deal with. When our world is rocked, however, the pain is bona fide and seems intolerable.

This reality was agonizingly shown to me several years ago. At 5 a.m. on New Year's Eve 1997, a severe pain in my left side and back abruptly awakened me. I have never felt such intense, constant, and indescribable pain. My groans were so loud that dogs down the street started howling. My wife called the doctor, who suspected that my pain was caused by a kidney stone. He recommended that she either drive me to the emergency room or call for an ambulance. Believing I would get treated faster if taken to the hospital by ambulance, my wife called 911. After what seemed like an eternity, the paramedics arrived, took my vitals, and carted me off to the hospital. As I gasped for air and writhed in interminable pain, a nurse joked that this condition was a man's way of knowing how it feels to have a baby. After a two-and-a-half-hour wait, I was finally admitted to the hospital. The urologist believed that it would be best to retrieve my "baby" rather than wait for delivery. I wholeheartedly agreed.

My wife knew that I was bad off when I showed no interest in my annual tradition of watching football games. In addition, the timing of this illness meant that our special New Year's plans would be scrapped. While that was unfortunate, football and New Year's plans were of very little concern to my preoccupied mind. Suffering is like that. The things that once seemed so important to us have a way of becoming less significant in the light of pain, illness, or heartbreak.

Prior to my illness, I had known other people who had kidney stones. While I was sorry that they were not well, my day was not negatively affected by their news. The reality of my own pain, however, moved me from mildly concerned spectator to frontline warrior. Not only was my life interrupted, but I wondered why I had to go through it. Admittedly, I did develop a whole new empathy for people with kidney stones.

Why This?

As part of our desire for control, we contrive a world that assumes that while certain things may happen to us, others things will not. For example, we think that divorce is something that will never happen to us since we are so deeply committed to our marriages. In addition to our belief that marriage is sacred and divorce is not an option, we may regularly attend marriage retreats. Not only do enrichment activities help to prevent problems with our spouses from growing, they deepen our intimacy so that the risk of emotional distance, let alone divorce, becomes negligible.

We can possibly imagine that one of us might have an incapacitating illness or die, but divorce? Never! The former tragedies are things that none of us can control; therefore, it is easier to accept the possibility of their occurrences. Yet we all know couples who seemed to share our beliefs and commitment to marriage but ended up divorced anyway. This reality is unsettling because we all want guarantees that our marriages will survive. We want to believe that divorce is within our ability to control and prevent, but if the truth be known, the possibility exists for any marriage to go awry.

Divorce may or may not be included in your "why this?" category, but there are certainly many other possible events that could forcefully shock you, such as financial collapse, death of a child, or becoming the victim of a violent crime. Whatever the random event might be, most, if not all of us, believe that certain things "could not happen to me."

Not only do we misunderstand why certain things happen or why they happen to us, we also struggle with why things happen when they happen. A young woman from Utah was only a week away from her wedding. The excitement, as well as the stress, was at an all-time high. In the midst of making the final arrangements for the wedding, the bride-to-be started experiencing awful oral pain. Though she was terribly afraid of dentists, her family convinced her to go. Once there, she was told she needed to have a tooth pulled. The dentist and doctors are still not sure what happened, but during the tooth extraction, the young woman stopped breathing. They rushed her to the hospital, but she was pronounced dead upon arrival. Several days later, she was laid to rest in her wedding gown.

It seems unthinkable that God could allow someone to die at that time and in that way. We will never know why God allowed her to die, but in our finite minds God's timing appears off. No matter how often the Bible speaks

in our finite minds God's timing appears off

of God's goodness, faithfulness, generosity, and mercy, it will never be enough to quench our tendency to question them.

Research shows that events that occur "out of season" are much harder to cope with.[1] Death of children, early onset dementia, and terminal disease at a young age are but a few examples of how timing is strongly linked to suffering.

Because we believe that things ought to be one way and are intolerant of a different outcome, we react adversely to crises. Such thinking fails to acknowledge what God's Word says about suffering. Too many Christians have beliefs that are not aligned with scriptural truth. It takes a traumatic experience to expose our actual attitudes. When our true beliefs are brought to the surface through calamity we can either strive to align them with Scripture or fight to maintain our view of life. As we will see throughout this book, God's Word helps us make sense of nonsense. If you can make sense of adversity—the emotional pain, the fear, the mental chaos, the faultfinding, the despair—you can move through the suffering without doubting your own sanity or ability to recover.

Before you make it through suffering, you need to have an accurate perception of the way things are; that is, you must do a reality check. Unfortunately, for many of us our reality checks bounce. The way that we think things should be does not fit the way things seem to be. In the next chapter we will examine five realities of suffering.

Chapter 2

NO ONE IS EXEMPT:
CHARACTERISTICS OF SUFFERING

When we fantasize about our futures, it's usually more like a daydream than a nightmare. We don't picture ourselves in the middle of crisis or pain. Instead, we have imagined prosperity, happiness, comfort, and joy. It is very unpleasant to consider the tragedies that could befall us. Yet suffering comes to all without prejudice—the Christian and the non-Christian, the destitute and the prosperous, the weak and the strong. Jesus said that God sends the sun and rain on the just and the unjust. Nothing will protect us from experiencing the suffering of this life, and when we are faced with the heartache of rejection, the emptiness of loss, the bite of physical pain, or the betrayal of being violated, pain is the natural result.

Reality #1: Suffering is Universal

Suffering is a timeless universal condition. A casual glance at the six-o'clock news or the daily paper provides ample evidence that people all over the world are experiencing hardships of many kinds. Since we live in a fallen world in which the sources of suffering are plentiful. Natural disasters, random accidents, and physical illnesses result in pain. Mental anguish, family dysfunction, and criminal behavior inject adversity into an otherwise peaceful life. Economic downturns, political unrest, and war bring distress, as does the fear that these things may befall us. Even the knowledge that we cannot ensure our future or control our destiny brings about suffering with greater force.

Not only does suffering abound worldwide; for many physical suffering is a constant. Every year 15 million children die of hunger.[1] By the end of the first decade of the twenty-first century an estimated 1,178,350 persons aged 13 and older were living with HIV infection in the United States, and 33.3 million adults and 2.5 million children worldwide.[2] Approximately 65 percent of world deaths resulted from natural disasters between 1985 and 1999.[3]

To others, suffering is experienced psychologically. Consider these alarming statistics: Mental disorders account for five out of the top 10 in the Global Burden of Disease and each year over 1 million people commit suicide worldwide.[4] Whether of physical or psychological origin, suffering raises the question: Where is God when "His children" are suffering?

Until the Industrial Revolution, suffering was assumed to be a constant of life. Today, with improvements in medicine, radical advances in technology, and significant progress in so many fields of knowledge, suffering has come to be seen as an anomaly. In spite of our accomplishments, the signature of suffering is written on every human heart. All people suffer, regardless of their race, gender, intelligence, financial status, or faith.

Reality #2: Suffering is Painful

There is nothing more central to the human experience than our capacity to feel, and no aspect of this is as deep as our capacity to suffer. The word trauma, which means "wound," uniquely captures the idea. Every person has experienced a wound or hurt. Yet as frequent as physical and emotional pain seem to be, we react as if trouble is unexpected and alien to our lives.

Sometimes there are no words to describe the excruciating pain that grips the soul. The agony is so intense it seems to envelop our entire existence. Pain can be like acid, rapidly eating away at us from the inside out. It's difficult to see beyond our own misery when we are consumed by the enormity of this kind of pain.

Emotional pain can also bring about a cascade of other symptoms: a loss of concentration, fatigue, changes in sleeping and eating patterns, profound sadness and depression, crying, agitation, and anger. Enduring such great pain would seem to be beyond the scope of normal human capability, and therefore it requires a supernatural Healer.

Suffering arouses pain and fear that are so intense that we naturally demand relief. The prophet Hosea saw this when he described God's people wailing upon their beds.[5] Sometimes the compounded effects of suffering produce a pain so intense that we feel desperate, wanting relief at any cost. When people are repeatedly traumatized—as hostages, victims of chronic family violence, or survivors of war atrocities—they may actually remain trapped in the trauma long after the events have ceased. So while pain may not go away, it can be anesthetized. Consequently, finding relief becomes our preoccupation.

Reality #3: Suffering is Personal

There is no correct way to suffer. Although certain aspects of human suffering are common, the experience is truly an individual process. Your reaction to pain is influenced by many factors, including the nature of the suffering, previous experiences with suffering, your personality and environment, and present circumstances. It is critical to remember that many of the situations that bring about suffering are outside the realm of normal experience, so there is no "normal" way to respond to them. Suffering is an intensely personal, privately lived, unique experience.

Of course, some people might have some notion of what you are feeling, especially if they've had similar experiences. But no one can fully grasp the reality of suffering in someone else's life—the plaguing questions, the pain, and the ongoing battles that only you can understand. But pain should not be experienced in a vacuum. Even when those around us don't understand exactly what we're going through, we can still share our hurts and our needs with family and friends who love us. Pain is personal, but that doesn't mean it should be experienced in isolation.

Moreover, we are not defined by the things that cause us pain. We are more than a label (e.g., a divorcee, a sexual abuse survivor, an alcoholic). Yes, pain is personal but it does not determine our identity nor does it denote our worth. Though other people might distort our true selves through the lens of the suffering, it is limited insight at best and a denial of who we are in Christ.

Reality #4: Suffering is Unnerving

Suffering often seems random; it has the power to turn our world upside down. The unnerving reality is that with one stroke of the clock, our worlds can completely change. From that one point in time, our minds, hearts, and bodies will never be the same again. In fact, research indicates that severe suffering can permanently change brain functioning. Seemingly cruel circumstances often leave us feeling stunned and blindsided, and we experience a shock to the system, a laceration of the soul, and a wound to the spirit.

Despite our attempts to devise a world where we can predict, contrive, and control the outcome, we find that our best efforts most often fail and we're reminded once again that life is beyond our control. We see the suffering of Christians who have perfect church attendance and seemingly perfect spirituality. However, the problems and turmoil they encounter seem to contradict their Christian lifestyle. How could such godly people experience such immense problems? To alleviate our confusion, we sometimes assume that beneath the righteous public persona there lurks a dark side. It comforts us to believe that as long as we are "good" suffering will not befall us.

Suffering is also unnerving because few people have any preparation for or understanding about suffering. To some extent, the shock of any trauma is a

we fear anything that is beyond our ability to control

function of its novelty and unexpectedness. Hence, the more unfamiliar the experience is and the more unprepared we are for it, the greater our shock and the greater our difficulties in working through the pain. In essence, we fear anything that is beyond our ability to control.

Suppose you are driving down a road when you happen upon a severely damaged area of pavement. Having expected smooth sailing on your journey, you are not ready for such an obstruction. Your car bounces about as you slow your speed to accommodate the perilous pavement. You might complain about high taxes and miserable roadways. You might belittle the government officials who seem to ignore the problem. If, however, a road sign had warned you about the impending problem, you would have curtailed your speed in preparation for the road conditions. Of course, you would not like having to deal with such conditions, but knowing that it was coming, you would have had a very different emotional response. Yes, you would still feel the bounce and jostle as you crossed the rough patch, but having anticipated the trouble, you would have readied yourself for the experience.[6]

Reality #5: Suffering is Mysterious

Suffering is a mystery, a puzzle for which we do not have all the pieces. Much like being in a disorienting maze, suffering produces the confusion and desperation of being trapped. Answers often seem to lie just beyond reach. Like a maze, it is difficult to find one's way out of suffering, and the inescapability of the pain can be overwhelming. Days seem to never end; the future is only an extension of the tormenting past. Hopelessness and despair often become our only companions. Our wills become paralyzed, constraining us to passivity. Although we yearn to feel normal again, we know normalcy is forever lost.

Initially, suffering produces a sense of disbelief. We think, This can't be happening to me, there must be some mistake! The experience feels unreal. It is more gratifying to swim in a vague sea of possibilities than it is to see reality clearly and face the deep hurts and fears of what is happening. Eventually, the unreality of the situation gives way to an overwhelming sense of bewilderment, and the suffering intensifies when it creates questions to which there are no ready answers. Confusion plagues the mind. Our gut-felt responses to suffering often override our theology. Our belief systems are undermined, and our faith is called into question. We doubt everything that we once believed about God. Oh, we know that He sent His only Son to die for us and that He has done miraculous things in our lives. But in the grips of confusing suffering, He is, in essence, only as good as His last benevolent action toward us.

Cries such as "Where is God?" and "Why is He not helping me?" seemingly fall on deaf ears. And when our faith in God is ruptured, we turn to our own reasoning in an attempt to make sense of the jarring turmoil. Such confusion is particularly disturbing when we believe that we do not deserve the ordeal. We are dumbfounded by the way things have turned out; it just doesn't make sense. How did I get into this mess? we wonder. What did I do to deserve such misery? We get caught up in the unending questions, but usually the repetitive, circular thoughts that bombard our conscious moments have no apparent answers.

While God seeks to use suffering for our benefit, Satan seeks to use suffering to create doubts about ourselves and the character of God. He convinces us that God is treating us unfairly. So in order to find answers to unanswerable questions, we tend to fill in the gaps. For instance, some people choose to find fault in someone or something else: He made me do it, or If I had different parents, this would never have happened to me. Sufferers attempt to understand the problem by ascribing the problem to something beyond their control; that is, they believe that they are victims. By attributing our calamities to forces outside of ourselves, we hope to protect our sense of order and control.

Some sufferers seek to make sense of the event by blaming themselves. Taking responsibility for suffering puts control in our own hands. But if this is only an attempt to make sense of the problem and not to resolve it, we end up feeling even more powerless. Of course, when we have brought about our own misery, we often become guilt ridden. Rather than having a God-given sorrow over sin that leads us to repentance and wholeness, we become intensely self-focused.[7] Compare the different responses of Peter and Judas to their betrayal of Jesus. Peter became broken and repented, but Judas was so self-focused that he committed suicide. This tendency to become self-consumed leads to hopelessness because it keeps us in bondage to our failures. In the end, blame only compounds the problem and confuses us more.

As we accept and acknowledge these unpleasant realities, they may collide head on with our understanding and view of God. In his journal of grieving the death of his wife, Joy, C. S. Lewis penned that in his loss and grief he was not ceasing to no longer believe in God, but that what he was learning about it was so unsettling. For that reason, we need to have a clear view of suffering that is rooted in the soil of God's Word.

Chapter 3

Many Christians have read the Bible and fashioned a personal theology that covers a collection of topics, including creation, salvation, the person of Jesus Christ, and other subject matters. While we believe that the Bible is without error, our theology is not inerrant. Theology is a human attempt to bring clarity to topics or texts that are found in Scripture. It is our theoretical understanding, hopefully based upon a careful scrutiny and study of God's Word. Thus, when thinking about a theology of suffering, the main question is whether or not we have one that is as biblically accurate and coherent as possible. We must methodologically cull out the truths that are scattered throughout the pages of Scripture and form them into an encompassing truth.

Throughout the rest of this chapter, we will examine eleven truths of suffering. These biblically bound precepts form the underlying foundation that helps make sense of suffering.

Truth #1: Creation and Humanity Will Suffer

God created man and woman with the capacity to transgress against their Creator. Hence, God programmed into His creation the possibility of suffering. Eventually, a world born by God's commanding Word defied Him, and consequently creation lost its perfect destiny and no longer operates by God's perfect design (Genesis 3).

The reality is that this world is broken, cursed, and fallen (Ecclesiastis1:15; 2:23). After the Fall, the perfectly created world changed in its state of being. All of creation groans from the impact of humans' sinful choices. Hurricanes, tornadoes, earthquakes, volcanic eruptions, floods, fires, drought, and insect infestations also take their toll on the human misery index. For Adam, the soil no longer yielded easily to cultivation. Instead, he experienced futility in his labor (Genesis 3:17). Eve experienced relational pain in her desire toward her husband, the fact that he would rule her, and in giving birth (Genesis 3:16).

Sin that originated in Adam's choice enslaved the earth (Romans 8:18-22). Creation that the sovereign God had declared good became corrupted. The resulting fallenness became one of the active forces in His new world. As we scan the horizon of this world we can become quickly confused, cynical, and even contemptuous.

Like the world, the human condition is broken. Each person's first commitment is to self rather than others (Genesis 3). Relationships are dramatically altered; humankind's personality and physical life were corrupted. At times those who are in positions of authority make choices that lead to exploitation and destruction. The sum of anger, rage and aggression is seen in acts of violence and terrorism. Countless people have lost their homes, businesses, and even loved ones as a result of narcissistic and sociopathic political leaders.

Since the first sin, fear and alienation have plagued us. Sadly, the resulting curse has affected everyone, the godly and ungodly alike. No one is exempt from pain; it is the common denominator for all of us. As members of the human race, we all experience suffering.

The introduction of suffering into this new world does not mean that suffering did not exist prior to creation. Somewhere in eternity past, Satan and his angels suffered the consequences of their rebellion. To strike back at God, Satan then plotted to destroy God's plan by prompting humanity to question and defy their Creator. The evil one devised a scheme to pass suffering onto the apple of God's eye—humanity. The insightful words of C. S. Lewis cut to the heart of our post-Fall situation: "There is no neutral ground in the universe: every square inch, every split second, is claimed by God and counterclaimed by Satan."[1] As such, there is both good and evil in the world. God created all things good, but evil has disfigured what God created.

Philosopher and atheist Friedrich Nietzsche said that his problem was not the suffering but the desire to ask, "Why the suffering?"[2] Because suffering is mysterious and unnerving, we all long for answers to the immense suffering that we see. The answers, however, are often elusive and hidden.

Although God's Word gives insight into His ways, He did not intend for us to comprehend everything, especially when it comes to His ways of dealing with the world (Job 38-39; Rom. 11:33-35).[3] Yet within our hearts we have a craving to be "in the know." Call it curiosity or interest, but even when something does not concern us, we desire to understand why things happen as they do. Adam and Eve illustrated this truth when they ate from the only tree that was restricted (Gen 3). The prohibition consumed their attention.

Scripture teaches us that God's ways are beyond our ways (Isaiah 55:8-9); His understanding is inscrutable (Isaiah 40:28), mighty in strength, unsearchable (Romans 11:33); and He alone is wise (Romans 16:25-27). God's plans for this world are simply too intricate, too complex, and too advanced for us to make sense of them. Yet, we believe that we can make sense of it all.

Over the course of 30 years of counseling, I (John) have repeatedly seen how many good Christians have an impoverished view of Christianity. One main problem when it comes to suffering may be that our theology is inadequate. After touring the United States, the well-known theologian and pastor Helmut Thielicke of Hamburg was asked what he saw as the greatest deficiency among American Christians. This great scholar said that we have an inadequate view of suffering.[4] We have allowed secular ideas to influence our theology. It is hard to find a desire to know God when we are suffering because our longing is for relief; nothing more, nothing less. Our desire for God is that He rescues us; in essence, we attempt to use God to deliver us from our suffering rather than use our trials to know God more intimately. Some assume that God will reward good with good and bad with bad. Other Christians believe that being a Christian includes a life protection policy. This assumption was the thinking of Hannah, a woman I (John) counseled several years ago. Born of Jewish parents, Hannah experienced a great deal of rejection when she converted to Christianity. In spite of her family's reaction, however, she became a student of the Bible. Her devotion to

Christ inspired her to excel in every aspect of her life.

Over time, however, her dedication to the things of God changed. Advancing in her career, raising two children, and maintaining a healthy marriage were more important to her life than serving Christ. Although God was still in her view of life, He was in her peripheral vision. Other pursuits consumed her time and interest. Her life revolved around the things of this world rather than the things of the Spirit. You probably would not fault her efforts. She was highly regarded in her profession and had two well-behaved, socially conscious children and a successful husband. Life was good. The blessings of God seemed evident in her life and family.

Unfortunately, her life would not remain so pleasant. Hannah's world collapsed when her husband of twenty years asked for a divorce. Soon, she was struggling to maintain a professional image, meet the demands of being a single parent, and put up a positive Christian front. Throughout the counseling process, I was unable to get Hannah to move beyond the question of why God would allow this suffering to happen to her. She was a good person—well respected, sincere, and diligent in her responsibilities. She thought the fact that she forsook her heritage and family's acceptance to become a Christian should have been enough to protect her from suffering. God owed her. Now, bitterness characterized her attitude. Since her beliefs about God were inconsistent with experiencing such pain, she abandoned her belief in God altogether. Sadly, she quit counseling, even more bitter than when she began.

The belief that a Christian will not or should not suffer is inconsistent with biblical teaching. As we've already seen, God allowed Job to experience seemingly unjustified misery. In the same way, many prophets and apostles were subjected to emotional and physical abuse, even death. And Jesus Himself, our Suffering Servant, endured substantial mistreatment. For the Christian, suffering is not an unusual experience; everyone suffers.

What ultimately drove Eve to eat of the forbidden fruit were the distorted words of Satan who said that it would make her wise (Genesis 3:1-6). The tree was not a tree of wisdom but of the knowledge of good and evil. As the fruit was being swallowed Adam and Eve did come to the knowledge of evil, but it came experientially. Moreover, what was truly evil could now be seen as good. As a result, we are now prone to see God's working as evil. We believe we know better than He. No matter how hard we try we will never plumb the depths of this mystery.

Our Western minds like to think logically. We love formulas and straightforward action steps. But God does not adhere to Western thinking. Thus, we should not think that God is only seeking to accomplish one purpose through our suffering. Any time we experience suffering, God may be challenging us to change in numerous ways. Yet, clearly no human can know the mind of the Lord. Whatever goals He has for you as you walk the path of pain are part of His divine plan, which He will make known to you at His discretion.

Truth #3: Godly People Will Suffer

If godly people do not suffer, how do we explain the fact that Jesus Christ suffered. Though His beatings and crucifixion were necessary in order for Him to accomplish His mission of redemption, God did allow Him to experience the physical suffering of crucifixion and the psychological suffering from abandonment and betrayal. The writer of Hebrews put it this way:

> *"For it was fitting for Him, for whom are all things and by whom are all things, in bringing many sons to glory, to make the captain of their salvation perfect through sufferings. . . . Though He was a Son, yet He learned obedience by the things which He suffered. And having been perfected, He became the author of eternal salvation to all who obey Him."* Hebrews 2:10; 5:8-9

These verses confront us with the reality that Jesus suffered and provided powerful insights into suffering. First, "it was fitting" for God to use suffering to perfect His Son. In other words, it is consistent with the character and nature of God to use pain and suffering to achieve His purpose. Jesus Christ became the perfect captain (literally, "leader" or "pioneer") of salvation because God was willing to allow it. It seems almost sacrilegious to say that allowing suffering is consistent with God's character. But before you turn your back on God, keep reading. Our goal is to know God; and if allowing us to suffer is indeed acceptable to Him, we must at least try to understand why.

The Bible makes clear that we can expect suffering. It cannot be avoided. We will hurt and be hurt. Pain will surround us. Though this sounds pretty bleak, there is hope. Though the basis of our hope is in the past work of Christ on the Cross, the realization of that hope is still in the future. God has assured us that His Son has overcome the world.[5] The grip of death could not hold Jesus.[6] In overcoming death, Christ defeated pain, sorrow, sickness, and suffering. Our hope rests in the truth that we will follow in His victory.[7]

Jesus said that life would not be easy. But we can take confidence and find delight in the hope that we have in and through Him. Christ's triumph over Satan is cause to find peace. Because Jesus conquered pain, He can use our pain to accomplish His plan in and through us.

The second truth from Hebrews 2:10; 5:8-9, that suffering teaches us obedience leads us to the next truth.

Truth #4: All Suffering has Meaning

For Christ, the path to suffering was obedience and the meaning of His suffering was to redeem the world from sin. Pain taught Jesus Christ obedience to the Father and submission to His will. It is an amazing thought to consider that Jesus, God Incarnate, could learn anything, but according to this verse, such was the case. Christ was not spared hardship and pain. Through suffering, He became our Redeemer, the High Priest who felt our infirmities, and through it He learned the costs of obedience. Moreover, because Jesus was wholeheartedly committed to do His Father's will, He willingly accepted pain as part of God's agenda. Perhaps there is no greater key to our ability to deal with suffering than to accept our circumstances and suffering as part of God's redemptive and transforming work in our lives.

Many of the early church fathers experienced suffering from following God's will and call.[8] The litany of horrific circumstances that Paul experienced are genuinely valid reasons to moan: imprisonments, beatings, shipwrecks, and deprivation. But Paul simply accepted them as part of his Christian walk. In fact, in the book of Philippians, Paul was bold enough to say that he deeply wanted to know the "fellowship" of Christ's suffering. Like readers today, the recipients of that letter may have thought, What is Paul thinking in saying that he wants to suffer? We're sure, however, that Paul knew exactly what he was saying.

Suffering has no value in our economy, except for those who profit financially from the hardships of others. We do not like the inconvenience and pain that trials impose, but God values suffering. In His economy, suffering is a wise investment because it bears the potential for greater things. Like any investment, it carries with it risks, but God knows that the advantages far outweigh the perils.

Suffering is not accidental, nor is it incidental. Suffering is not the result of randomness or chaos. It is allowed by God because suffering is purposeful. Thus, our responses to it are very important.

Personal trainers and athletic coaches are fond of asserting "No pain, no gain!" when you don't think you can lift another barbell or run another mile. In other words, there is no way to develop muscles without experiencing pain. We don't enjoy or take pleasure in the pain, but we do appreciate the results of the painful process. The same is true of suffering. It exercises our mental, emotional, spiritual, and theological muscles. In this vein, all suffering can make sense. Yet most of our struggles are due in part to our inability to make sense of difficult situations, trials, or adversities. That is, the real anguish of suffering is due to its perceived meaninglessness.

In our perceptions of the grand scheme of things, some experiences simply do not make sense. The famed Jewish physician Viktor Frankl was a prisoner in Auschwitz for two years during World War II. He spent most of his time in slave labor and near starvation. His parents, his brother, and his wife either died in the camps or were sent to the gas chambers. Except for his sister, his entire family perished. Frankl himself suffered torture and innumerable indignities, never knowing from one moment to the next if his path would lead to the ovens or if he would be among those spared to remove the bodies or shovel out the ashes of others.

On top of that, Frankl was a physician who was repeatedly called on to assist other suffering prisoners, thereby increasing the level of his own pain. It is reported that Frankl asked his suffering patients, "Why do you not commit suicide?" From their answers, he found threads upon which to weave a pattern of meaning. In his book Man's Search for Meaning: An Introduction to

Logotherapy, he describes how suffering and meaning are connected. Frankl accurately and perceptively wrote, "If there is a meaning in life at all, then there must be a meaning in suffering. Suffering is an ineradicable part of life, even as fate and death. Without suffering and death human life cannot be complete."[9]

Corrie ten Boom also understood the value of suffering. From the lice-infected bed of a concentration camp, Corrie penned, "We are in God's training school and learning much."[10] Solomon, who knew great pleasure, also learned that suffering is even better than comfort. Whereas suffering instructs, pleasure and comfort teach us little. We naturally prefer lavish comfort to deprivation and suffering, but in the long run, indulgence leaves us empty. [11]

Just imagine the pain of people like Viktor Frankl and Corrie ten Boom, who suffered incredibly, for long periods of time, in ways that only their fellow prisoners of war could even begin to comprehend. But their clear testimony is that meaning in life comes through suffering—even of the most intense kinds. Moreover, they realized that our lives are incomplete unless they include adversity!

Some things that happen to us are fairly easy to explain. We can have a good

meaning in life comes through suffering

sense of what God is doing or wants to do. Most situations, however, are less clear. One of the major problems many people, even Christians, have with Job's story is that the suffering he had to endure seems so meaningless. His trials do not make sense.

Suffering is somehow easier to endure when we can make sense of it—when we can make all the pieces fit neatly together. In fact, many people are willing to face suffering if they can find meaning. For example, in order to obtain a desired outcome, athletes and pregnant women volunteer to suffer. During her second pregnancy, my (John's) wife was confined to bed for over four months. Though some of our friends envied Denise for being able to take it easy, the constant bed rest was hard on the entire family. In fact, Denise found it particularly difficult to survive those four months of total inactivity. She saw all the things that needed to be done but couldn't help. Her ability to play with and care for our three-year-old, Katie, was limited, which pained her greatly. Church was out, along with dates with her loving and humble husband! What might sound like a blessing to many overcommitted people was really an ordeal for my wife.

We knew that she was going to have a boy. The confinement had purpose: to protect the life and health of the baby growing within. Though some things were outside of her control, this one thing, this stillness, was something she could do to bring order to a frightening time. As she visualized the birth of our first son, Stephen, she found purpose and meaning in her pain—enough to carry her through the four months of confinement.

Following the birth of his second son, a psychologist confided to me that he thought his wife had lost her mind. During both pregnancies, she had been hospitalized, almost died, and suffered long, arduous labors. After bringing their second miracle baby home, his wife told him that she wanted another child. Even with all his psychological training, my friend was dumbfounded that his wife was willing to once again subject herself to illness and possibly death.

Because God has a unique plan and purpose for each individual, no suffering is meaningless. To God, there are no puzzles with mismatched pieces. Suffering is one of the tools God uses to redirect our attention to what is really important because it mocks what we believe is important. We groan when we lose things such as comfort, order, and fairness—things we most depend upon. In struggling to understand our plight, we often demand that God explain Himself to us. We want God to make the pieces fit and then justify Himself for making life miserable. If for no other reason, God uses suffering to get our attention. As C. S. Lewis noted, suffering is God's "megaphone to rouse a deaf world."[12]

God roused Lewis through the death of his wife, and used the German concentration camps to shout into the lives of Frankl and ten Boom. These great writers were veteran sufferers. And if Frankl is right, nothing else will make us grow. Perhaps Christians can even learn and grow simply by hearing about the pain borne by others. In this way, their pain can work to inoculate us, even as a flu shot prevents or lessens our suffering. Is it possible that pain can even increase the quality of our lives?

Though there is nothing virtuous about suffering in and of itself, it does open the door to transformation. When we begin to understand that every painful ordeal has meaning and purpose, we can begin to see suffering for the precious jewel that it is.

It is foolish and even dangerous to pretend that we have a complete answer as to why God allows suffering. Regardless of the aim of suffering, however, we can rest assured that God has a definite plan in His divine mind! From that plan, meaning can be found. We can learn how to respond to suffering so that we not only please God, we grow.

Truth #5: Suffering Comes From Multiple Sources

As you search the Bible to determine the answer to the question, "What causes suffering?" you may walk away with mixed answers. In the Old Testament, suffering resulted primarily from Israel's rebellion, though calamity sometimes had other causes. In the New Testament, people seemed to suffer more for their faith than for any other reason. In essence, the Bible portrays suffering as coming from multiple sources. In the book of Job, suffering came upon him from the North, South, East, and West giving attention to the fact that poor Job was crushed from all sides. Likewise, suffering can come upon us from multiple sources. It is often important to recognize a possible cause or causes of your suffering in order to know how you need to respond.

Suffering comes because of a shattered and spoiled world. We encounter suffering because we live in a broken and fallen world. Philosophers refer to this as pain and suffering due to natural law. Because this world is not what God designed it to be, we will experience disease, disorder, disillusionment, and despair. A broken and fallen world produces disasters such as earthquakes, tornadoes, hurricanes, and other catastrophes. Sometimes these incidents are referred to as "acts of nature" or "acts of God." However, whether such incidents are sent by God to judge us, such as the enduring consequences of Noah's flood, or are simply the result of a fallen world, the devastation they produce is much the same.

A broken and fallen world will not allow for exact justice or fairness. You cannot extract logic from an imperfect world. Following the fall of Adam and Eve, this fact was predicted in the Garden. God placed curses on everything, including the earth.[13] Solomon despaired that we live in a world that is broken and cannot be fixed.[14] The apostle Paul also acknowledged that all of creation has been groaning like a woman giving birth as it awaits the day when it will be redeemed.[15] All sorrow and sickness result from the Fall. Everyone will suffer.

Suffering because of supernatural causes. Job's suffering was the result of Satan's intervention. Both Satan and his demons can create great discomfort in the human life. The Bible clearly attributes some instances of muteness, blindness, epilepsy, insanity, and deafness to the work of Satan.[16] For instance, Luke presents the story of a woman who was ill for 18 years. After healing her, Jesus states that Satan caused the woman's pain.[17] Because we are the image bearers of God, Satan seeks to destroy us by hurting, aggravating, and deceiving us. While Satan is certainly not the cause of every incidence of suffering, he does play more of a role than most of us are willing to admit.

During the Last Supper, Jesus shared some final words with His most intimate friends, the disciples. In His prayer to the Father, Christ asked that His people be protected from the evil one.[18] The word evil here can refer to an evil person or an evil thing. Jesus was not under the illusion that everyone would love those who love Him and follow His truth.

Although Satan's accusations may have led in some sense to Job's suffering, God allowed and permitted it. In fact, Scripture tells us that Satan sought permission from God to stretch out his hand against Job. God can allow suffering to come into our lives.[19] That is sometimes difficult to accept! The basic truth is that God permits and allows His children to suffer. Non-Christians, as well as many Christians, find it unthinkable that a loving God could permit— let alone cause—one of His children to experience pain. One psychologist, following the death of his spouse, said, "I've been a good Christian and have done what I can to serve God. Doesn't that amount to anything? I could never allow one of my children to be hurt; how can God watch me suffer and do nothing about it?" When we feel out of control, when life has treated us unfairly, we view God through a lens of victimization. The pillars that support our faith are shaken, splintered, and smashed. Ironically, the very weapon God has given us to persevere through suffering—faith—falls apart when we need it the most. No matter how we feel, the truth is that our supernatural God permits suffering. But that does not mean He is inattentive, indifferent, or callous about His children. While the idea that God allows our troubles may make it seem that He is heartless, in reality it shows just how much He treasures us. God is not unfeeling about our human misery. On the contrary, He is actively present with us in it. The truth of the matter is that when we face tragedy, God knows that we hurt and cares that we hurt.

A second truth is found in Job's suffering. While God does allow and permit us to suffer, He places limitations. Essentially, God told Satan that He would allow Job to be tested and tried, but Satan had to refrain from taking his life. God never tempts us beyond what we are able to bear. He places limitations on the extent and severity of testing and, subsequently, protects us.[20]

Suffering occurs because of the sinful choices of other people. Suffering may result from the choices and behavior of both Christians and non-Christians. In other words, sometimes we experience personal suffering through no fault of our own. In fact, the original poor choice of Adam and Eve has dramatically affected all of humanity. Later, Abel was murdered by Cain, Joseph was exiled because of his brothers' jealous rage, and Paul was tortured.[21] The cruelty these men suffered

God knows that we hurt and cares that we hurt

was not due to their own poor choices but the sinful choices of others.

We may be hurt either intentionally or unintentionally by other people. For most of us, the intentional wound is the worst. We simply believe that we do not deserve to be treated so poorly. But, whether harm is intended or not, the result is the same—pain. It doesn't matter whether a driver intentionally or unintentionally runs over you; broken bones are likely in either case. (Attorneys may see this metaphor differently.)

Sometimes you may be persecuted because of your desire to follow God. Paul remarked that people who desire to be godly will be persecuted.[22] Before his conversion, Paul was known as Saul, and he was a zealous persecutor of the church, making the lives of our early brothers and sisters miserable. Following his conversion, he became the target of others who sought to persecute the church. The role of unbelievers in the suffering of God's people can be seen from early in the Old Testament and throughout the history of mankind.

While Paul spoke of being a victim of religious persecution, there are other ways to be victimized. For example, criminals terrorize some people. Other people suffer from living with a raging alcoholic. Some children feel the pain of growing up in a single-parent home. We need only to recall the events of Hurricane Katrina, September 11, the Oklahoma City bombing, or the shootings at Columbine High School to see this truth. Consider the brutal acts of Ted Bundy and the faces of missing children on milk cartons to appreciate how extensively victimization occurs.

Both our families have been robbed more than once. My (John's) family was first robbed when we were in Florida during our first year of marriage. Though we did not have many possessions, the violation wreaked havoc in our lives. My experience happened in the driveway when our car was broken into and several valuables were stolen. In both cases, we experienced the feelings of any victim—fear, anger, grief, and confusion. Fortunately, neither of us allowed those acts to control us.

Perhaps more difficult to deal with is being hurt by other Christians. In particular, the pain is intensified when it's intentional. I once had dinner with a minister who had experienced incredible mistreatment by his congregation. Certain members of the elder body had sought to remove the pastor by making life miserable for him and his family. In two years' time, this group of church leaders successfully ripped the passion from this man's heart and destroyed his children's faith. His wife plunged into a black hole of despair. She was hospitalized on three occasions for attempted suicide. When visiting the home of parishioners, he was told, "Go away, Pastor, you are not welcome here!" After years of continued abuse, this pastor and his family left the church.

Christ said the world will know that we are Christians by our love.[23] Sadly, we too often send a contrary message. One unbeliever rephrased Christ's comment, "You will know they are Christians by the way they fight and the way they hate." It is grievous that, in this person's mind at least, our legacy is no longer sacrificial love but unrelenting hate.

Even though pain and suffering are sometimes attributed to the sinful actions or choices of others, it is always God's intent to use them for our benefit.

Suffering comes from our sin. In the Old Testament, God often described the sins of people like Jonah before pronouncing judgment on the Israelites. If the prophet had not disobeyed God's will, he would never have been swallowed by a fish.

Less dramatic is the story of Abraham, who chose not to believe God's promise that Sarah would give birth to his son and conspired to father a child his own way. Abraham slept with Sarah's servant, Hagar—a handmaiden from Egypt. Hagar gave birth to Ishmael. When the angel of the Lord visited Abraham years later, he reminded him that he and Sarah would have the promised son. Abraham begged for Ishmael to be that son. Like most fathers, he deeply loved his child. God had promised that Abraham's seed would be as innumerable as the sand and that the Messiah would be his descendant. Abraham desired this blessing for Ishmael. But it was not to be. Because of the choices that he made to defy God's will, Abraham had to experience the agony of losing a son when his wife demanded that Hagar and Ishmael be sent away.

Though our sin can produce suffering, all suffering is not the result of sin. Perhaps the best example of this belief is found in the Old Testament book of Job. We are given a behind the scenes tour of what sets the stage for his reversal of fortunes. According to Job 1:9-11, Satan's regular visit to heaven leads to a conversation in which God brags about his son, Job. As a result, Satan accuses God of being a Divine manipulator. Satan tells God that the only reason people worship Him is because He makes life so good for them. To paraphrase Satan, "Take their comfort away God, and You will see how people will turn their backs on You." Though Job is never made aware of the reason for his suffering, he is literally the representative of all human beings in responding to suffering. If Job fails to respond well, Satan's accusation has merit. Of course, Job doesn't fail...though his journey through the valley is horrific. After sitting with Job for seven days without saying a word Job's friends cannot help but respond to Job's declaration that he is suffering innocently. In short, his friends direct Job's attention to the fact that people only suffer because they sin (e.g., Job 4:7; 8:4; 11:1-3, 13; 15:20; 20:29; 22:4). Interestingly, Job likely held to a similar belief since it was the prevailing understanding of the problem of evil and suffering at that time.

Apparently, the prevailing perspective in Job's day was that suffering was connected with sinful living. This type of theology is known as Retribution Theology; that is, bad deeds are punished and good deeds are rewarded. The point is not that we are sinful or flawed beings, but that when we sin we are paving the way for punishment. The belief is that there is an exact correspondence between one's actions and one's consequences; righteous or good people do not suffer—only the wicked. Simply, we get what we deserve. It is a simple formula that makes some intuitive sense. Yet, it is deeply flawed. In fact, the book of Job proves that the view is wrong when God tells Job's friends that they have spoken lies about Him (Job 42:7). Lest one think that this view died in Old Testament times, it is also evident in the New Testament. In John 9, when encountering a blind man the disciples ask Jesus whether the sinner was the blind man or his parents. Jesus challenges their view with the fact that he is blind so that God's character may be revealed in Him; it has nothing to do with sin. Even Paul warned that we reap what we sow (Gal. 6:7-8).

The view that sin is the cause of suffering is still alive and well. Modern day Retribution Theology is often cloaked in terms of a person lacking faith or lacking the right faith, not trusting God, or sinful choices. If the sufferer prays for God to intervene in his circumstances and things do not get better, it seems logical to conclude that the sufferer has sin in his life and lacks faith.

Retribution Theory: Is God a Cosmic Punisher?

Kevin was a Christian when his college girlfriend became pregnant. Even though they both believed abortion was wrong, they made the decision, in their case, that abortion was the least negative choice. Kevin accompanied his girlfriend to the abortion clinic and nothing more was ever said about it. Within a few months he and his girlfriend parted ways, a rather common occurrence in such situations. Eventually, Kevin confessed the abortion to some friends and "made it right with the Lord." He would often share his testimony, encouraging others not to do what he had done. Years later Kevin married a wonderful Christian lady. After a few years of marriage they decided to expand their family but no matter what they tried, Kevin's wife could not get pregnant. They continued to ask family and friends for prayer; asking God to give them their own biological child. Over the course of time, Kevin and his wife were told by numerous members of their church that perhaps their inability to bear children was related to the fact that Kevin had aborted the first child that God had given him. Stories similar to this abound. Many people have been shamed with the belief that their suffering is directly linked to some sin.

It might be that you think other people could have such distorted notions, but not yourself. But think of how you may have responded when encountering a significant adversity. Perhaps you uttered, "What have I done to deserve this!" The idea that you are at fault is steeped in the belief that God is a cosmic punisher who creates adverse circumstances to keep us in line. It is almost as if we believe that God has set up a moral invisible fence; when we get near it we are shocked with volts of suffering in order to keep us in the spiritual yard.

In Romans 5:21 we are told that for the believer, grace reigns. Because of God's matchless love and grace, sin cannot abound more than grace abounds. No matter how big a sin might be, God's blanket of grace is more than sufficient to cover it.

Our personal and professional experiences tell us that the majority of suffering people's experience is brought upon themselves. With this assertion, we are not blaming the victim. Rather, years of counseling and interacting with people have taught us that we are often our own worst enemies. For example, when abuse occurs during childhood, the victim is not responsible for being abused. Each victim, however, is responsible for how other people's wounds, sin, and choices play out in his or her own life. Job was not responsible for the horrific events that befell him. Yet, his commitment and persistence that it was unjust did make his suffering worse. You cannot change what has happened to you, but you can change how you are currently dealing with it and how much you might be allowing it to play out through your behavior.

But accepting responsibility for pain is not easy. Flip Wilson, the 1970s television star, was known for saying, "The devil made me do it!" Even as we face the consequences of our own actions, all too often we point our finger at Satan, others, and even God, blaming Him for our pain. It is human nature not to take responsibility for our actions. But the truth is, the choice to defy God's will, defy common sense, or defy God's calling will inevitably lead to suffering.

Many people have felt the cold chill of reaping the consequences of their actions. For example, God's will is for sex to remain within the safety of a marital relationship. But when unfaithful marriage partners defy that original plan, they risk painful consequences: AIDS or sexually transmitted disease, broken families, damaged reputations. All of these circumstances are vivid reminders that we reap what we sow.[24]

Though most of us consider ourselves to be good, our dark undersides are innately sinful. The theological centrality of our need for redemption because of our sinful nature runs through the Bible. Rather than humbly acknowledging our sins, however, we attribute many of our sinful choices to others.

When we allow the flesh to govern us rather than following the will of God, we make sinful choices. Since the fall of Adam and Eve, our nature has been self-centered and self-serving. Let's face it, we are obsessed with ourselves. Our preoccupation is totally inward. Although Paul's instruction tells us that believers are dead to the old nature, those corpses have a way of repeatedly resurrecting themselves. Suffering is often the self-inflicted wound of disobeying God. [25]

Suffering comes from our stupid choices. Suffering occurs not only because of the sinful choices we make, it also occurs because of choices that interfere with the laws of nature. If we get too close to the edge of a cliff and fall off, our choice interacts with the laws of gravity and we experience a broken bone or worse.

I enjoy playing church softball; and while I am not a great athlete, I do fairly well for a man of my age. Unfortunately, I have a history of getting hurt in almost every game. The pain and suffering are not because playing softball is sinful. Rather, they stem from my foolish belief that I can still play as aggressively as a young man.

Choices that result in suffering may or may not be senseless. In other words, we may or may not deserve the consequence or their severity. But either way, we must choose how we will respond.

Suffering comes because of our godly service. Jesus experienced death, the ultimate in suffering, in order to do His Father's will. Christ did not want to taste the cup of death, but He chose to follow God's will even though He knew it would require suffering. There is a distinct difference between choosing suffering and choosing to follow God's calling, which may result in hardship. The former is a self-focused sign of masochism. The latter is a Spirit-focused sign of maturity.

Many American Christians typically view "suffering for Christ's sake" as a rejecting look, a lost relationship, a poor grade, or a legal dictate to remove a Christian symbol from public displays. While such things are hurtful and often unjust, they pale in comparison to the horrors other Christians have endured. Our response to suffering is traditionally self-focused: How can you do this to me? Too often, we lack the mature spiritual willingness to understand that God is truly involved in every aspect of our lives—even suffering. Because we view religious persecution as personal, we are not able to see that the evil one is really targeting Christ, not us.

While on a mission to persecute Christians, Saul experienced a supernatural encounter with the risen Jesus. Blinded by a brilliant light, he was asked a question that would drastically change the direction and course of his life: "Why are you persecuting Me?"[26] Saul realized that he was not only assaulting Christians but the Godhead as well. When God's children are abused, it is ultimately a slap in the face of Jesus.

Think of our brothers and sisters in countries such as Sudan. Because of their faith in Christ, these fellow believers are experiencing inhumane and brutal treatment. Many have been tortured, murdered, molested, jailed, sold into slavery, kidnapped, or raped. Their only crime, like that of the early apostles, is proclaiming the name of Christ.[27] As Oswald Chambers wrote, "God's way is always the way of suffering, the way of the 'long, long trail.'"[28]

Truth #6: There is no All-Inclusive Answer for Suffering

If you desire to have a single understandable passage that answers the question, why suffering? you will be extremely disappointed and disillusioned. You can search the pages of Scripture, and you will not find one verse that completely and fully explains God's purpose for suffering. But we are people who want answers; in fact, we want easy answers. Some Christians attempt to explain suffering by attributing it to sin, lack of faith, or some other cause. They offer quick solutions, a microwave theology. "Just trust God," we are told. Oh, if it were only that simple! The beginning of understanding suffering is the acceptance that we will not always understand it. Theologians have spent untold hours studying the Bible's teachings about suffering. While no one particular verse completely explains why God allows suffering, the Bible does offer some insight.

Job knew enough about God to trust Him in the things he didn't know. And like Job, we must learn to cope with pain and decide to accept as sufficient the things that God has revealed to us, even when we don't have all the answers. God's will is that we respond to His work so that He can accomplish His plan in our lives and the lives of those around us.

Truth #7: God is Not Obligated to Give us a Reason

When I (John) was in college, I experienced the loss of a significant relationship in my life. This loss produced great heartache that lingered for a long time. From the moment that it occurred, however, I knew exactly why God had allowed it to happen. As I reflect on that experience, I believe now, as then, that God was redirecting me back to Himself. Years later, rather than feeling the loss, I feel a deep sense of gratitude that God intervened in my life. At times like that, it's fairly easy to see what God is doing in our lives through a difficulty or tragedy.

Other times, however, it may take years to understand what God was trying to accomplish through a past difficulty. Walt and Lynn Wilson were a typical young married couple with two small children. Walt was a rehabilitation counselor, and Lynn was a dental assistant. Both had grown up in church, but over time they drifted away from the Lord. "I was playing church, one foot in the world and one in the church," he said. After nine years of marriage, the bottom fell out. "We were shipwrecked with no hope of reconciliation." Despair prompted Walt to return to the church. Eventually, God began to work a slow but miraculous healing of their marriage. Through the support of the church and the help of a counselor, Lynn and Walt began to rebuild their relationship. In time, they became involved in leading a support group for divorced and separated people and conducting marital enrichment programs throughout the state. Twenty years later, after taking early retirement, Walt was called to serve as the family minister in the same church that brought healing to their marriage.

It took Walt about two decades to understand God's purpose for his suffering. "It was the hardest thing I ever went through, but if it took this terrible problem to turn me toward a serious and committed life to Christ, it was worth it. It changed my family, marriage, and life for the better!"

Sometimes we may never know why God allows suffering in our lives. It may not be until we are in heaven that we learn from Christ Himself what He was doing through our ordeals. Our desire to know why us, why now, and why this, must be replaced with a stronger desire to know God.

The humbling reality is that God is not obligated to give us a reason. Biblical writers realized this truth. Solomon, the wisest man who ever lived, knew that his brilliance was not sufficient to comprehend God's ways.[29] The prophet Isaiah and the apostle Paul both remind us that we cannot tell God anything.[30]

God's ways and thoughts do not compare to ours. We think that we are wise, but compared to the eternal God, we have no wisdom. Trying to understand God from our vantage point is impossible—finite beings can never understand an infinite Creator. We simply don't have a large enough frame of reference from which to make sense of our lives.

Truth #8: God Knows Our Pain and is With us in Our Suffering

The First World War, which produced 40 million casualties, horrified people around the globe. Many soldiers died slow and agonizing deaths due to mustard gas and other poisonous gases, which hadn't been used before in modern warfare. The novelist H. G. Wells was angered by the carnage and wrote, "If I thought there was an omnipotent God who looked down on battles and deaths and all the waste and horror of this war—able to prevent these things—doing them to amuse Himself—I would spit in His empty face."[31] Because rewards and punishments, in the guise of happiness and discomfort, appear to be haphazardly distributed, many of us question either the goodness or the power of God.

Few of us may question God as H. G. Wells did. Yet if we are truly honest with ourselves, part of our confusion lies in not understanding what God's role is in our suffering. We simply do not understand how an all-powerful God could sit by and allow us to hurt. If God truly loved us, we believe He would protect us from problems, at least catastrophic ones.

Remember the old song that begins, "Nobody knows the trouble I've seen . . ." During times of suffering, we typically believe that to be true. Nobody can possibly understand what we are going through; nobody can sense how hard we are struggling to stay afloat; nobody can fathom the depth of our fear and confusion. Nobody, not even God, can understand how badly we hurt. If He did, we reason, He would do something about it.

Fortunately, that song does not end on the word seen: "Nobody knows the trouble I've seen . . . nobody knows but Jesus." Jesus, God's only Son, knows the extent of our suffering. The shortest verse in the Bible, "Jesus wept," conveys the truth that God Himself sheds tears.[32] Think about it: what is more incredible, a God who created everything or a God who weeps? He is not only aware of our suffering, He feels it. God is our fellow sufferer. Through His Son, Jesus Christ, He experienced suffering. No suffering has ever come to us that has not first passed through the heart and hand of God.

For most Christians, the fact that God is both present with us and knows our hurts provides at least some sense of comfort and assurance. But not everyone shares that belief. As a new counselor, I met with a godly woman who had been severely sexually abused as a child. As we examined her tormenting experiences, I commented that Christ did not leave her alone. He was with her the entire time. The lady's eyes became intense and her face stern as she remarked, "Then why didn't He stop it? Where was He when I was being abused?" As I sat speechless, I realized that I had exposed her anger toward God, but I had also cast God as the abuser. For her, knowing that God was present during her trials offered no solace. Instead, it confirmed her suspicion that God stood by and watched as she was abused. Clearly, He was indifferent to her suffering. My novice skills had created such a mess that I did not know what to do next. Unsure of how to respond, I asked God to give me wisdom. I believe He gave me these words: "He was in the same place that He was when they crucified His Son."

In time, this woman understood that God does not intervene in every appalling thing that we do to each other. In fact, His willingness to allow us to make harmful and wrong choices is not evidence of His indifference but instead an example of His long-suffering and grace. Once she dealt with her feelings of betrayal and abandonment, this woman soon found that God's presence could calm her inner turmoil and heal her wounds.

While He doesn't always intervene, we do see God intervening throughout history in the lives of people at different times and in different ways. In the Old Testament God appeared to be actively involved. Whether in the drama of Noah's ark, Abraham and Lot's journeys, the bondage of Israel, the fight to gain the Promised Land, or the judgment of Israel, God took an active and direct role. However, in the New Testament God made a transition. Although He was very involved in the lives of Mary and Joseph, the life of His Son Jesus, and in the development of the early church, He seems less involved than before. By the time of the Epistles, there is less mention of God directly intervening in people's lives as He did in the Old Testament. Just as in the Old Testament, suffering arrived via various avenues, but God's role in the New Testament was definitely different. When the time arrived for God to send a messenger to tell the people that He is actively involved, He punctuated His message with a baby.[33] That little Child was God's promise to move into the darkness of His children's lives and light an entirely darkened world. God had a purpose and would achieve it through an eternally designed plan.

Although the children of Israel thought that God had forgotten them, God reassured Moses that He knew His people were suffering.[34] And in the same way, God knows our plights and predicaments. He not only knows what is happening in our lives, God also understands our pain. According to the psalmist, He even counts our tears.[35]

Because He experienced what suffering is through Jesus, God knows the extent of suffering.[36] Through Jesus Christ, God took on the same body as ours, fully identifying with humanity. He saw and felt what the world was like through our eyes. In becoming like us, He felt rejection and incredible suffering. The prophet Isaiah, foretelling the agony of Christ, spoke of the sorrow that Christ would experience.[37] Jesus Christ knew suffering, temptation, and infirmities; He did not fit into the mold of this world.[38] At the end of His life, He endured incredible pain from the beatings and crucifixion. It was through Calvary that God succumbed to pain. Think about it—if God is responsible for suffering, He was at least willing to take His own medicine. Many religions have gods, but only one has a God who cared enough to become a man and to die.

Truth #9: God is Always at Work

Imagine how it would have been to live during the four hundred years between the Old and New Testaments when God was silent. How lonely the children of Israel must have been during those dark days. Their lives were governed by a foreign power, both politically and religiously. What was God up to during those years? Why had He stopped speaking to them as He had done previously?

Our experiences seem to parallel that of Israel's. At times, it seems as if God is silent. Because of our limited understanding, we think that He has become distracted. Or maybe He has too many irons in the fire to really watch over us. It is during these times that the pain of suffering seems greatest. God's presence during suffering is like a backstage worker in a drama—active, involved, and working to fulfill the ultimate thrust of the play, although usually hidden from the audience's view, He is just as involved as ever.

Perhaps you feel as if God is silent. Be assured, He is up to something. He is faithful to His Word. He has a specific plan for you and a timetable to accomplish His great work in your life.

Truth #10: God can Redeem Suffering

I have always found it intriguing that in the book of Job, God responded to Job's declaration of his own righteousness by pointing Job back to Creation and to the very character of God Himself.[39] The Creator asks Job, "Where were you . . . ?" The Lord declares that He created and sustains the universe. No one can duplicate God's acts of splendor, wisdom, and power. The all-powerful, all-knowing, and eternal God stands against the meager, ignorant, and mortal man, Job. Just as Job was unable to contend with God, we are incapable of doing so.

Nevertheless, God is still the Creator and Redeemer. There is no random event in God's world. God's original plan has been marred by sin, but all is not lost. Evangelist Ron Dunn has said that we gained more in the Cross than we lost in the Fall.[40] Suffering, along with all evil, was completely defeated at Calvary. Therefore, even suffering can have a redemptive purpose. Even in the midst of his own confusion and pain, Job contended that he knew his Redeemer lived.[41]

Since God created the world with structure and order, even suffering operates according to a set of rules and principles. Just as God governs us by His wise Word, so He also governs suffering in our lives. The Bible does not romanticize life. It provides a realistic picture of the human predicament and invites us with the hope of redemption. The day is coming when Christ will reign and destroy the greatest enemy, death.[42] Christians will be ushered into the new Jerusalem, where suffering does not exist.

But we live today between the Garden of Eden and the new Jerusalem. When you are hurting, redemption seems a long way off. As Christians, we need to realize that nothing, including suffering, is beyond the scope of redemption. Since suffering is a prominent topic in the Bible, we need to fashion an accurate theology of it to better understand God's purposes and promises. Such a biblical notion of suffering will help us avoid glib answers to such a complex problem.

TRUTH #11: There is an End to All Suffering as a Believer

As I typed out the preceding words on my laptop, I initially stopped with "there will be an end to all suffering." But as I prepared to elaborate on this point, I realized that statement was wrong. There is not an end to all suffering. There is only an end to all suffering endured by the believer. The Bible states very clearly that those who don't believe will perish and suffer eternal damnation. The apostle John conveyed a glimpse of what will happen to the unbeliever. Near the end of his revelation, John saw people whose names were not written in the Book of Life being cast into hell. For those without Christ, earth will be the closest thing to "heaven" they know. Believers, however, will experience something quite different; they will know the eternal comfort of God.[43]

Perhaps you have never taken the opportunity to turn your life over to Jesus Christ and ask Him to forgive your sin. This can be that time. Confess your sins to God and ask Him to be the Lord of your life, in light of His death and resurrection on your behalf.[44] Then you, too, can have the guarantee of where you will spend eternity and know that your suffering will eventually end.

For Christians, a time will come when every tear will be wiped away from our eyes. As the hymn writer says, "What a day that will be, when my Jesus I shall see, and I look upon His face, the One who saved me by His grace. When He takes me by the hand and leads me through the Promised Land, what a day, what a glorious day that will be."[45]

Chapter 4

LEARNING TO TRUST GOD...DESPITE PAIN

Many have commented that the problems of evil, pain, and suffering are the most difficult objections against religious belief in general and against the God of the Bible in particular.[1] It seems like all we need to do is turn on the television to witness the devastation that occurs to countless numbers of human beings. Tsunamis, earthquakes, famine, crime, and war are not far from any of us. Existential situations like these often overshadow more theoretical matters, as well. Undeniably, humans really do suffer. How could God allow all of this heartache and misery?

Our natural tendency is to make assumptions about what happens around us. When adversity hits, we attempt to make sense of it. We explain adversity by attributing either direct or indirect causes. In psychology, this process is referred to as "attribution theory," which explains the way we attempt to predict and control our lives. Research indicates that we rationalize our own behavior in terms of situational factors, while we explain the behavior of other people according to their intentions and dispositions. People assume that they have more control of their lives than they actually have. We hold tenaciously to this assumption, because if it is not true, then random events can happen to us. That is one reason the very belief in control is a strong predictor of physical and mental health. But when the illusion that we can control life is destroyed, we are likely to fall apart spiritually, psychologically, and physically. Like the story of Chicken Little in the introduction, we have arrived at the wrong conclusion.

Therefore, whether we attribute our suffering to our poor choices, the insensitivity of others, or supernatural forces, the bottom line is that we have to trust that God is good, trustworthy, and just. Suffering is not so much a problem to be solved as it is an opportunity to trust in God's ability to capitalize on our pain for greater purposes. Of course, our finite minds cannot (or will not) grasp the complexity of suffering. Many people find themselves in a crucible of choice. Some wobble back and forth between what they perceive to be the only options to explain suffering. Perhaps they think that God is either good and loving (so their suffering is from another source) or He is not good and loving (so He is responsible for the pain). The first perspective does not permit God to allow us to suffer in any way, because to do so would negate His goodness and love. The second view implies that suffering cannot come from anyone or anything else except God Himself. Yet the Bible is clear that while God is both good and loving, He does permit His loved ones to suffer; and we will never fully understand the matter.

In this chapter we will describe several aspects of the problem, along with a wide spectrum of commonly-suggested answers. A few critiques will also be given. Then in the following chapter we will examine why God allows so much anguish in the world.

One crucial point should be mentioned here. The problems of pain, evil, and suffering are many-faceted and we cannot deal with the complete issue here in all its complexity. Many of the individual features also extend beyond the interests of the average reader. We will address some of the outstanding issues, while certain others will only be mentioned briefly, or not at all. For the reader who is interested in pursuing additional aspects, including specialized issues, other treatments may be very helpful.[2]

Our Pain

To live is to hurt—life itself causes pain! Maybe you had an experience where you've worked through a particular issue, read a good book, or listened to a moving sermon, thinking you've grown in your ability to make sense of the world around you. Finally, perhaps you have learned the key that will tie your life together, and help you move on to the next step. Then boom—something happens and doubts arise. How do we reconcile these things with God caring for us and our particular needs?

Newspaper articles describe in detail various crimes and diseases in our society, many of them seemingly occurring in our own backyards. The headlines scream their bad news in our direction. Television and radio update the wars and hot spots around the globe. Reporters on location project anguish directly into our living rooms. Parents weep over the graves of their dead children, killed by marauders. Third-world famine rips at our hearts as small bodies are placed in the ground. *What is this world coming to?* has long been a popular question.

Sometimes it's not simply the pain itself that overwhelms us, but the sheer volume of it—what philosophers often call gratuitous evil. Some suffering seems to have a purpose—but this much? How do we account for the thousands of

nothing in Christianity is questioned as frequently as the point of evil, pain and suffering

innocent lives that are sometimes lost in wars or nature's mishaps?

To make matters worse, we are all emotional beings, some more than others. Our experiences sometimes wage war with our heads. Unfortunately, these experiences often weigh more heavily upon us than do the more theoretical truths that we learn. Pain and evil can upset our theological equilibrium. Suffering slams head-on into our most cherished beliefs.

It is perhaps true that nothing in Christianity is questioned as frequently as the point of evil, pain and suffering, including the nature of Scripture, the virgin birth, the deity of Jesus Christ, and His resurrection. Sometimes the question is posed like David Hume's fictional character Philo states it. Speaking of God and evil, Philo says it this way: "Is he willing to prevent evil, but not able? then is he impotent. Is he able, but not willing? then is he malevolent. Is he both able and willing? whence then is evil?"[3]

Formulations such as these often propose that the biblical view of God is incompatible with what we perceive in the world around us. Some even hold that the classical position is contradictory. For most people, evil undeniably exists.

Oddly enough, some philosophers and theologians think that there is a dilemma here, while others just do not. It seems to be what philosophers call a "person-relative" issue—one that is highly related to the individual who is doing the evaluating.[4] How do scholars usually respond? Perhaps surprisingly, besides Christians, even atheists struggle regularly with these issues.[5] Evil is simply a problem that affects us all, whatever our beliefs.

Responding to the "Why" of Pain

How have scholars proposed handling the quandary of pain and evil? Many philosophical and theological approaches have been suggested over the years. We will summarize a few of the more prominent responses.[6] Eastern philosophies frequently teach that pain and evil are, in some sense, appearances or illusions originating in ignorance. Changing the underlying cause eliminates the condition. For example, Buddhism holds that the origin of suffering is craving and that "the utter passionless cessation of this same craving" will cause the cessation of pain and suffering.[7]

Most philosophers, at least in the Western tradition, oppose positions that argue or assume that evil is some sort of illusion. Doubtless, as cognitive psychology has shown, a fair amount of suffering is the result of our outlook and thinking patterns. But at best, this is an incomplete explanation. After all, those who hold that suffering doesn't exist objectively still face the same ills as do others—they hurt, too.[8] Further, the data points to both more varied as well as more complicated solutions. Suffering is not just simply in our minds, nor does it stop by suspending all craving. Events in nature such as earthquakes and tsunamis do not suddenly cease just because we change our thinking patterns. Our chief question concerns the source of the pain. Even if some evil is due to ignorance and improper thinking, how did it originate? As Christian apologist Norman Geisler concludes rather pointedly: "Illusionism is no more than a 'beautiful theory' that is ruined by a brutal gang of facts."[9]

On the other hand, many naturalists argue that evil is quite real and its presence in the world argues against and perhaps even disproves God's existence.[10] But there is disagreement over the degree of seriousness presented by this problem. Sometimes the presence of evil is actually said to contradict classical theism, but this is increasingly rare. A softer position is that there is no formal contradiction, but evil still counts as a significant objection to orthodox Christianity. Naturalists consider this problem to be their "trump card" against theistic world views. Here we will survey some of the representative positions.

Albert Camus's book The Plague relates the story of a horrible epidemic spread by rats earlier this century in the city of Oran. With so many people dying of the sickness, the humanitarian thing to do, of course, was to support our fellow human beings in their plight. However, fighting against the disease meant that one was opposing the priest, who decided to do nothing, since helping the sick would cause one to fight against God, whom the priest believed had sent the plague in the first place. We are also supposedly faced with the same dilemma—be a humanitarian or be religious. One cannot choose both options.[11]

H.J. McCloskey's argument is somewhat related. He charges that theists cannot fight evil or else they would be guilty of interfering with the greater good that is supposedly achieved by suffering. So the theist is morally bound not to attempt to exterminate evil or the resulting good will not be attained.[12] J.L. Mackie has joined McCloskey in the contention that classic theism's basic beliefs in the omnipotence and omni-benevolence of God strongly oppose the belief that evil exists.[13]

If God exists, then, of course, atheism is gravely mistaken. But there is still more to say about the problem of evil. We need to make some comments here about Christians doing humanitarian acts. Naturalists like Camus and McCloskey are totally mistaken. Christians have every reason to fight against the pain, suffering, and injustice in the world. Even if greater goods were to come from every single evil, we still have numerous biblical examples of Jesus and others opposing evil.[14] The Jews in the Old Testament were commanded frequently to provide for the poor. Jesus regularly healed all sorts of sicknesses and fed the hungry. Paul took up offerings for poor believers.[15] Moreover, the Incarnation itself is the greatest biblical example of God opposing evil, especially in His work accomplished at the Cross. So believers are repeatedly encouraged and commanded to act in a humanitarian manner, whether or not good results from human suffering.[16]

Another critical response is that while God exists, the presence of evil indicates that He cannot solve the problem. Briefly, God is finite and hence limited in one or more of His attributes. Although Mackie does not take this view himself, he comments that one way for the theists to avoid the problem of evil is to deny one or more of the conflicting beliefs regarding God's nature. For instance, one might give up the belief that God is omnipotent or omnibenevolent.[17]

A number of philosophers, such as certain idealists earlier last century, denied one or more of God's traditional attributes.[18] Peter Bertocci states that "the creative Intelligence does not, or cannot, succeed in all his undertakings."[19] Edgar Brightman argues that God's inability to completely defeat the world's evil, especially unexplained, "surd" evil, indicates the presence of a nonrational element (termed "The Given") in the very nature of God.[20]

More recently, the best examples of those who believe that God is finite are probably the process philosophers, who generally conclude that God has both classical and non-classical attributes.[21] Schubert Ogden is an example. He holds that the traditional view of God cannot answer the problem of evil: "classical Christian theism ... cannot both admit the reality of evil and still maintain that God is all-good as well as all-powerful ... " So we must challenge the orthodox conception of God's attributes.[22]

Christians should point out that Jesus' brand of Christian theism was validated by the God of the universe when He raised His Son from the dead, and Jesus' views opposed finitism. There are far too many possible answers to the finitist positions without jettisoning God's attributes in the process.[23]

Process scholars celebrate the existence of God, as well as certain classical virtues, emphasizing his love. Yet, they especially challenge other classic attributes of orthodox theism like omnipotence, omniscience, and the immutability of God.[24]

Rather intriguingly, some prominent idealistic philosophers and theologians disagree with the conclusion of their colleagues and oppose the notion that God is finite. Multiple critiques have been offered against such a notion. Brightman denied that God had a beginning or ending.[25] How could finitists know exactly where or how God is limited? If God needs a cause for His existence, then this position is seriously handicapped, for existence requires an eternal cause.

Other idealists have argued that, even as scientific methodology often tables discussions while solutions are researched and addressed, philosophical discussions should also keep searching for additional information.[26] Other critiques are often mentioned.[27]

Another approach to evil tends to be much more deterministic in nature, and is frequently associated with some of the more extreme forms of Calvinism. This view holds that God actually created both good and evil, and that He is therefore the direct cause of both. We will also address aspects of this view in the next chapter.[28]

Lastly, probably the most common theistic approach to evil is that, while God does not cause evil, He allows it in order to accomplish greater goods, or to thwart greater evils. Often, this good is related directly to the free will of created beings. There are different angles on this view, to be sure, and it is held quite widely by thinkers who hold different concepts of God.

We will argue this last position in the next chapter. Why does God allow any evil at all? Are there adequate reasons to explain the kind of suffering we see in the world? What about the large amounts of evil that do not seem to accomplish any purpose? We favor the view that God allows evil in order to achieve a greater good, or to prevent greater evil.

Chapter 5

WHY DOES GOD ALLOW SUFFERING?

Philosophers and theologians from a number of differing viewpoints often agree that evil and suffering can be justified if there is a legitimate reason for it to exist. The most common responses are that pain may either exist in order to promote a greater good or to curtail an even greater amount of evil. In this book, we discuss the sorts of greater good that suffering often produces. We mentioned three such general categories: the existence of free will, the need for natural law, and what is often called "soul making," or the ability of persons to grow in a way that they would not otherwise were it not for their suffering. Much of this book concerns this third subject.

Of course, both critics and believers alike often grow cynical when this topic is discussed, especially when we are the ones who are suffering! It often seems that, the closer the problem is to our own backyard, the more frayed our nerves become. In this dialogue, we are going to pursue the topic of free will. Some scholars deny that it even exists, but we will not discuss that angle here.

Plainly, evil and suffering really exist. It is even rather difficult to imagine the denial of the personal reality of pain. Most people concur, often due to their own experience. Especially when it arrives at our own doorsteps, believers and unbelievers alike often ask, "Why?" In times like those, it is helpful to see some purpose behind our troubles. Theists are not alone in being interested in the reason for its existence.[1]

Scholars respond differently to these topics, to be sure. We viewed some of the major options earlier, providing critiques of several. We need to look in more detail at some of the intricacies posed by these issues. Here we will discuss two species of evil, concentrating on some of the reasons why God may allow its presence.

It is customary to distinguish two major kinds of evil—moral and natural (also termed physical) evil.[2] Moral evil arises from the free choices of finite creatures. By way of example, it might be said to be characterized as the sort of suffering that results from persons opposing persons, whether intended or unintended. Moral evil includes such common atrocities as war and crime. On the other hand, natural evil may be identified as the opposition between nature and persons, and includes disasters like earthquakes, tsunamis, hurricanes, and floods.

While general distinctions like these may certainly be helpful, this does not guarantee that it will always be easy to untangle one sort of evil from another. For example, while birth defects may at first seem to be of natural origin, we now know that medicine taken freely by a pregnant mother can cause serious problems for the unborn. Similarly, a famine may create havoc of a natural or physical variety, but the neglect of the affected persons by their fellow human beings afterwards may make it a moral issue as well.

To be a human being is generally thought to entail some freedom of choice. Even those who deny freedom will virtually always act as if they are truly making their own choices, such as ordering a good steak dinner! (Isn't it strange that even those who deny their own freedom always seem to end up with tasty meals that they really like, even without any choice on their part?) Moral evil results from the actions of those whose freedom conflicts with that of others, even if it was not anticipated. But it would seem that creatures are not truly free unless they have the possibility to make evil choices as well as good ones. These choices are the source of moral evil.

The atheistic response is often to assert that God could have created persons differently. Were better options available to God? Could He have created in a different manner? A few alternatives have been proposed, but one option gets more attention than the others.[3] Naturalistic philosopher J.L. Mackie is among those who suggest that it is at least logically possible for God to create free moral creatures who still always make proper choices, never harming others in the process. Since God could have created in this way without any contradiction, but did not do so, He therefore failed to act consistently with his omnipotence and benevolence.[4]

In response, Alvin Plantinga questioned Mackie's premise that God would do whatever is logically possible. In fact, God may not be able to perform these scenarios. For example, could God create morally free creatures that could not choose evil? If God creates beings that are truly free, could God guarantee that they would not act wrongly? But if they do not have free will, then this is a worse creative route.[5]

On this theistic rejoinder, Mackie's scenario is not a plausible option. In fact, it is not even logically possible for God to act in this fashion. To create free creatures that cannot choose evil is to deny the very freedom that they supposedly possess; hence, we are faced with a contradiction here. In his book Faith and Reason Ronald Nash applauds Plantinga's response to Mackie, by concluding: "In other words God cannot guarantee that significantly free creatures will always do what is good without depriving them of their freedom."[6]

The bottom line is that, in order to guarantee that creatures can act and choose more freely, God allowed His creation to engage in evil acts when it causes pain to others. While many think that God should not have allowed this suffering, presumably few would give up their freedom in order to get rid of it, as we will see. It seems that we value our freedom even more than we dislike our pain!

Others charge that since God is responsible even for what He allows, the reality of evil still ought to be laid at His doorstep. But it is absolutely crucial here that we appreciate the distinction between an infinite God causing evil and His allowing it. What is the alternative? To create without free will? Is that a better option? Again, I doubt that the majority of people would think so, even if they were suffering.

Further, Christian theists have long argued that God does indeed step into the process on many occasions, both causing more good as well as curtailing particular evils. The chief example is in providing His Son's death and resurrection as a potential path to eternal life, even for these same lawbreakers.[7] And many believers think that God is still quite active in the world today, as well.[8]

The fact that God does not intervene most of the time does not make

Him negligent, for to step in often so as to prevent evil is effectively to keep people from participating in the consequences of their own actions. The end result is to curtail individual freedoms. Here is the dilemma in a nutshell: how does God eliminate perhaps millions of hurtful choices every day and, at the exact same time, still allow His creatures to exercise true freedom? Even an omnipotent and omniscient being cannot act contradictorily, but He could guarantee just the right balance.

Arguably, the free actions of created, finite beings account for the majority of the pain and suffering in our world. As philosopher Elton Trueblood charges, moral evil "is far more serious than natural evil and yet it is the more easily understood." While physical catastrophes obviously can be catastrophic, to be sure, "these are almost trivial in their effects when contrasted with the unmerited suffering which comes as a result of the actions of wicked men." Trueblood explains that mental or emotional torment is the worst sort of suffering and people cause far more torture and anguish than does nature.[9]

Natural Evil

What about natural evils that position us against the world in which we live? Very regularly, we learn of disasters that devastate many thousands of lives. Trueblood comments again: "Natural evil is far less important, in the modern world, than moral evil, but it is harder to explain."[10]

Natural evil is more difficult to answer, especially from a theistic prospective, largely because it appears to have been birthed in God's creation, and seems to be disconnected from free will. So many have asked why God created a world with so many obvious imperfections? Theists usually respond that evil can be explained by God allowing it in order to either achieve some greater good or to prevent some even greater evil. So what positive consequences might result from natural evil?

The replies to these tough questions will be arranged in three categories.[11] It should be noted carefully that some responses, especially from the initial rejoinder below, will also apply further to moral evil.

We have already argued that the freely-made choices of created, finite beings probably account for the majority of suffering in the world. Emotions such as pride, greed, anger, and hatred provide much of the motivation for the atrocious acts that encompass many of the world's wars and crimes. Still, incalculable suffering also results from seemingly small choices--hurts that so often are largely unmentioned. Even our words are often designed to produce subtle wounds in order to get our point across more forcefully, or to keep others where we prefer that they stay.

There is another entire dimension to this problem that is often ignored entirely, even in the theistic literature. Scripture explains that Adam and Eve violated God's command in the Garden of Eden, introducing human sin into the world (Genesis 3; Romans 5:12-14). God answered the disobedience with punishments. Although believers are more familiar with the moral consequences of these choices, physical pain was also a direct result and the earth was no longer the same place it had been before (Genesis 3:14-19).

But we also read that the Fall of humans was orchestrated by Satan, who had likewise made the choice to sin at an earlier time.[12] This act introduced both moral and natural evil, since Satan and his demons frequently choose to inflict much pain, including both natural disasters (Job 1:12-16, 18-19) as well as sickness (Mark 5:1-20; 2 Corinthians 12:7).

Geisler argues that even the majority of natural evil may be explained by the Fall of Satan and the demons.[13] Arguably the most influential philosopher on this issue, Plantinga argues that "the free actions of nonhuman persons" such as Satan and his allies could feasibly account for much of the world's suffering. And Plantinga emphasizes that if this response is even possible, then it still serves its purpose as a potential explanation.[14]

The biblical witness testifies that it is more than just human sin that introduced moral and other evils into the world. Satan and his demons also utilized their God-given freedom to violate the Creator's laws. To be sure, this may not be a very popular topic among many of the philosophers and theologians who discuss this subject.[15] But for those who hold that there are good reasons to accept the reliability of biblical testimony, this adds an entirely new dimension to the subject of the free will of finite beings.

So humans, Satan, and his fallen angels may all have played major roles in the quandary of the problem of evil. Yet, the gift of free will is actually a blessing in disguise. Apparently since this is what God seems to have done, He must have concluded that it was better to create creatures with freedom, in spite of the results, than not to give His creation that right. In other words, to modify slightly the old saying, God decided that it was better to love and to lose than never to have loved at all. We have said that, presumably, few would trade their right of free choice even for the pain in the world.

Natural Law

The second category of potentially good results comes from the existence of natural law in the universe, a necessary condition for the fulfillment of divine as well as human objectives. At least three aspects must be noted here.

First, we live in a world that generally behaves according to natural laws. Such laws are essential for free creatures to function normally. Regularity is also crucial even when we consider miracles as God's actions, since they are usually contrasted with the normal order of nature.

But problems are immediately apparent. The same sun that is necessary for life on the earth can also burn. Likewise, while fire warms, it also consumes and kills. Water is absolutely indispensable to existence as we know it, but even relatively small amounts can also destroy life. Gravity is also necessary and usually taken for granted, but tensions in the earth's crust can cause untold devastation and destruction. It is also crucial to point out that pain serves us as a warning for worse problems, but it obviously hurts even as it also helps. Brian Hebblethwaite summarizes:

> *"There may well be logically necessary conditions which make it impossible to create an ordered physical universe containing organic creatures without the possibility of accident and pain. This line of argument can be reinforced by our increased scientific knowledge of the laws of nature . . . ."*[16]

If Hebblethwaite's assessment is correct, then an ordered physical world requires the possibility of pain and suffering. He then states even more forcefully, "God can no more create a balance of nature without the death of individuals than he can create a square circle."[17]

A naturalist may ask whether God could have created some other kind of world, with different laws, where evil would not result, at least in the same manner. But major problems emerge with such suggestions. Initially, such a proposal would probably have to invoke huge changes to the natural system. It is not even clear how such an enterprise could arrive at the desired goal. While isolated suggestions about this or that tweak might be helpful, the entire universe would have to be adjusted. It is doubtful that human beings could even conceive of the necessary amount and type of transformation that must be accomplished.

Additionally, the naturalist needs to proceed beyond the initial formulation to show how such an alternative world would actually increase the resulting balance of good versus evil. To whisk away potential suffering (or at least large portions of it) would not even be the highest goal if such would also curtail significantly the quality of life. Removing suffering may also remove the potential for growth as persons (see below) in a manner that is not a fair compensation.

Not surprisingly, no one has yet shown adequately how another world would have produced at least as much or more good and significantly less evil at the same time. If it is the case that a finite mind could not even comprehend the requirements for such an enterprise, it would seem that this makes the naturalist's challenge highly suspect, if not just plain impossible to prove.[18]

Should God intervene more frequently, perhaps by thwarting the evil even before it occurs? Should tsunamis and earthquakes be stopped immediately, or the weather changed before tornadoes ever form? (Over on the moral side, should bombs not detonate and knife blades simply turn to rubber?) This would require a massive number of miraculous interventions– enough that the natural world and its affects would be substantially altered. Irregularities in nature could actually become the norm. Further, it is still not at all clear that such scenarios would be sufficient to increase the long-term good in the world, as we will point out below.

Second, the greatest good result here may well arise if we are correct above about the affects of free choices even in the realm of natural law. The perspective of Scripture is that Satan and his demons are capable of perpetrating much suffering, including natural disasters. Many philosophers oppose such accounts, but Plantinga reminds us that even if this is a possible position, it maintains its force.[19] For God to curtail these choices would actually be to prevent regularly the normal consequences of free actions. We have said, too, that free will depends on a steady natural order. Once again, these limitations, especially on such a grand scale, would essentially return us to the problems that we noted earlier. The importance of this point, as Plantinga states, is that "natural evil significantly resembles moral evil in that, like the latter, it is the result of the activity of significantly free persons."[20]

Another component already introduced above might be mentioned relative to a natural law theodicy. Scripture teaches that the satanic and demonic Fall led to the human Fall. Besides the better known moral repercussions of sin, physical pain also resulted (Genesis 3:14) and the earth was changed (3:17-19). So there is theoretically a possible connection between these rebellions and the natural evil in the world.

Much later, the condition of life on the earth is described as having grown wicked, evil, corrupt, and filled with violence. So God judged the earth with the flood (Genesis 6:5-13). Depending on one's view then, the Fall and the flood would definitely have caused additional, far-reaching changes in the natural order.

Some frustrated folks, including believers who plead with God to answer all of their prayers, might counter that at least God could act once in a while in order to help them. But we have said that many Christian theists agree, to the point of maintaining that this is exactly what God does on certain occasions. Hebblethwaite adds that if this world was the only possible (or even the best) way for God to create finite beings, then these theistic responses are capable of explaining much. Once again, we are close here to the free will defense. Just as true creaturely freedom allows for the possibility and reality of bad choices, "so does finite free personal being require an ordered yet flexible environment . . . ."[21]

Third, naturalists should understand that they have to do more than simply object a biblical worldview. They must also disprove these theistic solutions to the problem of evil and suffering. Further, naturalists cannot simply assume the existence of the laws of nature without explaining them. For if the natural world is all there is, on what grounds do they even account for the very existence of these laws? As prominent philosopher and former atheist Antony Flew argued, the very existence of the laws in nature is a huge detriment to naturalism, which has no explanation for them in a chance universe. This alone favors the theistic option.[22]

In sum, biblical theism contends not only that the world was created with the natural laws intact, but that it was created without sin. As we have argued, the laws themselves can cause pain and suffering on their own. Further, the exercise of free will, both by angels as well as by humans, could have affected not only the cause of moral evil, but even played a pivotal role in producing natural evil, as well, including altering the physical structure of the world itself. Thus, free will can also lead to the suffering that ensues from natural disasters. Even as a possible response, this last point has much explanatory capability. Lastly, the naturalist needs to explain the laws of nature, rather than simply and automatically assuming their existence as natural phenomena in a chance universe, which seems quite unlikely. This appears to push us in the direction of theism from the outset.

Soul Making

Besides free will and natural law, a third general category of good results that are derived from the presence of evil in the world is the fact that human growth often occurs only from working through painful situations. Many have testified that working through painful situations is one of the best ways for us to increase in virtue. Moreover, such growth is the foremost way to prepare for eternal fellowship with God.

This "soul-making" position is perhaps most associated with philosopher John Hick's "Irenaean theodicy." The emphasis here is that God loves us enough to allow us to live life where "there are obstacles to be overcome, tasks to be performed, goals to be achieved, setbacks to be endured, problems to be resolved, dangers to be met... In this sense, life's challenges help to develop our characters."[23]

Hick's concept of soul-making is not the only way to configure these concepts.[24] Biblical insights teach some of the same truths, among other similar ideas. For examples, faith is refined in the fires of suffering (1 Pet. 1:6-7; 5:7-10). Pain can serve as a moral warning (1 Corinthians 11:27-32; 2 Corinthians 12:7-10), although such is not always its primary purpose. Personal suffering assists us in knowing how best to comfort others during their times of pain (2 Corinthians 1:3-7).

One of the most satisfying aspects is that, for the believer, earthly suffering may be rewarded. Pain and suffering are reconciled in the future state. Paul even encourages us to shift our thinking from our suffering to concentrating on its benefits in eternity (2 Corinthians 4:7-18; Romans 8:18). Peter gives a related encouragement: the resurrection of Jesus secures our heavenly blessings, which brings us profound joy even when we suffer for our faith (1 Peter 1:3-6). The author of Hebrews proclaims that this outlook characterized believers down through history (11:16, 32-40). The belief in eternal life for the Christian is an evidenced hope, as well. In the New Testament, this hope is connected firmly with Jesus' time-space resurrection, which is also central in some of the passages on suffering.[25]

One thoughtful objection to the soul-making defense is that evil often does not have this sort of positive outcome, but often overwhelms persons who are caught in its clutches. Individuals often respond poorly, or sometimes die without a chance to grow. And it is true that pain and evil often fail to provoke this spiritual sort of reaction. However, our three major categories are certainly compatible with one another and are not meant to be isolated. It is surely not being claimed that each one can (or should) stand alone. Insights from all three kinds of good should be combined. As a result, free will and natural law would also have to be considered in these cases (i.e., wrecked lives often result from the free choices either of the individual or of others).[26]

Moreover, combinations of causes can also come into play. For instance, another sort of free choice--our responses to our circumstances—can also produce perhaps even the majority of our personal pain. In other words, suffering very often stems not from what happens to us, but from how we react to these things and "download" them into our own lives.[27] This can provide an entirely different angle on the source of our suffering. As such, a circumstance that had the potential for soul-making could actually have been rerouted by the person to a very different and self-destructive end.

So we must be reminded, as we have indicated throughout, that real freedom does presuppose bad choices. Without this reality, individuals are not truly free. Unsatisfactory decisions and other problems can certainly lead to failure, defeat, and loss. The worst result of all is eternal separation from God.[28]

Chapter 6

GRATUITOUS EVIL: IS SUFFERING PURPOSEFUL?

A common and often repeated objection against suffering is that large amounts of senseless, gratuitous evil are far out of balance with any good that could possibly be attained through it. This can also be a thoughtful rejoinder. We will devote an entire section to this difficult question.

Atheists and some theists agree that there ought not be any purposeless suffering, or incidents where the type or amount exceeds what is absolutely necessary. This position seems rather common-sensical to some. But quite intriguingly, other theists have no problem with God allowing excessive amounts of suffering--what is often termed gratuitous evil.

Geisler states that "only a theistic God can guarantee man that unnecessary evil will not occur." He then makes a crucial distinction: "That the total amount of evil that does occur be no more than is necessary to the achievement of the overall plan to obtain the greatest good possible."[1]

A key in the discussion here is the emphasis on the sum total of evil, since we are not talking about an immediate knowledge of probable causes or a one-for-one reckoning. Geisler explains several additional points, (1) "No finite mind is in a position to press this point" regarding either the large quantities or types of evil and suffering. (2) Philosophical, historical, and experiential evidences for a Christian theistic world-view make it likely "that the right amount of evil is being allowed to accomplish the greatest good." (3) "The theodicy suggested here does not require weighing exact amounts of evil or measuring the degree of distribution . . . ." (4) Theism only needs to argue that there is more good than evil, not that the "most" good has resulted.[2]

Those who opt for a position against the presence of gratuitous evil often defend the related concept that God carefully controls everything so that no more evils are permitted than are absolutely necessary. According to this position, sometimes called the doctrine of meticulous providence, no single evil is ever meaningless.[3] In brief, God would never allow even a slight increase of evil than that which translates to actual goods.

In contrast, a growing number of theists seem to hold that it is unnecessary to require such a position. Given the foregoing discussion, it makes sense that God may have allowed created beings to make free choices to the extent that even great amounts of seemingly meaningless suffering does in fact happen. Both views have in common that large amounts of evil in the world are quite real, and both agree that there are good reasons why that is the case. But Nash makes the additional distinction that those who allow gratuitous suffering think that specific instances of evil may not have specific corresponding reasons, yet God would still have good reasons for the overall system.[4]

From the angle of the free will of created beings, since God seems to allow much evil for the sake of freedom, then would it not follow that creatures

Satan and death were defeated at the Cross and Resurrection of Jesus Christ

may well overstep their boundaries quite regularly, even greatly so? Many alternative options, in contrast to theism, tend to limit or even to deny human freedom. Does the notion of meticulous providence also limit human freedom? If only justified evil is allowed, and no more, does this not limit the range of our choices? Would Hitler, Stalin, and Pol Pot still have perpetrated their atrocities? For God to intervene and forcefully halt all gratuitous evil actions would then terminate a profound number of free choices. Therefore, between Christian theistic options, these considerations seem to argue in favor of gratuitous evil.[5]

But we must not forget that orthodox Christianity has long asserted that God has acted in order to limit the range of evil. God's intervention in the Incarnation is the chief example here. Satan and death were defeated at the Cross and Resurrection of Jesus Christ. The future will witness God's final victory and the ushering in of eternity. Do these considerations indicate the truth of meticulous providence? Only if it is concluded that all specific gratuitous evils can be explained, if there is no remainder of suffering. Otherwise, we are left with the notions of periodic divine interventions for which only God knows the ultimate reasons, followed by an eternity that puts wrongs to right for those who have responded to God.[6]

Regarding natural law and nature's disasters, defenders of meticulous providence would seem to contend that God intervenes often in order to nullify the worst evils. We have said that this limits the free decisions that may cause these events in the first place. Moreover, if a natural law approach makes sense, then "it is difficult to see why the same laws of nature will not also produce instances of gratuitous natural evil."[7] In other words, if both goods and evils result from necessary natural laws, why must the process be stopped at certain points? Lastly, the free will of Satan and his demons would have a direct impact on the multiplicity of natural disasters and diseases, as we find in Scripture, too.

The question of gratuitous evil is also correlated with soul-making. In spite of the amounts of evil and calamity in the world, many persons have grown through their experiences. This is not to assume that suffering always justifies the growth, for on the view that we are considering, some evil may have no such specific justification. But the point is that even gratuitous suffering could still produce much spiritual maturation.

A Dialogue on the Problem of Suffering

In order to make the theoretical practical, we are going to present the idea that free will is a benefit that offsets much of our suffering in a dialogue. Imagine two friends who hold differing views on the problem of suffering sitting down over a cup of coffee. Each has considered the problem from a philosophical perspective. We will begin the dialogue with the one who cannot accept the problem of pain as legitimate.

> "Religious folks so often try to explain how pain, evil, and suffering can all be explained by the wonderful benefits of life in this world, or by suggesting that God could be curtailing even worse evils in the process. But sorry--I just don't see it. Granted,

there are a lot of wonderful things in life. But are you trying to tell me there are enough positive benefits to offset all the suffering everywhere in the world?"

"I certainly realize that what we might call existential suffering can seem to be exceptionally difficult to bear, especially when we or our loved ones are the ones experiencing it. And I know, too, that both of our families have really been hurting in recent years."

"You're right; I know you understand. And I know that our family has really been 'up against it,' as they say. I've tried to give God a fair chance, I really have, but I just see the problem of suffering as too overwhelming."

"Okay, you and I have had many discussions over the years about the nature and existence of free will. And I know that you value it, just like I do. I've been thinking further about this subject recently. I propose that we see what happens if we pursue just this one area of what we might refer to as some of the 'blessings' in our lives that may just offset suffering. How does that sound?"

"You know I'm game. I always enjoy a good discussion, and I think we have both benefited from these times in the past."

"Agreed. All right, what do you include when you think of the benefits of free will?"

"What do I think about my own free will (smiling)? I consider the following everyday choices to be excellent things: the times I've been able to order a nice, juicy, medium rare steak instead of fried liver, to watch my favorite football team rather than watching yours, or, back in my teenage days, being able to make my own decisions about whom I wanted (and didn't want) to marry! How's that for a start?"

"Again we agree, except that I'll take barbecued spare ribs, my football team, and my dating choices back in the day!"

"Of course, there are also more theoretical choices such as whether or not to believe in God, or which political candidate to support. Sorry, let's not digress to politics again!"

"Fair enough. Let's think about some of our other choices. Do we also agree that free will likewise accounts for perhaps most of the suffering in the world—such as crime and wars? I'm thinking here of robberies, rape, drunken-driving, as well as wars and nonstop killing over what most rational people would judge to be small, nonsensical, often rather picky, problems?"

"Certainly, though I'd have to think about whether it accounts for most of the world's suffering. But it is at least a huge piece of the pie. Now it's my turn to agree. We are very close on these things."

"But we wouldn't want our free will stripped from us, would we?"

"Certainly not. Why should I miss my steak because somebody else cannot control their drinking?"

"Exactly. Then let's pose this question: would you trade all of your personal suffering in the world if, in the process, you would automatically lose all of your free will?

"Let's see if I have this right. You ask if I would get rid of all of my suffering if I also lost all of my free choices in the process?"

"Yes, and let's make it even more appealing: by all of your suffering, I'll include both mental and emotional as well as physical anguish. What do you say—wanna make the trade for your free will?"

"Very good question. I really don't know. I'd definitely want to get rid of all that suffering—especially with what has happened in our family lately. But that means perhaps that, when I go to order steak, no matter how much I hate it, I hear the words 'liver, please' come out of my own mouth! And I cannot change my order!"

"Yes, and instead of any football game, your TV only has a 'chick flick' on every single channel, 24/7!"

"Ugh! I'd rather cut the lawn! More seriously, I would have had no say in whom I marry, how many children we may (or may not) have, or if I am to be religious or have any political interests whatsoever."

"Yep, these are the sort of issues I had in mind. At least at this time, would you make the trade across the board? Right now? Or would you continue to take the suffering as long as you had all of your free choices?"

"You know, I think you got me here—at least for this moment. I want to think about this, to be sure. But right off the bat, I just cannot see myself making the 'free choice' to end all of my free choices!"

"So free will is a very positive good, even though it regularly leads to heinous evils?"

"Yes, surely. I think that's undeniable."

"And note that free will is not the sort of good that only religious folks can somehow appreciate. We might call it a 'natural good.'"

"Fair enough—I appreciate it, too."

"Okay, then I only have one more question. If free will is a positive that you, at least at this present time, would not trade for all your suffering, couldn't God have made that same decision when He created everything? Thus, couldn't He have decided that giving us free will is one of the greatest gifts that He could ever impart to us, knowing that, in the process, a lot of evil would still result?"

"I suppose. But I'm definitely going to have to think about all this."

Actually, something very much like this same scenario happened to me (Gary) during a philosophical dialogue with a skeptical unbeliever. Only we had an audience of exactly 50 people who, after considering the issue, indicated that they were ready to cast their vote on the same question that came up in the dialogue above: would you get rid of all your suffering if, in the process, you also lost all of your free will? In spite of the fact that most of those present were non-Christians, when the hands were counted, 48 of the 50 voted to keep both their free will as well as their suffering! Of the two exceptions, only one voted to get rid of both, while the other, a physicist with a Ph.D., couldn't make up his mind and kept putting his hand up and then down again!

For me, this had been an incredibly useful exercise. We were considering what we might call a "natural good" one that benefits both the religious and the non-religious alike. Yet, virtually no one, even among a group of predominately non-believers, would trade their free will for their suffering. God could have made that same choice.

SECTION 2

Can anything good come out of this?

CHAPTER 7: Refinement By Fire: Drawing Nearer to God Through Trials
CHAPTER 8: A Tough Mantenance Check: Recentering your Faith
CHAPTER 9: Collateral Impact: Suffering and the Church

Can Anything Good Come Out of This?

Diego had always been a good kid. His talent and self-assurance had impressed adults and peers alike. All of his pursuits had been aggressive and had met with success. Though a high school sophomore, his appearance and carriage gave the impression that he was older and more mature than his years. His youthful immaturity, however, was what got him into trouble. Like all teenagers, when Diego got his driver's license, he was anxious to test his independence. During a study date with a group of friends, Diego and Allison slipped off to have some time alone. The privacy of the dark car lent an air of romance and mystery to their actions as they engaged in sexual activity. Diego's world turned upside down the next day when a police detective informed him that Allison had accused him of rape. His secret flirtation with being grown-up was now a very public threat to his adult future.

Whether suffering comes as the result of our own choices or are an outcome of living in a fallen and broken world, it may seem to bring with it the death of hope. A well-intentioned quoting of Romans 8:28 (And we know that in all things God works for the good of those who love him, who have been called according to his purpose. NIV) may seem like a slap in the face. How could God possibly use this awful thing for anyone's good?

Chapter 7

REFINEMENT BY FIRE: DRAWING NEARER TO GOD
THROUGH TRIALS

Soul Sculpting

Lisa was 44 years old when she came to counseling. As a Christian, Lisa did not consider herself as someone who would ever need counseling. "Counseling is fine for others," she reported in her first appointment, "I just thought I was above ever needing it." The fact that Lisa believed she would never need counseling stood in stark contrast to the fact that her life had been anything but uneventful. Lisa grew up in a profoundly dysfunctional family. Her father, a mean alcoholic abused her physically and sexually throughout her childhood. Her parents divorced when she was eight, after her father's affair with the wife of another couple became evident. In response to learning of her husband's affair, Lisa's mother began a relationship with the mistress' husband.

Out of that background, Lisa somehow emerged fairly functional. She was an exceptional student; even finishing college in three years. In spite of her academic prowess, Lisa failed in her relationships with men. She seemed to pick narcissistic men who dominated and controlled her. Toward the end of college, Lisa came to know Christ as her Savior. For the first time in her life she had engaged in a relationship with a healthy "man," Christ. Lisa dove headfirst into her new faith. She started reading the Bible daily, took a Bible correspondence course, and invested her time in many church activities.

At her first job, Lisa met and married her husband, Glenn, to whom she had been married for 20 years at the time of her first counseling appointment. Although Lisa stated that she and her husband had a good Christian marriage, she was quick to mention that it had never been an affectionate one. Both she and her husband were active in church and continued to do so even with each addition to their family. It was those additions that became the most important part of their world: Kenny (15), Karen (12), and Katie (6). She and Glenn built their lives around their children. The family would spend many weekends camping at a nearby state park. Every three years the family made a journey to Disney World, where they would camp and spend time making memories with their children. Lisa stated that given the dysfunction of her own family life, her married family was "remarkably sane." Little did anyone in the family know that the saneness of her family was about to disappear forever.

About four years ago, their family was sent into upheaval when Katie failed to return home from school. To condense a long story, Katie had been abducted without ransom or word. About one year later, her body was discovered in a wooded area just outside of the city limits. Since Katie's abduction, the marriage had grown distant and cold. A family that once spent every free moment together now lived separate lives. Lisa reported that she was unable to function; along with the loss of her daughter she had lost her family and her faith. God seemed cruel. Lisa didn't give up her faith, but it seemed nothing more than "mindless rituals and practices." Lisa was lost emotionally, mentally, and most importantly spiritually. Her heart had become hard and unapproachable to a God who sought to give her comfort.

Fortunately, Lisa responded well to counseling. She worked hard at expressing her feelings in authentic ways, grieving the loss of her daughter, and rebuilding the family relationships. Over the four years of counseling, Lisa came to believe that God hoped to deepen her Christian walk through the loss of Katie. "I had a good relationship with God, but it never was really close. I think I kept God at a distance because I didn't know how to do intimacy and I didn't know how to strength my faith." Lisa stated that people at their church say that she seems to be the most well-balanced person in the church. She demonstrates a joy in her Christian walk and seemed like somehow who was just so comfortable in her own skin.

Sometimes the soul-sculpting of suffering comes in the form of refining our lives. As suffering works on us, we either become more like Christ or further from Him. In this chapter we will examine how suffering can enhance and enrich our faith. Our ultimate goal is to be like Christ, an objective that even the most formidable Christians also fall far short of reaching. Yet, suffering is a tool by which God can move us in that direction.

One cold day a hiker happened upon a logging site while walking the rough terrain and taking in the massive forest in the mountains of Oregon. As he made his way toward a river, he observed a lumberjack jabbing a sharp hook into logs that floated down the mountain stream. Some logs he let pass, others he hooked and separated into a different area. The hiker, perhaps curious or lonely for conversation, decided to inquire about the logger's work. Without taking his eyes from the floating logs, the man replied, "These may all look alike to you, but I can recognize that a few of them are quite different. The ones I let pass are from trees that grew in a valley, protected from the storms. Their grain is rather coarse. The ones I have hooked came from high in the mountains. From the time they were small, they were beaten by strong winds. This toughens the trees and gives them a fine grain. We save them for choice work because they are too good to be used for ordinary lumber."[1] Just as the wind and storms toughen trees to make fine lumber, suffering works to toughen us, thereby refining the quality and grain of our lives.

The book of 1 Peter was written to Jewish believers who were facing merciless persecution. The disciple of Christ wrote: "In all this you greatly rejoice, though now for a little while you may have had to suffer grief in all kinds of trials. These have come so that the proven genuineness of your faith—of greater worth than gold, which perishes even though refined by fire—may result in praise, glory and honor when Jesus Christ is revealed."(1 Peter 1:6-7; NIV)

One can only imagine their thoughts as they reminisced about what life had been like when they were practicing Jews. At one time they had been under Roman rule, but there was no persecution from their own people. Now, although Rome still ruled, they were experiencing cruel persecution from fellow Jews: slander, suspicion, violence, and hatred. They had no idea who could turn on them, fear was a significant element. If Jesus Christ was truly who He said He was, it seems inconceivable that He would sanction His followers to experience such appalling persecution.

Their response to suffering was probably not any different from ours today. As Americans we cannot comprehend persecution, but Christians in other countries can readily identify with these early believers.

Rather than responding to their suffering with despair and disillusionment, or even promising that it would end soon, Peter tried to encourage his readers to develop a proper response to suffering. To help them come to grips with their experiences, he attempted to foster a divine perspective on their suffering. He told them to rejoice because adversity tests the genuineness of faith. Peter's attitude was one of joy because he knew that Jesus' resurrection secured heaven for believers.[2] In other words, the Resurrection provides the foundation for our ability to cope with trials. Peter added that this heavenly hope cannot be taken from us or otherwise lessened.

As a student at Liberty University in Lynchburg, Virginia, I often heard Pastor Jerry Falwell say that a human's wealth or education does not determine his greatness; rather, a human's greatness is determined by how much it takes to discourage him or her.

Likewise, the apostle Paul knew the inward faith-building benefits of trials. Having endured tremendous suffering while serving the Lord, Paul realized that the end result of pain would be soul-making perseverance.[3]

A Life of Faith

God also allows suffering and testing to purify and increase our faith. Although Christians toss around the word faith with great frequency, many would be hard-pressed to define it. In essence, faith is a commitment to abandon all reliance on our own efforts. It is a complete trust and dependence on God that assumes He will be true to His word. Faith involves appropriating the promises of God with unwavering assurance. It is not so much the absence of doubt as it is experiencing uncertainty in such a way that we come to know and depend on God more deeply. Therefore, the process of increasing our faith is often contrary to what seems right, just, and purposeful. Corrie ten Boom said, "Faith brings us on highways that make our reasoning dizzy."[4]

In describing the accident that caused her to become a quadriplegic, Joni Eareckson Tada reported that she believed her injury was God's way of refining her faith so that it would not be based on her emotions but rather on God's character and nature.[5]

We also see this in the Book of Matthew in the Bible when Jesus and His disciples were crossing the Sea of Galilee and a great storm occurred.

The disciples, many of whom were experienced fishermen, quickly began to fret and despair. Panicked, they woke Jesus, who dusted the sleep from His eyes while they clamored to Him about the storm. In response, Jesus simply rose to His feet, stretched out His soon-to-be pierced hands, and calmed the storm. The bewildered disciples were speechless, but Jesus had something to say. Rather than simply returning to His nap, Jesus rebuked them for their lack of faith.[6] How I wish I could have seen the faces of the disciples at that point. Admittedly, my face would not have been any different. They were astonished by this Man's ability to eradicate a storm with His words. In spite of seeing Him do amazing things before, they lacked confidence in Him. Every difficulty seemed to shake the disciples faith.

The Blessing of Trials on Faith

The storms of this world tend to drench our minds and our spirits. The trials and tragedies we experience reveal our true "god," and crises have a way of exposing who or what we depend upon for life. A well-known adage says it well: "There are no atheists in foxholes." Certainly, in the midst of life's storms, we should cry out to God. But God expects His followers to trust Him, to have confidence in His will and plan for their lives, even in the storms. Failure to trust God in the alarming moments of life is evidence of a weak faith.

Sometimes God deals with self-reliant thinking by challenging it with something that requires us to rely on Him. Mac Cauley, a minister of a small, church, learned this when his world was turned upside down in a matter of seconds.[7] On a dark, and rainy evening, he and his family approached a red light on their drive home from the store. Before his vehicle came to a complete stop, the light turned green and Mac accelerated to the posted speed limit. Suddenly, he saw the face of a man directly in front of his car. Before he could react, the vehicle struck the man, throwing him against the windshield and then fifty feet through the air. After stopping and running to the man's side, Mac realized that the man was dead. Shocked and numb, he returned to his family. As a minister, he had worked to preserve life. Now he had killed a man. He knew that the accident had been unavoidable. But facts failed to remove the stark reality that this man was dead. The next hours, days, and months were difficult. At times,

Mac felt so desperate that he truly did not want to breathe another breath.

Eventually, the victim's family asked Mac to speak by telephone with the bereaved father. The conversation went well. The family held no contempt for him and had no desire to sue. But talking with the father made the young man he'd struck even more real. No longer was he simply a stranger, but a person with a history and a family who loved him. Once again, Mac found himself in the depths of another depression.

Throughout the ordeal, however, Mac never doubted the sovereignty of God. He knew that God was all-powerful. He knew that God had allowed this accident for some unknown reason. He tenaciously clung to the promise in Romans 8:28, that God could redeem suffering. And today he believes that his adversity strengthened his dependency on Christ. Mac does not believe God wanted him to kill the man, but he sees the ways that God used that tragedy. He had lived his life pursuing the will of God, but his suffering made him even more reliant on Christ.

Faith comes as the result of hearing God's Word.[8] Our faith is further shaped by our own experiences and by observing God at work in the lives of others. The Bible gives countless examples of faith, including Hebrews 11, which is a record of normal, everyday people who trusted God. Even though on occasion many of these people failed to believe God, their lives were characterized by faith rather than doubt. God counted them as men and women of faith because of their obedience. They were faithful, though they were tortured, mocked, scourged, imprisoned, dismembered, and forced to live as outcasts.[9] Their faith was evident as they trusted God to reward them for their endurance of hardships.

I will never forget the night my phone rang and I picked it up to hear my friend Ken's voice. I knew instantly that something was seriously wrong. Ken explained that his wife and two of their three children had just been diagnosed with a disease, one of the best-known killers in America. There was no cure. What were they to do? Having served his church well over the years, this Texas pastor calmly asked me why God would allow this to happen to his wife and children.

Over the course of the next several weeks, it became obvious that other issues were involved as well. On top of the horrible physical problems, Ken's wife was reacting against the Lord and no longer wanted to participate in their ministry.

This emotional element exacted an even heavier toll, adding to their already heavy burdens.

We continued to talk regularly, and as we did, Ken began to understand that there was a marked difference between what had happened to them and how they had processed that information. While there was no cure for the disease, the worst pain was being caused by the emotional aftermath. Quietly but forcefully, I pointed out to Ken a number of biblical truths. God had not broken His promises to them. Moreover, other believers had suffered even worse. After all, did Jesus' loving Father remove Him from the cross during His horrendous, prolonged torture? And isn't Jesus our example? Throughout the ages, Christians have grown in the process of such sufferings. Further, a wonderful eternity, full of heavenly rewards, awaits faithful believers.

As they began repeatedly reminding themselves and each other about these truths, Ken's family began to experience real change very quickly. Not only did they grow spiritually, but they also began to acquire information on how to cope with the dreaded disease. Today, they continue to minister together with peace of mind. While they cannot substantially change the physical sickness, they knew how not to heap emotional hurt onto the situation.

You might ask why faith needs to grow and why it is so important that God would allow His children to experience perilous circumstances in order to purify their faith. We will not deepen our trust in God unless we are forced to do so. No prudent person would choose suffering in order to become a person of faith. Yet God knows that faith is important because it gives us a greater perspective on life and eternity. God desires His children to have a genuine and purified faith, a belief that God is good no matter what we experience. Faith allows us to enjoy God's riches in spite of our pain or turmoil, to have a calm assurance and joy, and to know that God has everything under control.

Depending on the Provider, Not the Provision

The Prophet Elijah's ministry offers an intriguing story of the way God's provisions always point us back to the Provider. Perhaps Elijah is the Old Testament's best example of boldness. Before God used him to mightily defeat the prophets of Baal, He prepared Elijah by showing him His own sovereignty and character. Prior to telling Elijah of the coming drought, God miraculously sent him food delivered by ravens as Elijah hid near the Brook Cherith. Then the provisions stopped and the brook dried up. Imagine Elijah's confusion. But his training was not finished.[10]

God told Elijah to go to the home of a widow who would provide for him. Now Elijah must have been really confused. Widows were usually unable to care for themselves, let alone a stranger. Though God's plan seemed irrational, Elijah decided to obey Him and went to the widow's home. When he arrived, he discovered a woman whose outlook was as bleak as her financial state. The widow's savings and her hope had long expired. Her cupboards were bare. The only thing that she had left was one meal's worth of flour and a few drops of oil. Seemingly unmoved by her meager means, Elijah requested dinner. Although the widow had received instructions from God to feed His prophet, she wearily confessed that the handful of food she could barely provide her and her son with a final meal before they died of starvation. By human standards it would seem that this widow had a right to feel discouraged; after all, she had nothing left. The prophet told the anxious widow that God would make the bin of flour and jar of oil last until the drought ended, but first she must demonstrate her trust by providing dinner for him. Elijah was not insensitive to her plight, but he had learned that provision comes from the Lord. The widow took a step of faith and did as Elijah instructed. True to God's Word, the flour and oil jar were never empty. God multiplied the provisions because the widow had placed her faith in the Lord. Imagine the widow telling her son to gather all their old jugs to hold the blessings of God. Her former hopelessness had been rooted in the belief that her situation was hopeless. She had focused on what she did not have, rather than on what she did have.

Through His provision, God taught Elijah and the widow that in His hands little is much. The widow and her son may never have come to trust God's ability to meet life's darkest circumstances unless they had been on the brink of death. It is through our difficulties that we come to understand God's presence and power over despair.

Later, God allowed Elijah to raise the widow's son from the dead. This depressed and discouraged woman learned that even when we think all hope is gone, God continues to demonstrate His faithfulness. And the prophet Elijah was once again reminded of God's power to control substance, sustenance, and the inevitability of death.

Understanding God's power and character, the prophet was then prepared to take on King Ahab and his wife, Jezebel. He challenged the prophets of Baal to a contest on Mount Carmel, mocked them continually, and then, to win the contest, called down fire from heaven. With the victory in hand, he led an immediate attack on the so-called prophets in which they were all killed.

Queen Jezebel did not take kindly to her priests and prophets being killed and promised to do the same to Elijah. Though God had provided miraculously for him in the past, the evil queen's words were more than he could handle, and he was filled with terror. Afraid for his life, downcast and in despair, Elijah fled into the wilderness where the God who had proven that He is the miracle provider met Elijah. Once again God provided for Elijah's needs, even in this situation, continuing to teach Elijah about His character.[11]

It's easy to criticize Elijah until we realize that we are just like him. It is easier to depend upon our own resources rather than on the One who provides everything. Most of us rely upon what God does for us rather than upon God Himself. We judge His character, especially His goodness, by the things that He gives us. But only indulgent parents give gifts in hopes of being seen as a good parent. Wise parents know that indulgence produces indulgent children.

God, the perfect parent, knows that we need to trust Him, not His answers or provisions. When we become focused upon the things that God has given us, He may choose to remove those distractions so that we can see Him more clearly and redirect our attachment from the things of this world to God Himself. Although God may provide a brook of comfort, He may also allow it to dry up to see whether we depend upon the brook or upon Him.

Suffering reveals the insufficiency of our own resources. The apostle Paul saw that suffering kept him from trusting in himself.[12] His tendency had been to depend on his own resources, but suffering changed that. Affliction forces us to rethink the direction of our lives and to consider our priorities, values, dreams, pleasures, and what we depend upon for strength. Suffering redirects our attention to spiritual realities rather than earthly realities.

If you saw a picture of me, you would never know that I've been a long-term member of the YMCA. Though I'm not as faithful to working out as I should, I use the cardiovascular machines for my heart and weight machines for strength training. When you are overweight and not very muscular, it is quite intimidating to work out with members who look like a young Arnold Schwarzenegger. Over time, I've come to know some of these muscle-bound behemoths fairly well. Recently I asked one of them what I needed to do to improve my overall fitness. He told me that many people use the weight machines incorrectly, and that if I wanted to build muscle I needed to do multiple sets and sufficient repetitions so that the last several repetitions required significant strain. Well so far, this sounded fun so I asked him to continue. He told me that in order to increase muscle size, I first must break the muscle down and then build it up. "No pain, no gain," he told me.

God often uses suffering in the same way. In order to build His strength into us, He must first tear down our natural strength. Of course, this runs contrary to our natural philosophy of "No pain, more sane!" We wish to do the minimum amount of repetitions and sets possible, but God desires us to be spiritually fit.

My muscles' response to the prescribed torture was to become bigger and stronger. A similar process is what James, Jesus' half-brother, meant when he encouraged the persecuted Christians who were scattered throughout various regions:

> *"My brethren, count it all joy when you fall into various trials,*
> *knowing that the testing of your faith produces patience. But let patience*
> *have its perfect work, that you may be perfect and complete, lacking*
> *nothing." James 1:2-4*

No matter how much internal resolve we might muster, facing James's blunt challenge seems implausible. Harvesting the benefits of suffering is daunting enough without trying to find joy in it as well.

Several keys words in the Greek can help us better understand suffering. The word know (ginōskō) refers to experiential knowledge. James told his persecuted friends that in the midst of troubles there is something they could know with certainty. Most of us are so baffled by suffering, particularly what appears to be unjustified suffering, that we struggle to know what we believe anymore. But James assured his readers that they could have absolute confidence in the fact that patience always results from tested faith. The word patience originates from the word endure (hupomenō), which means the ability to live underneath something. In times of adversity, God typically doesn't deliver us from the problem. Instead, in order for us to experience His grace and strength, sometimes we must remain under a problem so that patience can make us perfect. The word perfect does not mean faultless; it means complete and fully mature.

Consider Jesus, who suffered in order to enter the fulfillment of His maturity and mission and learn obedience.[13] The following words of Scripture are amazing in relaying this truth:

> "Although he [Jesus Christ] was a son, he learned obedience from what he suffered and, once made perfect, he became the source of eternal salvation for all who obey him and was designated by God to be high priest in the order of Melchizedek." Hebrews 5:8-10, NIV

The word obedience means to follow someone who has greater authority. Jesus chose to remain under His Father's authority, even when it required pain and suffering. Jesus' response to His Father's will perfected, or matured, Him. It might be difficult to think of Jesus as needing to mature, but that is what we are told.

Much of Christ's suffering came from bearing the disgrace and shame of the Cross. We, too, are called to lose ourselves and take up His cross. Sometimes this involves suffering, but in the end, we know it's worth the price because through our pain, we can become the disciples of God we have been called to be.

It's human nature to want to avoid suffering. We often seek to minimize pain even if it means that others will suffer. As Victor Hugo said, "Adversity makes men, and prosperity makes monsters."[14] When I am lifting weights, I don't always notice any changes in muscle development. However, with time and consistent training, it becomes obvious that the muscles have strengthened. The same thing happens to our spiritual muscles when God uses problems and suffering to strengthen us.

James suggests a second benefit of trials—they help us to grow so we will lack nothing—or become "entire." The word entire means to be in balance. Whether it is a ceiling fan, vehicle tires, a checkbook, or scales, balance is critical. My muscle-bulging friend suggested that in addition to changes in my strength-training program I should vary my aerobic workout to include activities other than jogging. Apparently, runners build their hamstrings more quickly than they do their quadriceps. This imbalance can lead to knee problems since the muscles behind the legs are weaker than the muscles in front of the legs.

God wants us to have every area of our lives in balance. To help us mature spiritually, God knows what buttons to push, what trials to bring, and what crises to put into our lives. As we are spiritually toned by suffering, the character of Jesus Christ is bred into our lives, and we become more spiritually balanced. Paul recognized that spiritual maturity resulted from problems, and Peter also spoke of God using suffering to make us spiritually mature.[15]

Transformation is Mandatory

Imagine yourself as a lump of coal, part of a rich vein in a cool, dark mine. Suddenly, the brutal force of picks and hammers separate you from the rockbed and tear you away from the security of the mine. You are shoveled into a wheelbarrow with other pieces of coal. Your life has been turned totally upside down. But things are about to get worse.

You will be forced to endure incredibly hot temperatures that will exert great pressure on you. If you could talk to the men handling you, you would scream, yell, argue, plead, and perhaps even fight them in order to avoid this fate. If the handlers heeded your pleas, the pressure and pain would be relieved. But while it is true that you would avoid a horrible experience, you would also miss your transformation into a diamond. Synthetic diamonds, the strongest, most beautiful jewels in the world, are not born; they are made, the result of extremely high temperatures and pressure applied to carbon.

Even if we knew that in the end we would become priceless diamonds, most of us would still refuse to undergo that process. It might help you to know that the word diamond is a derivative of the Greek word adamas, which means "unconquerable."

Suffering has a way of honing our character like nothing else. As a young girl, Helen Keller became very sick. Although she recovered from her illness, she would never again be able to see or hear. Isolated from the voices and images of everyone she loved, Helen became overwhelmed by her life of darkness and filled with rage—life was surely over.

But Helen's parents hired a gifted teacher, Annie Sullivan, who taught her to communicate by reading words written on her hands. Eventually, Helen was even able to attend college and write her autobiography, The Story of My Life.[16] She became a world-famous speaker, and her story inspired many because of the great obstacles that she had overcome. Truly, Helen Keller knew of suffering, but rather than being embittered by her loss, she learned to recognize suffering's character-building effects. She once said, "Character cannot be developed in ease and quiet. Only through experiences of trial and suffering can the soul be strengthened, vision cleared, ambition inspired and success achieved." Even though Keller was both blind and deaf, she could honestly say she was grateful:

> *"The struggle of life is one of our greatest blessings. It makes us patient, sensitive, and Godlike."[17]*

God wants to transform rough, sullen, and sin-shaped people into grateful, joyous, and holy men and women of God. Yes, God loves and accepts us unconditionally. But because He loves us so much, He wants to make us the very best that we can be. He calls us to the highest standard: to be perfect like Him.[18] His love requires that we become spiritually transformed.

Perhaps one of the verses most often quoted—and misquoted—in times of trials is Romans 8:28-29:

> *"And we know that all things work together for good to those who love God, to those who are the called according to His purpose. For whom He foreknew, He also predestined to be conformed to the image of His Son, that He might be the firstborn among many brethren."*

The passage's promise carries a condition: all things work out for our betterment if we love God and if we are called according to His purpose. This promise is not given to the unsaved; it is only for those who belong to God.

God's sovereign purpose is that our pain and suffering be transformed from bad to good. Our Redeemer specializes in making huge profit from what seems like obvious loss. In God's economy, bad often possesses the power to accomplish God's ultimate good. In this famed passage to the Romans, Paul defines good as being "conformed to the image of His Son." We are the chosen people of God, called to prepare the world for the returning King. To accomplish this mission, we must become like Him. The work of conformity changes not only the outward demeanor but the inward character as well.

In speaking about people with disabilities, Howard A. Rusk of the Institute of Physical Medicine and Rehabilitation wrote, "You don't get fine china by putting clay in the sun. You have to put the clay through the white heat of the kiln if you want to make porcelain. Heat breaks some pieces. Life breaks some people. Disability breaks some people. But once the clay goes through the white-hot fire and comes out whole, it can never be clay again; once a person overcomes a disability . . . he has a depth of spirit you and I know little about."[19]

If this process is true for those who don't know God, imagine how much more Christians can benefit from trials because of the transforming nature of a Christ. Consider the apostles Peter and John, who were arrested for preaching the gospel of Jesus Christ in the Temple. This injustice provided an opportunity for Peter to preach to the Jewish ruling council, the Sanhedrin. They experienced more than a message that day; they experienced the very power of God. Peter and John's response to suffering was so radical that it unnerved even their unbelieving audience.[20]

Brussels is well-known for its fine lace shops. A man visited one of these shops with his wife, and while she was shopping, he spoke with the shop owner about the lace-making process. The owner led him back to a small room that was used for the production of their finest, most delicate lace patterns. To his amazement, he saw that the room was completely dark except for a narrow stream of light from one very small window that fell directly upon an artisan and his work. The owner explained that the most delicate and expensive lace is made when the worker is completely in the dark with only his pattern in the light. Similarly, God uses the darkness that accompanies problems as a means of transforming us into His pattern—Christ's image.[21]

God's Transforming Purpose

When followers of Christ were first called Christians, it was not a compliment. Just as Plato's followers were called Platonists, those who bound themselves to Christ were credited with His name. The believers in Antioch were known for leaving all to follow Christ. Their critics mocked their lifestyles by referring to them as "Christians." The label didn't dismay them; in fact, they couldn't have chosen a better name for themselves. Perhaps the name was part of a divinely conceived plan, and God's intention was for His followers to be given His name because they were to be like Him. Even though we know that becoming like Christ is accomplished by God's work in our lives, it runs counter to our self-serving human nature. The following poem clearly depicts the difference between our natural self-orientation and a Christlike orientation.

"For He was a man of sorrows and familiar with suffering; I prefer to be familiar with comfort.

He was a man despised and rejected; I prefer to be honored and accepted.

He took up your infirmities, disabilities, and sickness; I prefer health, strength, and wholeness.

He was pierced, crushed, and oppressed; I prefer no injuries, no smashing, or injustices."[22]

There is no escaping the fact that as we go through the process of becoming like Christ, we will experience hardships. Our responses to those painful experiences will indicate our progress toward that goal. The Bible says that being corrected may not be welcomed, but if we learn to be obedient through it we will live in peace.[23]

Chapter 8

A TOUGH MAINTENANCE CHECK:
RECENTERING YOUR FAITH

When the movie Titanic was released, it broke box office records. The multimillion dollar movie follows a fictional couple through the reality of the maritime tragedy. While the movie contains many moving scenes, perhaps none is more moving than the one that takes place in the waning moments of the ship sinking. As passengers were frantically trying to get into the limited number of lifeboats, the band played music on deck. In the final moments before the ship was completely submerged, the bandleader thanks his friends for the privilege of playing with them over the years. As the band members begin to disperse, the leader takes his violin and starts to play "Nearer, My God, to Thee." Hearing their leader playing the classic hymn, the band solemnly returns to accompany him. Truly there was not a more fitting song in those final minutes. Tragically, many passengers were approaching an eternity without God.

As it did for the bandleader, grave adversity often prompts us to assess our relationship with God and eternity. God's purpose is to draw us into a more personalized faith relationship. Oswald Chambers poignantly professed, "Why shouldn't we go through heartbreaks? Through these doorways God is opening up ways of fellowship with His Son. . . . He comes with the grip of the pierced hand of His Son, and says—'Enter into fellowship with Me; arise and shine.'"[1]

God's passion is for His children. He longs for us and wants us to long for Him. Engulfed in the pit of anguish and depression, the psalmist longed to draw closer to God because he realized that only God's character could help him.[2] And through adversity, he experienced a deep longing for God.

Because Job's initial response to his affliction was humility and worship, many Christians presume that Job never swayed in his attitude. But chronic suffering takes a toll. Consider Job's comments and accusations in the aftermath of his suffering:

"I desire to speak to the Almighty and to argue my case with God." (13:3, NIV)

"I will surely defend my ways to his face." (13:15, NIV)

"Can anyone bring charges against me?" (13:19, NIV)

"[I] know that God has wronged me and drawn his net around me. Though I cry, 'I've been wronged!' I get no response; though I call for help, there is no justice." (19:6-7, NIV)

"Let God weigh me in honest scales and he will know that I am blameless." (31:6, NIV)

The man who had initially not charged God with wrongdoing changed his opinion. Job demanded his day in court before God, and he got what he asked for, God showed up.

In the concluding chapters of Job's biography, we find Job silenced by the cross-examination of God. In chapters 38 through 41, Job and God were engaged in a battle of words over God's justice and goodness. Every time Job thought he had God on the ropes, God landed a powerful blow to Job's argument. In the end, God's opposition sapped the fight from Job, and the struggle was soon over. At one time, Job had stood before the Creator of the universe a prideful man. Finally humbled, however, Job was unable and unwilling to get up from the mat, but humility does not equal defeat.

God hadn't declared the depths of His power and greatness in an attempt to defeat Job, but to give him a special understanding of Himself. Though God knocked Job down, He did not knock him out. And as he lay stretched out before God, Job exclaims that though he had heard about God from others, he has now seen Him with his own eyes.[3] For the first time, Job understood the ultimate prize, an enriched and personal relationship with a generous, loving, and lavishing God.

Prior to his trials and travails, Job thought he knew God, but he had only known about Him. Like many of us, Job held traditional assumptions about what God was like, how God should act, and what God could do. He had probably heard about God's goodness, grace, mercy, and sovereignty from the

Job understood the ultimate prize, an enriched and personal relationship with a generous, loving, and lavishing God

testimonies of others. After his own battle with the Almighty, however, Job had a more personal knowledge of God, as well as a changed life. Suffering had opened an opportunity to experience God in a way that Job would never have chosen, yet he could now say something like, "God, I have experienced you in a deep and personal way. I no longer have secondhand knowledge of you but firsthand experience."[4]

Many believers have a traditional understanding of God. We go to church, where we learn about the Lord's nature and hear messages and testimonies about His power, love, and justice. Such instruction is good and necessary in developing us as believers. But it is only as we battle with God that we are brought from a head knowledge to an experiential knowledge. Then, like Job, we can testify to what God has done personally for us.

Drawing Near to God Through Prayer

The great English preacher Charles Haddon Spurgeon once said, "The best style of prayer is that which cannot be called anything else but a cry."[5] Sometimes our hardships are so great and our futures so bleak that we are driven to our knees. There we can do little else but cry out to God, but it is from that position that we draw near to God and learn to rely upon Him in the most personal way.[6]

When the pain is greater than our ability to tolerate it, we find ourselves much more willing to pray. No longer does prayer seem like drudgery or an obligation. Instead, in pain, we fall on our faces before the Lord, pleading and begging for His help. When our needs weigh heavily upon us, our prayer lives reflect a personal sense of urgency, and we come to understand that prayer is more than an activity. It is a relationship with the Creator of the universe.

Therefore, prayer goes beyond simply asking God for help. It becomes a means of seeking communion with God so that we can experience His power and presence to sustain us. When Moses was on Mount Sinai receiving the Ten Commandments, God informed him that the people of Israel were committing grievous sins. God told Moses that because of their rebellion, He would destroy Israel, but Moses prayed desperately for their deliverance.[30] And because of his prayer of intercession, God agreed not to harm His people.

Perhaps the children of Israel never knew that the warrior efforts of their leader protected them from God's hand of discipline. Clearly, the people benefited from Moses' prayer. What might be less obvious is that Moses benefited more than anyone from battling with God. Being informed of God's plan to punish His people, Moses knew that he was the only one who could intercede. But imagine being in Moses' sandals. How could one man possibly get the Lord Almighty to change His mind? Confronted with the fear of what would happen to him and the people, Moses fell to his knees and did what only a desperate person can do: he pleaded for mercy. Though the people did not come to a more personalized faith through that ordeal, Moses did. His spiritual understanding of God's power and grace improved through hours of fervent prayer.

In desperate times, knowing what to say and how to pray can elude us. We may want to pray, but like Moses, we do not have a clue about how to move the heart of God. In thinking about our struggle to know how to pray in times of suffering, I was reminded of a story. A mother was working in the kitchen preparing an evening meal when she saw her little boy sitting in a corner of the room saying, "ABCDEFG."

"What are you doing?" she asked.

"Mom, you told me I should pray, but I don't know how. So I gave God the alphabet and asked Him to make a good prayer out of it."

This anecdote illustrates an important point about our suffering. Like the boy, there are times when life's difficulties make it nearly impossible for us to pray. There are simply no words to describe the longings of our hearts. Or maybe we've been hurt and we don't want anything to do with prayer because that means having to deal with God. In such times, being told to pray to God is about as inviting as being forced to interact with someone we're fighting with. The last person on earth we want to be around is the one we blame for our problems. The fact is, we'll do just about anything to avoid the discomfort of being around that person. We know that if we speak, our words will be polluted by hurt and self-defensiveness, creating even more distance between us.

Just as communication is the lifeblood of a relationship, prayer feeds our spiritual lives. Most people blame a lack of communication for relational problems, but in reality, it is simply the by-product of a much deeper issue. Communication is only a vehicle we use to share what is inside our hearts with someone else. The vehicle is not the real problem; it's what's inside us that's the problem. When a relationship is in trouble, those involved often become impassioned in their communication: "I can't live without you," "Just give me one more chance," "I'll change," "I'll do anything to make things right." In the same way, when we face troubled times in our lives, our passions flow out toward God. Whatever we're feeling—desperation, anger, fear, or shame—is reflected in our communication with the Lord.

During times of tragedy or distress, our willingness to pray does not always become greater. We cannot wait until we feel like praying; we must pray whether we feel like it or not. God wants us to communicate with Him. Since He knows our hearts, He knows what we are thinking and feeling anyway. Our words will not surprise Him. Regardless of what we have to say, God longs for us to open up to Him in prayer.

It is through prayer that we find God.[8] It is through prayer that we harness the power and sustaining grace to face any trial. Christianity's uniqueness is found in this truth. We believe in a personal God who desires to have a relationship with us. Moses captured this truth in the following words:

> "What other nation is so great as to have their gods near them the way the Lord our God is near us whenever we pray to him?"
> Deuteronomy 4:7, NIV

A dear friend of ours went through many months of dark depression. She simply could not find an end to her gloom. Like the little boy praying the alphabet, she knew that the Holy Spirit promised to intercede on her behalf, but she wondered if He had forgotten about her. Then one day, her pastor explained that when we can't pray, not only does the Holy Spirit say to the heavenly Father what we are not able to say, He also burdens the hearts of other Christians to intercede for us as well. The Comforter comforts by understanding our hearts' cries, giving them words, and then speaking the passion of our hearts to the heavenly Father.[9] This woman was broken by the reality of God's love for us, and in particular His love for her, and this realization was a key factor in her recovery.

I still remember the day Lynn came into my office, took a seat, and spoke rather caustically: "I'm going through severe problems that are beginning to affect my marriage and family, as well as my business. I've read your two books on Christian struggles, and I need some help. But if we're going to talk, I want to have something understood from the very beginning. Don't say that my problem starts with me, and don't just tell me to go pray or read the Bible. I've tried these things ever since becoming a believer and they simply don't work."

What an introduction and challenge! But Lynn was right—she needed someone with whom she could talk, and once we worked past her initial barriers, the conversation started to flow more easily. Over the next few months, I met weekly with Lynn, concentrating on the problems that had caused her so much pain. In spite of her initial proclamation, Lynn began to see that her own perception of her struggles was indeed the chief culprit in her suffering. She began to dispute her false views, and after less than two months, she was doing wonderfully.

Soon, Lynn made a personal discovery—having worked again through her faith, she realized both that it was real and that it had been there all the time. She simply had to learn how to appropriate the truths that God had long before set forth. Years later, she called me and declared that not only had her faith survived the rocky times, but that God had become more real than she had imagined. She had been liberated!

These experiences are not unique. Many of us struggle to pray at times. Any attempts at prayer seem futile and unproductive. Yet God longs for us to pray, even when forming words seems more than we can manage. As we struggle with the loss of a desire to pray, seeking His face in whatever way we can, we begin the journey of drawing near to Christ.

When we are suffering, prayer may seem impossible. But no matter how we feel, we need to set aside familiar patterns and get down to business. As we do so, we become drawn into a deeper fellowship and personal intimacy with God. Prayer teaches us that we cannot depend on ourselves, that we need God's strength. God reaffirms the promise that His power is made perfect in our weaknesses.[10] In light of your suffering, consider the following promises found in this familiar hymn:

What a friend we have in Jesus . . . all our sins and griefs to bear!
What a privilege to carry everything to God in prayer!
O what peace we often forfeit,
O what needless pain we bear,

All because we do not carry everything to God in prayer.[11]
Corrie ten Boom sang those words from solitary confinement in the Ravensbrück prison camp. Finishing the verse, she heard the voice of another woman in an adjoining cell reply, "O what peace we often forfeit, O what needless pain we bear, all because we do not carry everything to God in prayer." It was the voice of a woman who had just watched as their Nazi captors shot and killed her husband.[12]

Faith and Religious Doubt

Religious doubt and uncertainty seem to plague a high percentage of people. This applies to both unbelievers and believers alike. Jews and Christians who may question this may not have to go any further than an examination of the Old and New Testaments. It is well known that Job's life is virtually synonymous with pain, suffering, and doubt. But too few seem to realize that Abraham, called the man of faith, and David, nicknamed a man after God's own heart, both struggled throughout their lives with their faith as well as their behavior. In the New Testament, John the Baptist wondered if Jesus was the Messiah or if they should look for someone else (Lk. 7:18-28). Paul sought God about his own thorn in the flesh but it was not taken away (2 Cor. 12:8-10).

Quite frequently, doubters think that their questions are factual in nature. So they often conclude that all they need to do is to finish studying one more book or working through one last crucial issue. They often think they are so close to solving the problem, but they simply never seem to get there. Sometimes they conclude that they have concluded their study of the problem, occasioned by a sharp rise in positive emotions, only to see this elevated mood dissipate over the next few days. This process is often repeated frequently. Also, it seems to be the most common with males.

Below is a sample dialogue that provides an example of how religious doubt can intersect faith:

"So you're experiencing questions about your faith?"

"Yes, I'm having factual questions about whether some key elements of Christianity are actually true or not."

"Okay, let's discuss this, using the New Testament Gospel message as our focal point, since it is definitely at the center of the Christian faith. If the factual content of the Gospel includes at least the Deity, death, and resurrection of Jesus Christ, which are you struggling with? Do you have serious questions about the Deity of Christ?"

"No, I think I'm pretty solid on that. There are certainly good reasons to believe that Jesus Christ claimed to be Deity."

"Then how about Jesus' death, including His atoning for our sins?"

"Well, all men die and I know that I'm a sinner or I wouldn't be talking to you now. So I don't think I struggle too much with Jesus' death for my sins."

"Okay, then what about the resurrection? Do you have any questions about it?"

"Well, I'm not denying that I have had questions about the resurrection before. After all, it would be a pretty incredible historical event. But I have studied this subject a fair amount and I know that the evidence for the resurrection is also excellent. So I have to say that this really isn't my problem either."

"Then what makes you think that your doubt issues are primarily factual in nature?"

"Well, just about the time I start thinking that I have these questions solved, sometimes I start getting a little nervous. Then I usually think, 'What if it's all somehow untrue? I mean, how do I really know that that's what actually happened?'"

"But if it is really factual doubt that you are experiencing, wouldn't the good evidence that you already recognize solve the issue?"

"Sometimes it does--at least for a little while. But then I start asking the 'What if?' questions all over again."

"Let me ask you another question: does it ever seem to you that you never quite get to the end of your questions, even when you have great factual responses? And is that sometimes painful in itself?"

"Actually, it's funny that you should ask this. Just a few months ago, I was remembering when pursuing my questions was all a lot of fun. I couldn't wait to talk to my friends, turn the next page of a good research book, or think through an important issue. But then I realized that my doubts had taken a more painful turn in recent days. I have now begun to wonder if I will ever solve them. There always seems to be more questions, more 'What ifs,' and a growing sense of never getting to the end of all this. I have to admit, I'm a little anxious that I am not going to solve this. Yes, that does hurt a lot."

"You know, I've had a lot of discussions with doubters, and the process you are describing is actually quite common."

"Really! Actually, it's quite exciting to find that others are in the same boat that I am. I tend to think that I am alone in this."

"Well, I can assure you that that's not the case."

"So then, if I hear you correctly, this isn't some form of blaspheming the Holy Spirit? To be really truthful, that's another thing that I have been bothered about lately, as well."

"All I can tell you is that I'm not hearing anything that sounds like blasphemy of the Holy Spirit. But why don't you seek the lord's wisdom on this? Perhaps He will show you that you belong to Him."

"Wow, that's really encouraging, too! You have really taken some worries off my mind!"

"You have probably noticed that we have moved a long way from the original assertion that you have been experiencing factual doubts. The 'What if?' questions, the move from 'exciting research' to painful episodes, along with the blasphemy question are all indicators that what was originally a factual question has now migrated to an emotional one. We can come back to this issue, but I just wanted you to know that I think we have crossed a crucial line here. It now seems that perhaps you have been 'barking up the wrong tree' so to speak, and you now need to seek a different sort of salve--something to counteract emotional doubt."

"I deeply appreciate your insights. I don't feel like I'm very knowledgeable about treating emotional issues. By I just have one last, quick question. Are there remedies for these sorts of emotional issues?"

"Yes, I'm pleased to tell you that there are numerous good treatments for emotional pain. I'll glad to work through some of these with you."

"Thanks! I feel like I have reached a new plateau today. I definitely want to pursue all this further with you."

As in the case of the doubter in the preceding dialogue, most problems of languishing faith are rooted in emotions rather than the intellect. Stress, wounds, and losses can quickly erode the stability of one's faith. The formula is something like:

Existing Faith - Afflicted Emotions = New Faith

Our existing faith can become undermined when life stirs up powerful emotions that call into question what we believe. The degree to which our emotions become afflicted can over-ride a life of faith more rapidly than most people believe. Though emotions are the culprit, most express their level of skepticism in intellectual questions. Like the doubter in the dialogue, when we can recognize that our emotions are undermining what we truly know to be true we are more likely to doubt our doubt.

You've likely had the experience of traveling downhill and being passed by heavy trucks as their speed and weight propelled them past you. At times it seemed as if they would run you off the road! Their ability to intimidate you was short-lived, however, when they attempted to climb the next hill. The ease with which they had traveled down the road was lost; momentum subsided and these beasts of the road slowed to a crawl. To maintain their normal speed, the drivers must be able to accelerate in order to compensate for the steep incline. Without the speed and momentum to carry them up the next hill, the weight of the trucks negates having the pedal to the metal.

Sometimes Christians experience similar acceleration and deceleration patterns. When traveling down level roads, they maintain their acceleration, feeling particularly empowered in their commitment to grow in Christ. Maintaining speed and forward momentum is no problem as long as the conditions around them are favorable. However, like the heavy trucks when they

To become like our Lord, we must move forward in the good times and the bad

encounter the steep ordeals of life, forward momentum sometimes diminishes. Then they either crawl or stall. They are fair-weather Christians. Such people believe that their momentum is dictated by road conditions, not their ability to increase their speed. They view suffering as a logical justification for their dark attitude. After all, how can one move forward in their spiritual life when things are so difficult?

Consider the early church. Common sense says that the persecution the early church endured should have minimized its growth. Not so. Nothing—not arrests, not beatings, not imprisonments, not threats—seemed to deter these followers of Christ. Instead these challenges accelerated the growth of both the early believers and the church as a whole.

Like Job's faith, our trust in God is to be based on what we know to be true about God and His character. After all, our dependency and confidence in an object are only as sound as the object to which we have committed ourselves. When it comes to God and His character, we have good reason to place our trust in Him, even in the midst of suffering. The truth of God's character is that He who holds the future also holds the present. He is the same yesterday, today, and forever.[13]

To become like our Lord, we must move forward in the good times and the bad. In the process of sculpting the image of Christ into our lives, our souls are remade into the image of the One who created them. The apostle Paul graphically described it this way: "My dear children, for whom I am again in the pains of childbirth until Christ is formed in you . . ."[14]

Suffering is not always virtuous, but what it produces is. It all works to mature our souls and build inner beauty. May God use your struggles and trials to propel you forward so that you will develop fully and completely in Christ.

Chapter 9

DEMOLISHING SIN AND RECONSTRUCTING A GODLY LIFE

Perhaps you have seen old casinos in Las Vegas being demolished so that modern, contemporary, and more alluring casinos could be built on the old site. In the building industry, engineers make sure they strategically place their explosive material and time its detonation so that a structure will collapse on itself in such a way that it minimizes any physical damage to the immediate surroundings.

At times, parts of our lives need to be demolished so that something better can take there place. In the words of Joni Earicksen Tada, sometimes God allows that which He hates to bring about that which He loves.

*God Uses Suffering to Demolish Sin and
Strongholds in Our Lives*

Spanking, time-out, and grounding—when I was a child, such words were enough to make me shudder. Whether treated appropriately or regularly exposed to maltreatment and abuse, all children have an aversion to discipline. It is never an enjoyable experience.

Just as we received discipline from our parents, we also receive discipline from our Father God. Unlike the imperfect judgment of earthly caregivers, however, God's discipline is perfect. And because of our sinful choices, God may even allow suffering as a form of discipline.[1] Hebrews 12:5-6 tells us that God rebukes those he loves and "chastens everyone he accepts as his son." The fundamental principle of obedience is that we will reap what we sow, and our actions are never without consequence.[2]

Biblically, consider Miriam, who was stricken with leprosy after challenging the God-given authority of her brother Moses.[3] And David, who suffered the death of his son following an adulterous affair.[4] And Ananias and Sapphira, who were killed by God for lying, cheating, and hypocrisy.[5] Not all suffering is the result of sin, but sometimes there is a clear link between sinful choices and the suffering that follows.

God Dares to Discipline

Parents responsible for the training of their children understand the need and value of sound, effective discipline. But seldom would any parent dare to discipline someone else's child unless given permission to do so. In the same way, God disciplines only His own children. So if you are experiencing God's hand of discipline, there is good news: you can be sure that you are His child.

At times God may delay His discipline, giving us the opportunity to return to Him on our own. But if we continue in our sin, God may need to bring the sting of pain into our lives in order to get our attention.[6]

Our challenge as a child of God's is to learn not to despise His discipline, but to see the pain and affliction as a good thing. Suffering is an opportunity to learn the ways of our Father; such an attitude is impossible without a passionate desire to serve God.

Three different words are used in the Bible to describe the way God disciplines us: chasten, rebuke, and scourge.[7] The word chasten (paideo) describes God's goal to train and instruct rather than punish us. The word rebuke (elegcho) means to convict, refute, or to reprove; in particular, it describes a conviction that results from having a wrong exposed. God will use suffering to cause us to see our wrongs and repent. The third word, scourge (mastigoo), was used to describe Jewish beatings.[8] This word is used in a metaphorical sense to reveal that we have transgressed God's law and need to be punished. God sometimes uses the actions of other people to accomplish this purpose.

Just as parents want their children to become healthy and mature adults, God also wants well-behaved children who will mature into spiritually stable and healthy adults. So, while God's primary way of dealing with His children is unconditional, nurturing love, when a spiritual spanking is needed, God will discipline us. His goal is not to harm us, but to bring about repentance.[9]

Most family experts recommend that parents set limits. God seems to agree, providing clear boundaries and telling us the consequences for stepping over those lines. As humans, we may tend to be overly strict or overly permissive in our parenting. But our heavenly Father is always balanced and just in His parenting, tempering justice with mercy and always working for our good.

The Old Testament provides many examples of God's children experiencing the consequences of their choices. In Leviticus, for example, the Lord clearly outlines to Moses at Mount Sinai that continued disobedience by the Israelites would result in persecution and plagues.[10] We might assume that such stern lessons would cause the people of Israel to look long and hard at their choices, but the Old Testament is filled with stories of the continuing rebellion of God's people. In the book of Judges, we see a cycle that begins with the people serving the Lord. After some time, however, the people forsake the Lord, and God raises up an enemy to discipline them. In pain, the people then cry out

while God's primary way of dealing with His children is unconditional, nurturing love, when a spiritual spanking is needed, God will discipline us. His goal is not to harm us, but to bring about repentance

to God for help. God hears the cries of His repentant children and, with great compassion, delivers them.[11] For a time, the people serve the Lord, but then the cycle begins again.

Perhaps that cycle sounds familiar to you. So often, we are walking intimately with God but for some reason turn aside to do our own thing. After a period of time, God uses adversity to discipline us. We recognize the hand of the Lord on our backsides and cry out to Him. Thankfully, God, who is rich in grace and mercy, has already raised up the Deliverer, Jesus Christ, and through Him we are restored to a right relationship. And so the cycle goes.

The point is clear: our disobedience hurts God and He will not tolerate it forever. Following the great repentance of Nineveh, the prophet Jonah whined a prayer to the Lord, acknowledging His gracious and merciful heart.[12] The pouting prophet knew that God did not want to punish Nineveh but would grant to them His mercy and grace. God abounds in compassion both to the repentant and the unrepentant. God will, however, use whatever is necessary to get our attention and turn our hearts toward Him.

Why God Disciplines Us

In Hebrews 12:5-11 we find five specific reasons why God may choose to discipline His children. The first two reasons are primarily aimed at reorienting our wrong behaviors, whereas the last three are targeted to positively motivate us. God disciplines us:

1. To teach us obedience
2. To bring about confession and repentance
3. To demonstrate His love
4. To help us know Him in a personal way
5. To make us holy

1. God Disciplines us to Teach us Obedience

Sometimes suffering is God's way of taking us to obedience school. In other words, God seeks children who are mindful of Him, and suffering has a way of helping us to become obedient. As we saw in chapter one, even Christ learned submission to the Father through suffering.

When the prophet Samuel learned that King Saul had sinned, he rebuked the defiant king on God's behalf. Unmoved by Samuel's reproof, Saul continued to justify his actions by insisting that his disobedience was a way of making an offering to God. But the unrelenting prophet explained that God valued obedience more than worship.[13]

God's discipline is an invitation for us to return to His ways and character. As parents we can appreciate our heavenly Father's desire to raise dutiful children. We want our children to respect authority, to adhere to our heartfelt convictions and values, and to learn to choose right. God longs for the same character from us.

It seems a stretch to think that suffering and pain can help us learn God's laws; but apparently King David found this to be true. Perhaps he was thinking about his sin with Bathsheba and the subsequent misery that befell his house when he admitted that through his affliction he had learned God's statutes.[14]

2. God Discipline us to Bring About Confession and Repentance

When my family was ready for a pet, we decided to adopt a retired racing greyhound. The adoption agency told us that greyhounds hunt by sight, not smell. Therefore, when they see something interesting, they will take off after it. (And, boy, can they take off!) For safety's sake, the agency required "adoptive parents" to enclose their backyard. This sounded like a relatively simple task since our front yard was already lined by a split-rail fence. All we had to do was stretch a fence line from the house to the existing fence and then cover it with wire.

Though we had never put up a fence, we decided to tackle the job. We eyed the spot on both sides of the house that seemed to make a straight line, and off we went. That was the day we discovered that our yard was a shallow disguise for an acre of rock. So we made logical choices. When we hit rock, we would move a few inches to the left or right and dig again. When we were finished, the fence looked as twisted as a radio wave! That evening, as I rested my sore muscles, I saw a home improvement show on how to put up a fence. What timing! A day late, I learned that to lay a straight fence, you have to figure a three-by-four-by-five triangle with the house and the end of the fence line.

God intends for us to use His Word the way builders use the three-by-four-by-five triangle: to keep us straight. The book of Amos was written during a time of economic prosperity in Israel. Everything was going well for the people, except that they had drastically strayed from God's Word. The problem with getting offtrack is that we often do not realize how far and how quickly from the truth we have strayed. Though the people maintained a form of religion, worship had become only a perfunctory ritual. Amos, a farmer-turned-preacher, was called by God to warn the people of God's impending judgment. In a vision, Amos saw a plumb line from which the people had departed as they lived by their own standards. The newly anointed prophet urged the people to repent and realign with God's standards.

The Greek word for repentance is one of the better known Greek words. It is the word metanoia, which means to perceive afterward, to go in another direction, or to change one's mind. Repenting, therefore, occurs when we become unsatisfied with the direction in which we are heading and determine to change course. Consider the Prodigal Son, who was no longer satisfied being at home on the farm. Borrowing from his future, the young man took his inheritance to find "the good life." And that he did! Perhaps he mused to himself, Life can't get any better! But the laughs did not last long; when the money disappeared, so did the pleasure. Broken by prolonged hardship, the prodigal returned to his father and repented.[15]

Misery is a good teacher since it presses us to do something to change our predicament. That is one reason why painful experiences are valuable to God. They compel us to stop, consider our circumstances, and change our ways.[16] Fortunately God is rich in mercy and grace. The Prodigal Son knew that he had sinned, but he failed to recognize the grace and mercy of his father. God wants close fellowship with His children, so He will do whatever is necessary to bring us back to Himself. He knows that we are committing spiritual suicide, destroying our testimonies, and missing out on His blessings when we stray from Him.

The book of Habakkuk deals with the wickedness of Judah. As the book opens, we find the prophet asking God how long He will allow their sinful ways to continue without discipline. When God tells Habakkuk that He plans to use the brutal Babylonians as His rod of judgment against Judah, the prophet can't understand why God would use such an evil and corrupt nation to punish His people.[17] But God is willing to take whatever action or means is necessary in order for His children to accept His ways, confess their sins, and repent. And when the Lord directs the world to be silent before Him, Habakkuk comes to know and acknowledge the glory, power, and holiness of God, finally affirming his trust in God's salvation.[18]

3. God Discipline us to Demonstrate His Love

Do you remember your parents telling you that the spanking you were about to receive was "going to hurt me more than it is going to hurt you"? I always had a hard time understanding such sentiment. If it did hurt them, it certainly did not hurt them in the same place it hurt me! But now as a parent myself, I have a better idea of what my mom and dad meant. Although I do not tell my children that their punishment hurts me more than them, I do tell them that I would prefer never to discipline them. I do not like being the bad guy. Yet I'm willing to accept that responsibility because I want the best for my children. Parents understand that sometimes discipline brings sadness both to their children and to themselves. However, they know that the lesson learned will outlast the unhappiness and discomfort of the moment. Even research shows that children who are not disciplined do not feel loved by their parents.

The author of Hebrews tells us that God disciplines those He loves.[19] We may sometimes feel like telling God not to love us so much, but in truth, His discipline is not just for wayward children, but for the best of us as well. We all made mistakes as children; and we will make many more mistakes as spiritual children. We will do the wrong thing, say the wrong thing, or go in the wrong direction. But God knows that when we are spinning our spiritual wheels in the wrong direction our prayer lives are hindered and we are hampered in our ability to minister and serve. Like any parent, when God recognizes that His children are playing near a cliff or strolling through traffic, He seeks to draw us to safety. Through discipline, God reaches out to bring us back into balance and in line with His character.

4. God Disciplines Us to Help Know Him in a Personal Way

Hebrews 12:5-8 teaches us that those who are not disciplined by God are not part of God's family. In fact, the writer chooses some very strong language to convey this point. The King James Version captures the intensity of this thought when it uses the word bastard to describe those people who go without discipline. God chastens every son; not a single child is exempt from His lovingly administered discipline. Only those individuals whom God receives through faith in Jesus Christ are God's children. Many people may profess to be in God's family, but the lack of discipline by God's loving hand indicates that they are not His rightful children. Discipline affirms that we are God's legitimate sons and daughters.

5. God Disciplines us to Make us Holy

Parents desire to rear their children so they will become solid citizens. Christian parents strive for more—raising children who love, honor, fear, and serve the Lord. Godly parents want children who will be citizens befitting a heavenly Kingdom. God's ultimate aim at parenting us is much the same.[20]

As we'll see in the next chapter, one of the blessings that emerges out of suffering is sharing in God's holiness. God longs for us, His children, to be holy as He is holy![21] The passage makes clear that our holiness is not measured by the way others live. We are not to compare our lives to those around us, but rather, we are to use God's own holiness as our reference point. Holiness doesn't mean having holy behavior. Instead, a holy man or woman is a person whose inner being reflects God's character. Holiness is revealed from the inside out. Our heavenly Father seeks children whose character reflects His. And as we've already seen, God is willing and able to use whatever it takes to generate holiness in our lives, even if it means putting us through various ordeals.

God Uses Suffereing to Produce Humility

Perhaps you recall the story of Eustace in C.S. Lewis's work and the movie *The Voyage of the Dawn Treader.* On a stop for repairs and resupply, Eustace Scrubb sneaks away to avoid a day of hard work. As he wonders through the mountains he finds himself stuck in a valley, unable to crawl out because of the slippery sheer sides. A noise draws his attention and he turns to see a dragon, who dies before his eyes. As a storm approaches, Eustace runs into the dragon's cave for shelter. It is there that he discovers the dragon's treasure. As his field of vision is filled with gold and jewels, his heart became filled with greed. Eustace puts on a golden bracelet and while sleeping he is turned into a dragon. What now? A boy to a dragon is quite an enchantment, but how can he possibly become a human again?

Though horrified by his transformation, his dragon wings allow him flight out of the valley, giving him the illusion of power. However, the isolation of his life as a dragon reminds him of how cruel he was as a human. Though outwardly an ugly dragon Eustace is beautifully transformed inside; he has learned to think far less of himself and more of others. He wishes to become a boy again so Aslan, the great lion and son of the king beyond the world's edge, takes Eustace into the mountains and tells him to undress. After great effort Eustace is able to shed some of his dragon skin but not completely. Though he scrapes off his scales and steps out of the skin, he is dismayed to see that another layer of dragon skin is underneath. Eustace makes several attempts to shed the skin but continues to fail at peeling it away. His own efforts to change himself are ineffective. Aslan tells Eustace to lie down and warns him of the pain that is to come. With his great claws, Aslan cuts deeply into the dragon's flesh and peels away the dragon skin. It is the most painful experience Eustace has ever felt; as if Aslan has cut right to his heart. But in the end, Eustace is once again a boy; restored by the work of one who is greater than himself.

Like Eustace we need God's presence and transforming power to remove the thick and endless layers of pride and self-sufficiency. Indeed it is painful, often far too painful and unnerving for us to bear. But in the end, we are restored by the One who can bring about lasting change.

The Blessings of the Thorn

Paul learned that God uses suffering as a means of eliminating pride. Even though Paul wanted his thorn in the flesh to be removed, he knew it had value.[22] God had revealed Himself to the apostle Paul in a wonderful experience. But with this special blessing, he received a painful reminder not to see himself as more blessed than others. Paul believed that his agony was a gift from God to redirect his focus and to keep him humble.

Due to our forceful flesh, we readily exchange a focus on God for a focus on what we believe is important. We have become more concerned with knowing ourselves than with knowing God. Paul's thorn in the flesh taught him that God detests self-absorption. Since our lives are littered with distractions to an intimate relationship with Christ, God may need to introduce suffering in order to redirect our attention back to Him. Like the church of Ephesus, many Christians have lost their first love for God.[23] Jesus Christ has been displaced as the central figure in their hearts and lives.

When I first begin counseling patients, I ask them to identify their most important goal for therapy. Typically, there is little difference in the priorities of believers and nonbelievers. More than anything else, they simply want to feel better. No client has ever asked me to help him take up his cross daily. No one sets as her goal to become more like Christ. As we saw earlier, our deep-seated beliefs are revealed through times of suffering. Adversity has a way of revealing what is most important to us. There is nothing wrong with wanting to be rid of a problem. Yet when our primary motive is self-improvement, we fail to see how suffering can help us know Christ more deeply. Given our attitude of wanting control, predictability, and fairness, we experience the same emotional turmoil as the unredeemed. When our dependence is upon Christ rather than on how we feel, we find that His grace is enough. The apostle Paul knew that he should brag only about the Cross of Christ, never himself. Only when our self-pride is crushed are we broken and humbled so that we must rely on God rather than ourselves.

Not only does suffering remove self-absorption, it also allows the power of God to be displayed in our lives.[24] Paul was able to see God's power and grace manifested through him because his times of suffering were not joyless. He found a deep sense of joy in giving God the glory, even in the midst of affliction. Just as the power of God rested upon the Ark of the Covenant, the shekinah glory that Paul experienced during his suffering was witness to God's presence in his life.

I can still remember the day that Randy arrived in my office. Randy was a brash young man who was an excellent university student as well as an exceptionally gifted athlete. And Randy knew he was special. But he also had experienced a pretty rough life. Suffering physical abuse as a child, Randy still bore the scars on his face. Rejected by his parents, he had entered military service and now sought other ways to gain attention. A young Christian, he wanted above all else to be absolutely sure of his salvation.

At first, Randy promised to be an eager learner. He studied the theory behind several of the assignments that I gave him. But he steadfastly refused to attempt any application to his own situation. After many visits, Randy decided not to pursue our discussions. The results were a bit demoralizing for me—why wouldn't a person who had suffered so much take advantage of substantial pain relief?

Years later, I was speaking in a California church and discovered that Randy was in the audience. Not only was Randy married and doing very well as an engineer, he had gone back to the lessons that we had discussed so many years earlier. I was thrilled to learn that Randy had gained victory over his lack of assurance and now taught classes in his own church on how to think and live biblically! Thus, many more students had benefited and gained victory over their own pain. Somewhere along the way, Randy had shed his pride. God had replaced it with a humility that was itself very inviting.

It is easier to act spiritual when all is going well. When our families are healthy, friendships are warm and comfortable, and the bills are paid, we tend to take our blessings for granted and regard them as benefits of our own hard work rather than God's provision. When life is good we think that all we have was gained by our own power, that we are in control. But one phone call, one doctor's visit, or one unexpected turn can knock the props out from under us. Our self-assurance is gone and we find ourselves like children, small and helpless. We are unable to make things work on our own power, and we must be dependent upon God.

We can learn never to take things for granted. We can begin to see each day and each circumstance as a gift from God. In essence, we can learn gratitude. As we confess our weakness to God, He releases His power in us. Our weakness is exchanged for His divine strength.

Pain and heartache are God's prompting to turn our focus on Christ. By learning that our resources are insufficient for life, we learn that, without Him, we are nothing. As we realize our total dependence on Jesus Christ for every good and perfect gift, our suffering might even lead to a genuine sense of humility.

A story is told of two artists who were putting the finishing touches on a church ceiling. One of the artists was older and a master of his craft. The other artist was his young but very talented apprentice. After working tirelessly all day on the painting, the young artist stepped back on the scaffolding to admire their work. Captured by the beauty of the painting, the young man didn't realize that he was standing dangerously close to the edge of the high platform. The master artist knew that his pupil would plunge to his death if he stepped back any farther. Fearing he would frighten his student by a warning cry, the master quickly grabbed one of the paint buckets and deliberately splashed paint across their masterpiece. Stunned by the master artist's apparent insanity, the young artist lurched forward screaming, "What have you done? Why did you do that?"

Upon hearing the reason, the young artist's anger and confusion melted into tears of joy and thankfulness.[25]

God sometimes uses suffering to protect us from ourselves, especially from disastrous choices that could destroy our testimonies, our families, and ourselves. Moreover, God grieves when we sin because it means that He also loses out on fellowshipping with us. In love, He may even need to pick up a can of paint and splash it across the sinful masterpiece we are creating in our lives. By being confronted with the reality of our hearts, we can allow God to remake our souls for His glory.

Chapter 10

We doubt that Job gave much consideration to the fact that his story of suffering would impact millions down through the centuries. Yet many people have been challenged and encouraged by his story of loss and recovery. Job's is a story of paradise lost and paradise regained. Everyone finds connection to some aspect of his story; regardless of how we experience the book we are impacted in some way.

Our suffering impacts other people. Sometimes that influence comes from observing our journey through tragedy. Sometimes, it is a direct byproduct of our response to the difficulties we encounter. Far too often our impact on others is harmful rather than helpful. Sufferers may vent their afflicted feelings on other people. Some do so through criticism, others by rages, and sadly far too many do so by being physically abusive.

Because our lives are intricately woven into the lives of others, the repercussions of our suffering can be profound. In this chapter we will see how our suffering may be a vehicle for positive change in the lives of others. That our pain may be the reason that someone comes to Christ puts our suffering into a different context. Suffering may also be used to enrich the church. Other believes can be called to come alongside of us to walk with us on the journey of pain. We don't have to go at it alone but can help other believes in the body of Christ learn to demonstrate love, mercy, and grace to those in pain. Finally, suffering can prepare us with the knowledge and skills to minister to others. There is no school more trying than the school of hard knocks, but it can be the basis upon which a ministry is built. We will first advance the idea that suffering can be a witness to non-believers.

Truly, our walks speak louder than our talk. Yet when we experience deep tragedy or affliction it is difficult to exhibit hope, joy, and peace. The story has been told about a missionary whose wife and child died of disease while they were ministering overseas. For many years, the missionaries had been striving with little success to introduce a primitive tribe to Christ. Following the death of his family, the missionary began to see a great work of God happening in the lives of the people. Pleased but confused about this turn of events, the missionary questioned one of the tribe's leaders about the reason for their change of heart. The leaders told him that following the death of the missionary' wife and child, the people observed him very carefully. They watched him walk quietly to the grave, exhibiting a sense of hope and confidence. The leader said, "We don't understand your religion, but we like the way you bury your dead."

Paul Walked His Talk

The apostle Paul did not write the book of Philippians, known as the "book of joy," while he was on vacation. Giving instructions on a life of contentment and peace would have been easy to write if he had been sitting alongside a sparkling pool or dangling his feet in a hot tub. But Paul penned these words from a very different venue.

On Paul's second missionary journey, he and Silas ministered in the city of Philippi, located in the Roman province of Macedonia. While there, they were beaten and imprisoned. Later, following his third missionary journey, Paul was taken to Rome and put in prison. Scholars believe that the letter to the church in Phillipi was written from that Roman prison cell. It is that setting that forms the backdrop to this book of joy. Ironic as it might sound, it was while he was incarcerated that Paul found greater purpose in his own suffering.

> *But I want you to know, brethren, that the things which happened to*
> *me have actually turned out for the furtherance of the gospel, so that it*
> *has become evident to the whole palace guard, and to all the rest, that my*
> *chains are in Christ; and most of the brethren in the Lord, having become*

confident by my chains, are much more bold to speak the word without fear.
Philippians 1:12-14

Sometimes suffering opens up a door for others to see Christ at work in our lives. In fact, from a prison in Philippi, Paul and Silas introduced the jailer and his entire family to the Lord.[1] Paul saw times of tribulation as opportunities to share his faith. He may have been imprisoned, but he used his incarceration as a means of evangelism. In the original language, the word furtherance is a military term. It refers to those soldiers who went ahead to prepare the way for the advancing army, ensuring safe and easy passage. These men would cut away all the underbrush, clear all the obstructions out of the path, and if necessary, build bridges so that the army could advance. In this passage, Paul was saying that his imprisonment was accomplishing the same kind of work as these soldiers—it was clearing out the debris and building bridges so that the gospel of Christ could progress. His suffering did not prevent the gospel from going forth, but actually promoted it. Though the authorities had intended to hinder the gospel by persecuting the early church, their actions had the opposite effect on believers.

Paul recognized that his trial would advance the gospel and also help him reach government officials who typically would not have an opportunity to see a Christian in action. He commented that his incarceration was known throughout the whole palace.[2] For the kingdom of Christ to advance, he was willing and able to bear any trial.

Adoniram Judson, the renowned missionary to Burma, endured untold hardships in his attempts to reach the lost. For seven years he suffered hunger and deprivation. During that time he was thrown into Ava Prison and for seventeen months was subjected to the most horrific mistreatment. In fact, for the rest of his life he bore the marks of the chains and shackles on his arms and legs. Upon release from prison, he asked for permission to enter another province to continue his ministry. After hearing Mr. Judson's request, the godless ruler indignantly denied it, saying, "My people are not fools enough to listen to anything a missionary might say, but I fear they might be impressed by your scars and turn to your religion."[3]

In the same way, Daniel's three friends, Shadrach, Meshach, and Abednego, illustrated the power of a testimony formed in the face of a fiery trial.[4] King

Nebuchadnezzar commanded all the people of the land to bow down and worship his statue, threatening to throw anyone who refused into a furnace. The three Israelites, however, stood firm in their conviction that God alone is worthy of worship. It was not their desire to be seated in the smoking section, but if forced to dine at a table in that section, they knew it was of little consequence. They understood that God could rescue them from the furnace and determined that, even if He chose not to do so, they would remain loyal to Him.

When he realized that Shadrach, Meshach, and Abednego had defied his orders, the king ordered that they be thrown into a furnace that had been heated seven times hotter than usual. But when the king went to check on the three Israelites, he was astonished to see four men in the furnace, and exclaimed that the fourth looked like the "Son of God."

Wouldn't it have been interesting to know what those four men were talking about? Perhaps Shadrach started singing a chorus, "Give me oil in my lamp, keep me burning, burning, burning. . . ." Our imaginations will have to fill in the details. But since they were fellowshipping with the presence of Jesus Christ, it's probably safe to assume they weren't in any hurry to get out.

Nebuchadnezzar's life was transformed when he saw the way these three men faced their ordeal. He proclaimed that their God was the one true God and decreed that anyone who spoke against the God of Shadrach, Meshach, and Abednego would be put to death.

When we get a promotion, when the bills are being paid, when the children are behaving, and when we have good health, our neighbors and friends see us as being no different than them. If in the midst of adversity and suffering, however, they can see that there is a difference in the way we cope, they conclude that something—or Someone—is making this difference in our lives. When we endure suffering in a way that demonstrates our eternal hope, God is magnified and people see that there is no other god like ours! As they see our joy and hope in spite of the worst of circumstances, they may even be compelled to say, "I want what they've got!" It is through our scars and hope-filled lives that people may come to accept the Savior.

Years ago, I knew a couple who had recently lost a son in a horrible car crash. Their son was among the many thousands of innocent victims whose lives are lost or changed forever by an intoxicated driver. Even while this husband

and wife were in the middle of their own grief recovery, struggling with the rawness of their pain and suffering, they started a ministry to others. They used their child's photo as the means of drawing attention to the problem of drunk driving, and today, they have distributed more than fifty thousand pieces of literature! While they don't believe that God caused this situation in order to promote the work of His ministry, they know He has certainly blessed their message. You might be thinking, But why must it fall on me and my family? Aren't there other ways God can accomplish His purpose?

This kind of thinking is the result of an attitude that demands comfort, fairness, and predictability. Since we are self-serving, anything that is not to our liking will evoke negative emotions, passions, and behaviors. God's call is to redirect this attitude so that it begins to accommodate His will. Think about what it took to redeem us. If there were any other way to accomplish our salvation without requiring Jesus to die, God would have done so. But Jesus had to sacrifice comfort and fairness to bring us eternal life. Though committed to God's will, even in His final moments He asked God to spare Him from facing the torture of the cross.[5]

Often, it is only through our pain and suffering that people see the grace, hope, and joy we have in knowing Jesus Christ. Remember as you go through suffering that God may be opening a door of opportunity through which you might share your faith.

Paul recognized that his suffering not only opened a door to witness to unbelievers but also gave him a chance to be an example to fellow believers.[6] His outlook was much different than ours often is.

One of the well-known early church fathers, Polycarp, lived just after the apostle Paul. Polycarp made significant contributions to the early church. In prayer, he believed he had a vision in which he was martyred for his faith. His vision did not alter his message or ministry. Eventually, Polycarp would be confronted with an opportunity to either fulfill his vision or escape martyrdom.

As an elderly man of eighty-six, Polycarp was summoned by governmental authorities. They required him to call Caesar "Lord Caesar," but Polycarp declared there was only one Lord and it was not Caesar. The officials told him that he could spare his own life simply by saying those words, but Polycarp held his ground. He contended that he had served God his entire life and that God had never let him down. How then could he possibly blaspheme the One who had saved him? At first, the authorities threatened to unleash wild beasts on him, and Polycarp told them to go ahead and do so. Figuring that the sting of fire might better capture Polycarp's attention, they threatened to burn him at the stake. Polycarp's response? Such fire only lasts a short period of time and then it burns out, but the fire of hell burns forever. Again, he told them to do with him whatever they wanted.

History tells us that Polycarp was burned at the stake, but his body was not all that caught fire. His testimony so ignited the early church that the gospel spread like wildfire.[7] It takes a selfless attitude to view suffering as an opportunity to benefit another individual. Yet when we use our suffering to reach out to others, we benefit as well. Despair will never become our companion when our eyes are securely focused on Christ.

The furtherance of the gospel was the heart's passion of Paul's life. Suffering not only provided an opportunity to advance the gospel but also to advance his soul. American Christians cannot appreciate how suffering and winning others to Christ are connected like those in countries closed to the gospel. I have made several trips to Romania with a mission organization. While there I met pastors and lay leaders who understood what Paul was speaking about through personal experience.

Before Romania came out from behind the iron curtain, believers in Christ had to worship and share their faith in secret. The gospel was not publicly promoted, yet the church continued to grow. Pastors and believers were beaten and thrown into prison for doing nothing more than telling people about Christ. I felt so unworthy to be teaching these men and women anything. Following one of the seminars I was leading for these heroes of the faith, I was dining with a pastor and his wife. Though his English was broken, the pastor shared about the suffering he endured for being a preacher of the gospel. The pastor smiled as he shared story after story of people being saved through his suffering. The conversation ended on a most unusual note. When freedom was brought to the Romanian people, he said that while he rejoiced in the opportunities such freedom would bring, he feared that the Romanian church would become complacent and soft without the constant threat of persecution. The pastor knew that the lack of persecution could actually have a negative rather than a positive impact upon the church. Over the years, the pastor has seen many good things result from the country's newfound freedom. At the same time, his fears have been realized as well. Many in the Romanian church have lost their fervor.

Our own suffering has an outward impact on others. To sweeten the pot, our souls are revived as we watch others come to Christ by seeing the hope and joy in our lives amidst the pain.

Suffering Illuminates the Value of the Body of Christ

During World War II, the German government sought to find the best method of torture for extracting information from prisoners. They conducted numerous experiments and eventually concluded that solitary confinement was the most effective option. After only a few days alone, most captives told all that they knew.[8] This supports our understanding from Scripture that we were created with the need for relationship. At no time is the need greater than when we are suffering. As this German torture technique proved, in order to persevere we need other people to emotionally support us through tough times.

During periods of testing and suffering, it's important to turn to other committed Christians for support and encouragement. Without it, we are easy prey for temptation, despair, and abandonment of faith. Sometimes God allows us to go through suffering so that we may experience the loving care of God's people, the church.

God calls the church "the body of Christ." This description portrays Christians as a unified group of people whose lives are intricately woven together. The Holy Spirit indwells each Christian and is, through Christ's body, an extension of His presence on earth. Though each individual makes a unique contribution to the body, we all work together to fulfill Christ's mission for the church in the world.[9]

Unfortunately, many church folks act as if they have no problems. Rather than honestly and genuinely revealing personal struggles, we assume we can open up only after we have navigated the rough waters. Our testimonies tend to be stories of recovery and triumph rather than honest admissions of current pain and struggle. The fear of looking like a "poor excuse for a Christian" compels many hurting people to go into hiding. Because they fear being criticized, some people even stop attending church.

One of my recovering alcoholic friends once told me that the great thing about Alcoholics Anonymous (AA) is that it "reaches out without reaching down." Of course, there are times when judgment is necessary, but judgment alone is not sufficient. People long to be loved and accepted. Without unfailing love, it is difficult to truly hear truth. Quite honestly, most of us do a poor job in relaying truth to hurting people. Consequently and sadly, some Christians end up being undeservingly judged or treated harshly by other Christians when love is what is needed most.

I once overheard a conversation between two women about another church member whose husband had left her after the tragic death of their son. The two women wondered what this woman had done to "cause" her husband to leave. Eventually one of those women faced similar problems and, because of her skewed perspective on suffering, struggled to determine what she had done to drive her husband into the arms of another woman. Whenever we can attribute irresponsibility to someone else's behavior, we convince ourselves that as long as we are vigilant we can avoid such adversity. We thus fabricate a view that life must be orderly, controllable, and manageable. As a result, sufferers live in isolation. True feelings are hidden from others so that no one suspects how deep the pain and struggle are. The isolation reinforces the lack of Christian unity and validates the soul shame. Unfortunately, it also makes sufferers easy prey for those promising comfort from a source other than God.

The human body is designed so that wounds generally heal spontaneously with remarkably little medical interference. A thorough analysis of the body's response to injury is beyond the scope of this book. Yet it is important to know that when someone is hurt, a physician depends heavily on the body's own ability to repair any damage. For instance, when your finger is cut, the whole body is affected, including loss of blood and fluid, pain, and the release of cellular products into the bloodstream. In response to the injury, the body depends upon a highly dynamic, integrated series of cellular, physiological, and biochemical events, exclusive to itself. In fact, medical scientists are unable to reproduce the entire process of wound healing in a laboratory setting. Many physiological adaptations are at work to fight off foreign material or bacteria, remove any cellular debris and injured tissue fragments, and redirect blood flow. As the body goes through various phases of the healing process, the individual begins to notice increased strength, vigor, and appetite. All of these are signs that healing is taking place within the body.

The biblical design for the body of Christ is much like the physical body. Just as the body seeks to heal an injured member, so the body of Christ should minister to other members who need healing. As Christians, we are to promote restoration, which also means that we are to protect the wounded from the additional pain of insensitive words and thoughtless actions. Callous comments have no place in the body of Christ. They break the heart of God and violate His command to love, encourage, and care for one another. Because we share the same Father, we are to feel the affliction of others and respond in ways that promote healing.[10]

This truth was evidenced in the early church. People who may have been strangers prior to conversion went to great lengths to demonstrate love and concern for each other. Believers provided mutual support by sharing their resources with those in need.[11.] In the same way, we accurately reflect the love of Christ when we embrace and actively support our fellow believers.

Gary first met Chris when he was a graduate student. Chris was a gifted musician—one of those rare students who had so distinguished himself from his classmates that he was constantly being sought out, not only locally, but around the country. Very few people knew that Chris had been diagnosed years before with a very serious personality disorder. Although he had been treated by a physician, he decided on his own to discontinue the treatments.

Chris first contacted Gary to ask if he could speak with him about his personal assurance of his salvation. His lack of assurance was taking a tremendous toll, affecting both him and his ministry. Not being a trained physician, psychologist, or counselor himself, Gary referred him to a Christian psychologist. Chris faithfully kept his appointments and placed himself back under his physician's care. After learning to recognize the signs of his illness and to change his thoughts as well as his actions, Chris made great strides. With the full support of his physician, he later received permission to stop their visits. Through it all, Chris turned his personal struggle and victory into an avenue to help others who are hurting similarly. Today he is a nationally recognized musician, frequently performing in churches and giving his testimony. Whenever they talk, Gary always checks in with Chris on how he is doing. Over the years, he has remained a wonderful example, not only of how suffering can be treated, but also how the body of Christ can benefit from the lessons we learn.

The Ministry of the Body

Many church members ask how they can help someone who is going through the valley of suffering. As members of Christ's body, we are the physical representation of Christ to others. You can minister to others who are going through a time of suffering in the following ways:

Pray for the Hurting Members

One of the more humorous stories in the New Testament depicts the church responding to suffering through prayer. Following James's execution, King Herod arrested Peter and threw him into prison. Herod was so angry with Peter that he had him guarded by four squads of soldiers. These circumstances motivated the Jerusalem church to pray continually for Peter's release. Even as they were diligently praying for Peter's freedom, he was miraculously released from prison and arrived at their door. When the servant told them that Peter was standing at the door, their response was, "You are beside yourself!" To put it in present day terms, "Honey, get a grip!" While believers debated whether or not God had answered their prayers, Peter had to keep knocking until someone finally let him in. When the door was opened and they saw Peter standing there, "they were astonished."[12]

When our brothers and sisters in Christ hurt, Christians should pray—fervently. Do you remember the story of Nathan in the Introduction? Prior to Nathan's surgery, members of his church gathered throughout the week to pray. When we pray for others, we are saying that we will intercede to the Father on their behalf. In essence, we dedicate our time and energy to them through prayer.

Encourage Hurting Members

Many recovering alcoholics say that the key to recovery is spending time with others. Interestingly, this camaraderie is one of the reasons many go to bars, and it is one of the very things used to sell alcoholic beverages. The reason such advertising is successful is that it caters to a critical human need—namely, the need to belong and feel accepted.

People are less interested in being part of a "friendly church" than in having genuine friendships within the church. Friendships require spending time and getting involved in people's lives. The writer of Hebrews framed this point as follows:

> *And let us consider one another in order to stir up love and good works,*
> *not forsaking the assembling of ourselves together, as is the manner of*
> *some, but exhorting one another, and so much the more as you see the Day*
> *approaching.   Hebrews 10:24-25*

The word for stir up above is the same Greek word as the word for provoke, which is used in Ephesians 6 where fathers are told not to provoke their children to wrath. In other words, Christians are to provoke one other to love and do helpful things.

Affliction often provides fertile ground for establishing friendships. By reaching out with helpful hands, empathetic ears, and willing feet, we can provide practical help to those who are hurting. This type of help is what Paul had in mind when he spoke of bearing the burdens of others.[13]

Help Hurting Members

In the days and months following Nathan Sours's death, Dave and Nia's church family provided practical support. The grass was mowed, meals were prepared and delivered, and cards and calls poured in for almost a year.

Solomon recognized the value of friendship at times like this when he said, "A friend loves at all times, and a brother is born for adversity."[14] Literally, the passage means that a brother is born for "a time of adversity." True friends prove themselves by helping in whatever way possible. During such times, genuine love is revealed. Truly, they will know we are Christians by the way that we act out our love.[15]

It is our pain, not our blessings, that touches people. This is another reason God allows us to suffer. Through suffering, His people are drawn together to respond to the needs of a hurting member. If you are deeply hurting, knowing that your pain could benefit others might offer little solace. While God may not specifically orchestrate a trial for this purpose, it is His desire for the church to be bolstered by the suffering of others.

If you ever watch football games on TV, you have likely seen an injured player or two. Sometimes someone is hurt so severely that he can't even move. At times like this, the crowd falls silent, and even the opposing team becomes somber as the medical responders come out onto the field. When the problem is very severe, the players sometimes arrange themselves in small groups to pray there on the field for their injured colleague.

The Christian life is not a spectator sport. We actively participate with one another on the field of play. When a fellow player is wounded, it's up to us to spring into action in whatever way we are led or are able. Pain and suffering often have healthy effects upon the sufferer and others alike. As the body of Christ, when we are aware of others who are hurting, we are to respond to the wound with love, comfort, encouragement, and support. In this way, the benefits found in pain move outward into the lives around the sufferer, validating our need for each other.

Suffering Illuminates a New Ministry

Tom and Maria Whiteman were high school sweethearts. In addition to their love, they also shared a commitment to serve the Lord through the local church. They attended Bible College together and were married during their senior year. After a romantic honeymoon and graduation, they packed their few possessions and moved back to their home state where Tom became the youth pastor of a conservative church. It was a storybook beginning for a young Christian couple, deeply in love. But Tom and Maria did not live happily ever after.

After four years of marriage and ministry, Maria told Tom that she was no longer happy in their marriage and that she no longer loved him. She confessed that for the past six months she had been involved in another relationship.

Tom's shock was complete; he had been blindsided. Perhaps he should have seen the warning signs, but he didn't. "It was like a bad dream, listening to my wife's explanations and reasoning. I kept thinking, This can't be happening. She must have had a bad day. Tom had never considered that his marriage might fail. He had grown up in a Christian home, committed his life to the Lord, attended Bible school, become a minister, and maintained a regular devotional life. "I had a formula all worked out: As long as I committed my life to God and put Him first, He would bless me. God would surely protect me from anything serious," said Tom. Sadly, when put to the test, his formula for life failed. His beliefs about an orderly and predictable world were shattered.

Now Tom was alone. Not only had he lost his wife but, as a divorced man, he was no longer eligible to serve as a minister in his church. Confusion, fear, and hopelessness characterized Tom's life. "My ambitions were dashed. I had no future. I was convinced God could no longer use me." As he endured the harsh comments of those who blamed him for failing as the head of his home, feelings of loneliness and denial gave way to anger. Perhaps the most addictive and intoxicating of emotions, anger gives a euphoric burst of power and energy. Like unspent fuel, anger can keep feeding on itself, shielding a brittle self-image from potentially damaging revelations.

Guilt and gnawing shame mounted beneath the shallow veneer of anger. For Tom, there was no escape from the gut-wrenching questions that penetrated his flimsy defense. "What have you been doing wrong? What secret sins do you have in your life?" Wounded by those to whom he had turned for comfort, Tom left the fellowship of the church. "If this was Christianity, I wanted nothing to do with it," he said.

After about a year, Tom decided to come out of his spiritual desert and give the church another try. He searched for a church that would be less judgmental and more open-minded than his former church. Tom found one that offered a divorce recovery program. He joined, hoping that people in this congregation would treat him differently. He was pleased to learn that although these believers treated him more lovingly, they did not compromise on biblical doctrine.

With the help of the divorce recovery group and other Christians, Tom began to move through his grief. He realized that God could still use him to minister in ways he had not yet explored.

Tom returned to school and earned a master's degree in counseling and a doctorate in psychology. He began to minister to others who had suffered the pain of separation and divorce. Along with several other people who had experienced divorce, Tom founded Fresh Start Seminars. Today, there are Fresh Start offices throughout the United States, England, and Australia. This ministry provides hope and healing to broken people all over the world. Tom learned that God could use his personal tragedy to witness to others. "He took the worst thing that ever happened to me and used it for His Kingdom," he said.[16]

Godly Comfort

In 2 Corinthians 1:3-6, we find a wonderful promise: there is no trouble that we go through in which the comfort of God is not available to us. The word comfort comes from the Greek word paraklesis, which means "to encourage or console." It has the idea of sighing with another—walking along with the person who is suffering and sharing God's love through support and encouragement.

The perfect manifestation of God's comfort is the Holy Spirit, the constant presence of God in a believer's life. While a friend may lighten a burden for a time, God's Spirit journeys with the Christian through the trial, understanding the pain and communicating the unwavering love of the Father.

In this second letter to the Corinthian church, Paul spoke of the "sufferings of Christ," which he endured in obedience to the Father's plan. In fact, Paul noted that God comforts us in all tribulation.[17] The present tense of the verb assures us that the God of all things is willing to comfort us continually and constantly throughout the duration of the trial.

But notice, too, that God provides comfort in all our troubles. Even when our miseries are the result of our own poor choices, God offers Himself as our Comforter. When our disobedience and selfishness bring about suffering, healing can begin only with confession and repentance. At that point, we begin to know God's comfort.

A Ministry View

When problems are plentiful in our lives, the comfort of God abounds even more.[18] Paul further explained that suffering teaches us about God's comfort. Without experiencing trials, it would be impossible to personally know how

God can minister to a broken heart. One of God's expectations, however, is that we not become preoccupied with ourselves during times of suffering. He desires that we share His comfort with others who are also in need, giving out of the resources that have been provided to us. The passage says consolation is given "that we may be able to comfort those who are in any trouble, with the comfort with which we ourselves are comforted by God."[19] Paul had suffered much, and consequently had experienced the comfort of God. He then was able to share that solace with the Corinthian believers. Such action reminds us that those who are continually experiencing the comfort of God are well suited to minister to others in need of support. C. S. Lewis knew of this truth when he wrote, "Think of me as a fellow-patient in the same hospital who, having been admitted a little earlier cd. [could] give some advice."[20]

Paul emphasizes that we need not have experienced the same problem in order to be helpful to a person in need. Because we ourselves have experienced the ministry of God's comfort, we can comfort those in any trouble. Author and evangelist Ron Dunn poetically describes this ministry by saying, "Sometimes the tears we shed water the flowers in other people's gardens."[21]

One day I received a disheartening call from Jason, a middle-aged, philosophically minded evangelist who desired some advice. This servant of God was deeply troubled by the problem of suffering, so much so that he was beginning to question his own salvation. Jason had graduated from a prominent Midwestern seminary and had published a couple of very helpful books. He wished to keep up his nationwide ministry, but his struggle over the issue of suffering was beginning to affect his ability to preach and teach. He confided that he even felt somewhat suicidal.

I recommended that Jason contact a Christian counselor in his area. Through that contact, Jason learned that he was creating most of his own struggles. He was a quick study and made rapid progress. His questions were answered, and most importantly, Jason was able to come to grips with his own emotional issues. After completing a university doctorate while pastoring a church, Jason realized his lifelong dream of teaching. For several years now, he has been a seminary apologetics professor. With God's help, Jason moved from being suicidal and desperately wanting to leave the ministry to equipping others to pastor and teach. As in the New Testament days, God still changes lives and uses our struggles to help others.

By providing comfort to God's children, Paul himself was blessed and able to avoid self-pity. He realized that finding God's comfort in the midst of adversity allowed him to minister to others more effectively.[22] Mac Cauley, whose story we read in chapter 7, discovered that his car accident actually helped him to develop a keener sensitivity to hurting people. "Throughout my ministry, I was always sensitive to depressed and hurting people, but now I have a whole new appreciation and different understanding for those who are hurting," he says. Mac is a better shepherd because he experienced the profound comfort of God during his own time of suffering.

In an interview regarding his role in the movie Tootsie, Dustin Hoffman described the experience of being disguised as a woman. One of the makeup artists told him that it was impossible to make him look like a pretty woman.

God will take the greatest pain and suffering of our lives and use it as a springboard for ministry to others

Hoffman says that he went home that night and cried as he recalled how many women he had rejected in his past. Regardless of how smart, kind, or talented they were, he had rejected them solely on the basis of their physical appearance. Because he had now been judged on appearance alone, Dustin Hoffman could now be more empathetic toward these women.

Similarly, suffering allows us to identify with others and provides us an opportunity to testify about God's comfort to a broken soul. Someone has said that encouragement is like peanut butter; the more you spread it around, the more it sticks to things. As Christians, we need to spread our experience and comfort to others so they may come to know the God of all comfort.

Like Tom Whiteman, we may find that God will take the greatest pain and suffering of our lives and use it as a springboard for ministry to others. Of course, this doesn't mean that each of us will develop an internationally known and respected Christian ministry. However, it does mean that through our difficulties, God has equipped us to share His hope and comfort in our own particular corner of the world.

Think back to the story I (John) told earlier about losing my fiancée. When she broke up with me, I was studying and preparing to become a missionary. In the aftermath of the loss, however, I started taking psychology classes in order to better understand my hurt. Through the painful sting of rejection, God redirected my career pursuits from missions to counseling. Prior to this loss, I could not figure out why anyone would want to see a counselor. But as I wandered in my own desert of loneliness and abandonment, I learned the value of the helping relationship.

Today, nearly thirty years later, I have had the opportunity to share that story with countless clients who have experienced similar losses. My suffering taught me the value of obedience, depending upon God, helping others, and becoming more like Christ. The messages hidden beneath my clients' pain have been different and unique to them. But they've been encouraged by hearing how my own suffering has been redeemed. The opportunity that God has given me to comfort others through my own loss demonstrates that God does not waste His comfort. He has redirected my suffering outward to other people who are hurting in one way or another.

SECTION 3

ARE YOU THERE, GOD?

How can one family sustain so much loss? All three of the Gordon sisters had fought breast cancer, two of them battling it twice. Maggie, the middle child, was crippled by childhood polio. Susan, the oldest had lost her husband to a sudden massive heart attack and, a few months later, her son to a drug overdose. Betty, the youngest had battled the demons of her own son's addiction and the loss of her once prosperous business. The aunt who had raised them was dying of Parkinson's disease and a beloved cousin had recently been murdered by an obsessed boyfriend. In a world of so much pain and sorrow, how does one trust God? Where is the stable foundation upon which one can build a firm and lasting faith?

Chapter 11

IN HIS PERSON:
PUT ON THE GOD-COLORED GLASSES

Belinda, a thirty-eight-year-old woman, cried her way through her first counseling session. Her dress and mannerisms proved that she was trying hard to present an image of someone who had it all together. However, her recent hospital admission for severe depression revealed a different story. It took several sessions to get Belinda to share her experience. Obviously, trust was not something that came easily to her, so establishing rapport was a painstaking process. But eventually the walls were let down enough for me to see inside.

Belinda grew up in the Midwest and attended a very conservative Bible-believing church. She was active in her youth group as well as other church activities. By all standards she was a model child. Like most teenage girls, she dreamed of meeting the right person to marry. Until then, however, she vowed to keep herself pure.

A youth pastor joined the staff at Belinda's church and quickly got to know this young lady through her willingness to serve in any way that she could. Perhaps he recognized her need for affirmation, because before long he was sexually abusing her as often as he could get her alone. In addition, he was also abusing several other girls in the church. Belinda's innocence was shattered. No longer could she see "godly men" as trustworthy.

After several years of the abuse, one girl finally told her parents, and the minister's sin was exposed. The elders and staff members decided it was best to keep the ordeal quiet since they thought nothing good could come from having "a man of God" and a Christ-centered church in the middle of such a horrible controversy. Not only would the church's reputation be tarnished, they reasoned, it would also cause great upheaval within the church. In order to avoid a scandal, the minister was asked to resign. Unbelievably, he was offered a favorable recommendation. Belinda's parents told their daughter not to speak about the "episode," and for years, this child of God had nowhere to go with her inner pain. Because Belinda saw herself as "spoiled goods," her self-esteem plummeted. She felt terrible, blaming herself for allowing the abuse to happen and for letting it continue for so long. She truly believed there was something wrong with her.

She married after graduating from college, but her sex life never lived up to her expectations. In fact, she tried to avoid intimacy at all costs. Sex left her feeling dirty. Her confused and hurt husband withdrew, leaving Belinda to battle feelings of abandonment and rejection all over again. Who could blame him? she thought. I am not worthy of such a good man.

Spiritually, Belinda did not fare much better. She was active in the children's department of her church, served as chairperson for the benevolence committee, and worked tirelessly in the drama ministry. She was even involved in a local crisis pregnancy center. Everyone considered Belinda to be a godly wife and a wonderful lady. But no one sensed the growing emotional and spiritual unrest in her soul.

Belinda viewed God as someone to be appeased. Of course she believed in grace, but she had a hard time applying that grace to her own life. Her spiritual journey was little more than repeated attempts to gain God's approval. No matter how much Belinda tried to feel peace in her relationship with God, His approval always seemed beyond her reach. Her resolute efforts only left Belinda lonely, fearful, tired, and depressed. Like a field officer, she marshaled her forces in an effort to reclaim a sense of control in her life, but in spite of her resurgent resolve, she could not withstand the powerful assault of her internal turmoil.

Combat fatigue eventually resulted in an inability to fight any longer, and unable to overcome her overwhelming feelings of shame and despair, Belinda surrendered to her emotions. She experienced a debilitating depression that necessitated a prolonged hospitalization. Belinda, like so many other sexual abuse survivors, felt incredible inner pain. She could see no redeeming value in her experiences.

Through counseling, however, Belinda began to realize how many battle scars she bore. Some were the result of her past wounds, but others had been caused by her own ineffective tactics to control the pain. As her sense of safety increased, she began to lower the walls that she had erected to hide her pain and protect her already depleted reserves. Energy she once used to avoid her feelings was now channeled into therapy, and eventually Belinda was able to move through the issues of trust, fear, control, abandonment, and acceptance. Her marriage improved beyond her imagination. The shame and fear that once paralyzed her was replaced with comfort and enjoyment. Belinda now speaks to groups on sexual abuse and counsels with other women who have experienced sexual trauma.

Most importantly, Belinda came to see God in a different way. No longer is she bitter at God for allowing the sexual abuse to occur. She is finally able to worship God deeply.

What was true for both Belinda in the 21st century was also true for Job thousands of years ago. Following his discourse with God, Job was left practically

God changed Job's preoccupation from explanation to worship

speechless. His arguments had proved agonizingly insufficient. His attitude was exposed as arrogant.[1] He realized that God alone is in the position to decide what is best for any of His children.

Job responded to God on this issue one last time. In the final chapter of the book, we find Job with a new outlook on life, as he realized that God can do everything. His mind had been opened to see his ignorance before the Almighty God, and he finally understood that his terrible experience had allowed him to see God in a bigger way.[2] Humbled by the hand and words of God, Job exclaimed that he now had a fresh grasp of the power of God. His burning question of "Why me?" was never answered. Rather, God changed Job's preoccupation from explanation to worship. His new understanding of the vastness of God settled Job's confusion and eliminated his demand for answers. Sovereignty was no longer just a theological concept to Job but a firsthand reality because God used suffering to enlarge Job's capacity to know Him. Job once saw God as oppositional, but he learned to see His sovereignty in a new way.[3] Knowing that he had an all-powerful and glorious God, Job could now live in triumphant confidence.

Thousands of years after the penning of Job's words, the prophet Jeremiah found himself in the king's prison for preaching God's message. As God tested Jeremiah's faith, the weeping prophet declared that there was nothing too hard for the Lord.[4] In response to his prayer, the Lord told Jeremiah that he was correct; nothing was too hard for Him.[5] Just as suffering had changed Job's understanding of sovereignty, Jeremiah's heartache unclouded his perception of God's nature.

We are similarly encouraged today by those who have walked through deep waters with God and have emerged, not only relatively unscathed, but as brightly shining individuals whose relationship with God has clearly matured. I (Gary) met one such saint during a speaking engagement at a Midwestern college. Charles was seriously handicapped and found it quite difficult just to walk. On top of that, he had also been recently diagnosed with a severe emotional disorder that required constant medication. To further complicate his situation, a rare blood condition plagued him from time to time. Combined with repeated mistreatment and neglect as a child, Charles lived constantly with pain. One bout with illness brought him to the threshold of death. Many would wonder about the fairness of someone suffering from such severe physical and emotional hurts.

Charles often struggled with nagging doubts regarding his salvation. Sometimes this would erupt into anger at God, as he lashed out at Him for his myriad of problems and blamed God for not intervening or taking them away. As we talked, Charles and I developed what has become a long-term friendship. I helped him identify his errant thoughts and substitute God's promises in their place. It took some time, but over a few years, Charles achieved very significant victories over his religious doubts. Later, he used similar techniques to make major strides in dealing with his emotional condition, as well as with the wounds of his past. While his disability and blood disease remain incurable, Charles today has grown to such an extent that he has been able to bless others in their struggles. Having completed his college degree, Charles now works with people with disabilities and has also published several items in apologetics, his chosen field of research. Incredibly, in spite of a serious speech impediment, Charles now teaches an adult study group.

Above all, it was his personal, detailed study of God's attributes that changed Charles's attitude He often tells me he cannot wait to go to be with his Jesus, who has transformed his daily existence in ways that would seem impossible to everyone who knows him and his handicaps. He constantly works on applying these truths to his life. God's grace and mercy have triumphed, infusing Charles with a joyful attitude that has become obvious to those whom he meets and with whom he works.

When we suffer, we typically see it as an attack, and the God who allowed it as the enemy. We're quick to point a finger at some person or some circumstance. Ultimately, we have a deep sense that God could have prevented us from experiencing the calamity if He had really wanted to. No responsible parent would let his or her child proceed into harm's way without doing everything to stop it. God seems too irresponsible, if not downright cruel and callous, to be trusted. The pain is compounded by the sense that God has wronged us.

I (John) counseled a forty-year-old widow named Olivia, whose pain was immense. Her husband had been killed by a drunken driver, and Olivia's joyless and gloomy existence cast a shadow on all who saw her. Though I did not believe it was warranted, her family wanted her in the hospital. She was grieving deeply, but her grief was compounded by a pessimistic and melancholic personality.

From the onset of therapy, Olivia recognized that she was angry at God. She couldn't pray, have devotions, or sing in church. In fact, it was a struggle for her even to go to church. After about seven months of counseling, I told her that she had the right to be angry at God. After all, God had cheated her out of a future with her husband. She did not deserve that kind of treatment from a God who was supposed to be loving. At first she agreed with me. Then I went a step further, continuing to "shake my fist" at God, so to speak, in an attempt to help her see the irrationality of her perspective. Finally, I hit on a key phrase. "God has wronged you," I said. "He has wronged you, and He had no right to do so!" It was as if the floodgates of her soul opened, and she began to weep uncontrollably. Though she had said similar things in many of our previous counseling sessions, this time it was different. Through her tears she kept saying, "No, no! God didn't wrong me. God can't wrong anybody." Her anger and resentment toward God began to melt. And though her grief did not disappear, her faith was rekindled.

In contrast to most of us, Betsie ten Boom's unwavering faith gave her a greater appreciation of the wonderful inexplicability and sovereignty of God. Before her arrest, Betsie stoutly affirmed, "But if God has shown us bad times ahead, it's enough for me that He knows about them. That's why He sometimes shows us things, you know—to tell us that this too is in His hands."[6] Betsie was able to see every evil and jarring plight as an opportunity to praise God and share the good news of Christ.

When Betsie and her sister, Corrie, were placed in the filthy conditions of Barracks 28, Betsie found comfort in 1 Thessalonians 5:15-18. Reading from a Bible that had been safely concealed from the prison guards, she told Corrie that regardless of their circumstances, they were to praise God. She even thanked God for the fleas since the guards avoided entering the barracks because of them. Betsie's unflinching assent of God's personal involvement in her suffering encouraged Corrie to rethink her own understanding of God's character. And on her deathbed, overcome by the awesomeness of God, Betsie envisioned the remarkable opportunity their imprisonment offered: "We must tell [people] that there is no pit so deep that He is not deeper still. They will listen to us, Corrie, because we have been here."[7] Despite the horror of a concentration camp, the Ten Booms were able to see the glory of God. Just like Job, Corrie and Betsie learned that God was the God of their worst situation, even in the German concentration camp Ravensbrück.

When we experience the storms of this life, we are prone to fear. We clamor, act impulsively, or slump into despair and depression. But Jesus is in control, waiting to demonstrate that He has power over the storm. We will never know of God's power over the tempest unless we go through the storm and experience His capacity to calm it. Because Jesus was and is the Creator God, He is able to speak to His creation and bring peace and restoration.

When we, like Job, see God for who He is, we can stop blaming Him for our pain and suffering. We learn to accept both good and bad from the hand of the Lord. We come to know God's power when we see Him move in an impossible situation and meet our personal need. Possibly St. Augustine had this in mind when he exclaimed, "In my deepest wound I saw your glory, and it dazzled me."

Chapter 12

IN THE GIFT:
DOES SUFFERING HAVE REWARDS?

What is the best gift that you have ever received? As I thought about that question, I remember a number of things that I received from my parents over the course of many birthdays and Christmases. The one gift that stands out, however, was given to me when I was teaching at a small Bible college in Florida. It came after my wife and I were robbed. Though we didn't have much, the thief took the few valuable items that we did have. Ironically, we were in the process of photographing our possessions for an insurance policy and our 35mm camera was stolen. Though we had just signed up for renters insurance, we didn't have the money to pay the $250 deductible. I had mentioned the robbery and our financial hardship to a colleague but I never dreamed of what would follow. At the next chapel service, the president of the student body came to the podium and, to my surprise, asked that I come to the platform. He told me that they had heard about the robbery and our financial difficulty. The students had rallied together and raised nearly $375. He told me that they knew that was more than the deductible but that they wanted to bless me with it. I stood there stunned, dumbfounded, and in absolute humility. Tears poured from my eyes as I accepted the gift.

Regardless of the culture, all people like to engage in some form of gift-giving. I could tell that the joy the students received in giving me that financial gift was greater than the joy that I had in experiencing their generosity. Even more than the students at that small Bible college, God is a giver. God is a lover of humanity. Like most lovers, He delights in giving gifts. The Bible is full of many verses that reveal the generosity of God. He gives simply because it flows from His character. God desires to enrich and bless His children.

Yet, when we think of God as the giver of gifts, we do not put suffering into the same sentence, let alone paragraph or chapter! Suffering is the last word that comes to mind when we think of God's generosity. God, however, does grant us gifts through our heartaches, brokenness, and pain. In this chapter we want to unwrap a few of the gifts that come out of suffering.

God's Gift to Job: Earthly Blessings Through Trials

The story of Job has always intrigued us. In its pages we find another purpose in suffering. When we arrive at the later part of Job 42, it is easy to simply skip over it. By the end of the book, we realize that Job's steadfastness in suffering was not only meaningful but also recognized by the heavenly Father as worthy of reward. Job declared early in his biography that he would bless the Lord's name no matter what happened to him.[1] And because of this faithfulness, he was able to receive blessings from the Lord—more than what had been taken from him. In fact, Job had experienced loss, but he also understood what it meant to obtain grace.

Indeed, God blessed Job by giving him double what he had had before his adversity began. He was given twice the number of livestock, sheep, camels, and donkeys. Though his seven sons and three daughters had all been killed, he and his wife had seven more sons and three more daughters. Finally, Job lived another 140 years and was allowed to see his descendants for four generations. In the long run, Job's suffering was short lived when compared to the years he was given to enjoy his family, wealth, and health.

Once again, life looked promising for Job. But his new life was the result of a changed heart. Because of his ordeal, he had discovered that God is more than a concept or an impersonal being, and that nothing in his life had occurred outside of God's watchful eye. With a humbled heart, Job realized that God could be trusted. And because of Job's changed attitude, God knew that He could trust Job with a double portion of blessing.

Imagine the gossip that must have surrounded Job. After all, people of his day believed that suffering was punishment for wrongdoing. Perhaps they considered him a first-class hypocrite during his suffering. In the end however, God silenced Job's critics. The blessings that Job received communicated to his accusers that he was a just and upright man. But it wasn't Job's goodness that earned him a reward, it was his broken and contrite heart that brought about the blessings of God.

Of course, it is very difficult to know what God has planned for our futures. Often it is even tough to make sense of our present struggles. About twenty years ago, I (Gary) got to know one of my philosophy students well. Al seemed to have a very promising future, but a short while after I met him, he was diagnosed with cancer and quickly underwent surgery. Al's future was put on hold, and the next few weeks and months included further tests, treatments, more tests, and more treatments.

Al knew he needed to pull his life back together. He just wasn't sure the best way to do that. Should he finish his studies even though he couldn't be sure that he would live long enough to graduate? Should he do something else while he waited for his treatments to be finished? Living his life from day to day, Al decided to go back to school and finish his bachelor's degree. Every three months, he had to travel to a hospital for more specialized tests to ascertain whether or not the cancer

How often we miss the blessings of God because we have chosen to pursue our own way

had returned. Once he received his degree, he went straight to graduate school and finished his master's degree. Then he completed his Ph.D. and a lengthy residency.

Today, Al is a well-known Christian psychologist. He has a private practice, is an adjunct professor at a prestigious Texas university, and so far has written four books and many journal articles. He is constantly in demand as a speaker. Moreover, he married his college sweetheart and thoroughly enjoys their three children. Incidentally, three of his books address various issues of pain and suffering.

When Al was on his back in more than one hospital, God could very well have been preparing him for a future blessing. It is certain that his struggles prepared him to be a blessing to others!

How often we miss the blessings of God because we have chosen to pursue our own way. The blessings we receive will not necessarily be like those of Job; yet suffering can prepare us to receive greater blessings. Consider Joseph's story in Genesis. He told his brothers that while their hateful actions had been meant to harm him, God had used them to accomplish good.[2] We can now see how God redeemed Joseph's trials to bring incredible blessings to the nation of Israel. In the film Star Trek: Wrath of the Khan, Mr. Spock sacrifices himself to save the Enterprise. As he's dying, he exchanges a few words with Captain Kirk:

> *Spock: The needs of the many outweigh . . .*
> *Kirk: . . . the needs of the few.*
> *Spock: Or the one.[3]*

Joseph's trials were unfair and unjust if the few, or in this case the one, is more important than the many. But Joseph was not greater than the nation of Israel. As God's child, Joseph knew that God could use him in whatever way He deemed appropriate to attain a greater good. Joseph's ability to accept that truth gave him not only the power to endure but also the ability to forgive his offenders.

After an initial reading of Job's epilogue, some may think that God is restoring Job's losses twofold in order to apologize. It almost seems like God is blessing Job to make up for all that he had to endure. But, God doesn't do wrong, nor does He need to apologize. If we dig into this passage more deeply, we may finally realize the richness of those concluding verses. Job's epilogue is a vivid illustration of Solomon's words: "The end of a thing is better than its beginning."[4] Job's life had been full prior to his suffering; still he emerged a "new and improved" Job. Suffering had personalized and purified his faith, tested his faithfulness, matured him, and prepared him for a greater blessing than he could ever have imagined. His enhanced financial portfolio likely paled in comparison to the new sense of life he now experienced. Though his wealth increased greatly, the changes in his life loomed even larger. Job learned that there is a God above and beyond the suffering, a God who is incredibly grand, gracious, good, and generous. Knowing a God like that was Job's true reward. The blessings of God were not a payoff; they were only the manifestation of how our outrageous and extraordinary God operates.

The character of God compels Him to be a generous lover. He deliriously desires to bless His children. His blessings are never to be seen as indulgent. No. At the same time, our God knows that an ungrateful heart is ill prepared for His unimaginable blessings. Unless He prepares our hearts and remakes our souls through the sting of suffering, we might selfishly bask in His blessings without any sense of humility or gratitude. Those who have either never faced serious suffering or who have reacted to their pain in less than constructive ways may find it difficult to get past Job's actual circumstances. But when we meet people like Charles (introduced in chapter 11) who are so marvelously transformed as a result of their suffering, we get a small glimpse of what wonders God works through those who are willing to grow.

God's Ultimate Gift: Heavenly Rewards

In addressing the problem of pain, C.S. Lewis keenly observed, "A book on suffering which says nothing of heaven, is leaving out almost the whole of one side of the account. Scripture and tradition habitually put the joys of heaven into the scale against the sufferings of earth, and no solution of the problem of pain which does not do so can be called a Christian one."[5] It is this hope of heaven that is the prime ingredient in a theology of suffering.

The biblical writer James knew that heaven played a significant role in helping people find meaning in suffering. His book is addressed to Christians who were suffering due to their faith. In order to direct their eyes from the sorrows of this world to the joys of heaven, James wrote, "Blessed is the man who endures temptation; for when he has been approved, he will receive the crown of life which the Lord has promised to those who love Him."[6]

Heaven and an eternity with God truly are rewards for those who suffer. But this reward has a condition: we must endure. As we saw earlier, the word endure (hupomenō) comes from the word patience which means "to live or abide underneath a problem."[7] Patience doesn't mean living without anxiety but rather enduring adverse circumstances without letting them sour our attitudes.

In a world of instant gratification, we typically expect God to respond immediately when we pray. Some Christians even preach spiritual formulas that, when properly applied, guarantee quick and effortless results. When these formulas work, we feel great. Things have gone our way, and the notion that God can be manipulated is reinforced. But when the formulas don't work, and that is often the case, we may either be bitter toward God for not giving in to our demands or experience incredible guilt, thinking that we are not worthy to gain His favor.

Paul assures us that earthly suffering cannot compare with the glory that we shall one day experience.[8] This passion for heaven helps to explain how Paul could characterize his immense hardships as "light affliction." In spite of such adversity, he was able to see this life of suffering not as a sprint but as a marathon. He realized that the ultimate reward awaited him if he remained steadfast and faithful to the task of following Christ.

The Coaster

During graduate school, I and one of my friends decided that we needed a break from our studies and made plans to go to Kings Dominion (an amusement park in Virginia). The big day finally arrived, bringing with it record high temperatures. But that didn't stop us. With the foolish arrogance of youth, we decided to brave the heat and head to the park.

Eager to be the first in line for the park's new roller coaster, we arrived early. Unfortunately, so did a thousand other people. We grabbed a map and huddled to devise our strategy. With a confident battle cry we sprinted through the park, pushing through hedges and hurdling small children, always being sure to offer a hurried "excuse me" along the way. Near the back of the park, the gray-green skeleton of the snaking coaster consumed the skyline. Victory was in sight! Judging the goal to be a mile away, we paused to catch our breath. Instead, our breath was taken away when we saw a sign that stated, "The line for the Anaconda starts here." Even worse was the realization that we had to backtrack three hundred feet to find the end of the line. Still, in spite of the heat, we took our places for the three-hour wait. I thought we would never make it. By the time we got to the roller coaster, we were sick from the heat and soaked with sweat. But at long last, we climbed into the coaster and strapped ourselves securely into the seats. Then off we went! And for the next forty-five seconds we experienced the ride of a lifetime!

Why would anyone endure such a long, tortuous wait for such a short ride? Simply because we knew that once on the ride we would experience exhilaration. As enlivening and thrilling as a ride on a roller coaster can be, heaven is far, far better.

Living in this world is like standing in a long line for a roller coaster. Sometimes it's uncomfortable, chaotic, and trying. Some days seem as if they will never end. Yet we continue to struggle on, day by day. We can endure this world of pain and suffering because we know there is a glorious and wonderful ride beyond comprehension waiting for us on the other side. The trials of this world are nothing compared to the ride ahead. Our suffering is to be endured only momentarily, but the crown of life will be worn forever.

Too often we try to make living in the world the ride itself. But lines are only a means to an end. Of course there's nothing wrong with making the wait as comfortable as possible. In fact, some people have the capacity to turn waiting into a party. They bring sleeping bags, chairs, and countless other things to entertain themselves while waiting to purchase concert tickets or to see their teams play. But without the ultimate payoff of purchasing that ticket or seeing the game, the waiting is futile. Reasonable comforts are understandable. But when we focus more on worldly comfort than on heaven, the situations that seem out of our control become nearly intolerable.

Viktor Frankl wrote, "The prisoner who had lost faith in the future—his future—was doomed. With his loss of belief in the future, he also lost his spiritual hold; he let himself decline and became subject to mental and physical decay."[9] God wants us to live for what is on the other side. As we strive to gain God's perspective, we will learn to see beyond our present circumstances and focus on what is in store for us in the life to come. In dozens of New Testament texts, we are told to live in the present with an eye to the future. When we apply the truths of heaven to our earthly issues and problems, suffering takes on a whole new meaning. The great heroes of the faith (such as those whose credentials are recorded in Hebrews 11) considered the future promises as present realities, thereby transforming their adversities into hope. There is no greater understanding of suffering than to live with a future hope.[10] The hope of heaven allows our present sufferings to be covered in the peace that God provides for those who are at rest in His sovereignty, promises, and faithfulness. God has the power to transform suffering into a glorious expectation for the faithful Christian. And when we reach heaven, not only will we receive rewards, but the immediate presence of God as well.

I met Jennifer when she stopped by my office to ask for help choosing a research paper topic. Because of her tremendous leadership abilities, Jennifer had served in several influential capacities. For example, one summer she had led a team of students into an impoverished area of the country to feed and provide shelter for the needy. She had earned a reputation as a very caring person who truly loved others, as well as someone who was willing to spend her own time and energy in helping to make real changes in people's lives.

In spite of her excellent potential, however, Jennifer grew angry with the Lord. She was tired of always being the one who volunteered to work for others. "Haven't I done enough already?" she would ask. When I first worked with her, Jennifer's anger affected her spiritual walk with the Lord. Desiring to see her return to her previous level of commitment, I encouraged her to write an essay on the subject of ways God might use to motivate believers. She agreed to do research in this area.

Sometime later, she turned in a wonderful essay, which concluded that God uses both negative and positive motivation in the lives of Christians. During the process of writing the paper, Jennifer realized that she had mistaken God's intentions. Scripture is clear that negative motivators are not always punishments. They are often used to keep believers from wandering further from God's blessings. On the other hand, Jennifer saw that God also promised positive motivators: rewards that are designed not simply to "force" us to obey, but to help us enjoy more fully both this present life and eternity. Once she realized the error in her thinking, she worked on changing her attitude about God. She realized that in growing angry toward God, she had actually been selfish and sinful. She needed God's reminders against wandering, but she also wanted to enjoy more peace in her life as well as God's heavenly reward. Jennifer responded by repenting, and she resolved to follow God wholeheartedly. In so doing, she recovered her first love. She discovered that God had her best interests in mind.

As the Suffering Servant, Jesus has a special interest in all those who have suffered in this life. In the description of Stephen's stoning in the Book of Acts, Jesus is pictured as standing and waiting to lead the ovation of heaven as His followers are about to come home.[11] Surely, He held the crown of life to adorn the martyred saint for his faithfulness. For Stephen the best was yet to come.

The following story beautifully illustrates this promise.

> Audrey often spent time visiting with an old bedridden saint
> and was always amazed by her cheerful disposition. Audrey was

also friends with a very wealthy woman who always seemed to view things from a negative perspective. Although her friend professed to be a Christian, she always seemed downcast, and Audrey thought it might do her good to meet her other friend, the bedridden saint.

The saint lived in a garret, five stories up. At the bottom of the stairs, the wealthy woman looked around, drew up her dress, and said, "How dark and filthy this is!"

"It's better higher up," said Audrey. When they got to the second floor, however, things were no better, and the woman again complained. But Audrey only replied, "It's better higher up."

The third floor actually seemed worse than the first two, and the woman again complained, but Audrey's response was the same: "It's better higher up."

At last they reached the fifth floor, where the saint's bedroom was located. As they entered the room, the wealthy woman looked around at the thick carpeting, flowering plants in the window, and little birds singing in their cages. And there she also saw the bedridden saint—one of those saints whom God is polishing for His own temple—simply beaming with joy. The wealthy woman said to her, "Isn't it difficult for you to just lie here?"

The saint smiled and said, "It's better higher up."[12]

Suffering is certainly not a gift that we like to receive. Yet our Lord knows what we need. Whether the suffering is the doorway to give us earthly blessings or not, we are guaranteed heavenly rewards. Crowns symbolize royalty, authority, honor, victory, and reward. God, the ultimate Promise Keeper, has promised a crown for those who endure suffering. The symbolism is not lost on us when we consider the fact that God's Son, Jesus Christ, wore a crown of suffering.

Chapter 13

LIFE IS THE WAITING ROOM

The subject of death and dying touches everyone at one time or another. A group of researchers found that even preschoolers have ideas about what it means to die. One young boy named Jimmy shared his view of death: "When you die, they bury you in the ground and your soul goes to heaven, but your body can't go to heaven because it is too crowded up there already." Judy said, "Only the good people go to heaven. The other people go where it's hot all the time like in Florida." John responded by saying, "Maybe I'll die someday, but I hope I don't die on my birthday because it's no fun to celebrate your birthday if you're dead." (Indeed). Marsha offered another perspective on death. "When you die, you don't have to do homework in heaven, unless your teacher is there."

We will all die someday, but only God knows how and when. Thinking about one's own death is not pleasant for many people, but for the believer, it should not be the cause of fear. Through death, we walk into the presence of God.

Paul's Waiting Room

The apostle Paul seemed to always know how to make the best of a bad situation. He found himself in the waiting room of prison, awaiting the strong possibility of his own death. Yet, Paul viewed his imprisonment as a means to advance the gospel, sharing his story with those who might not have otherwise heard it. When jealousy and envy created a competitive environment in the church, Paul simply rejoiced in the fact that the Good News was being preached.

Paul was able to use bad circumstances for good because he was preoccupied with honoring Christ. He was willing to esteem Christ, even in death, which he thought was better than earthly life.[1] Through his life, he desired that Christ would be magnified—brought into sharp focus. Not only did Paul want to glorify

Christ through his words and deeds, but even in his own body. This concept might be what Paul meant when he told the Roman church to present their bodies as living sacrifices.[2]

Like Paul, we should be devoted to honoring and magnifying Christ. In the face of suffering or adversity, this is possible only as we die to ourselves, take up our crosses, and follow Him.[3] But what does it mean to take up our cross and follow Christ? For readers in Paul's day, the cross was a symbol of death, a painful death, a death that robbed the cross bearer of dignity. Paul used the analogy to exhort Christians to consider the things we desire from this world as dead. Taking up our crosses means viewing those internal desires of our hearts as having no value, as if they could—or more accurately should—be thrown away. We must yield the demands of our hearts and allow God to have the right of way. In other words, we are to view our desires for comfort, financial security, good health, status—things that are not bad in and of themselves—as buried and gone.

What do you desire most in life? Very few Christians would earnestly hunger to glorify Christ through their lives if doing so meant torment. As we have already seen, though it pains even the most devoted believer to admit, our central passions are for ease, comfort, predictability, and fairness.

For Paul, his central passion was Christ. Whether he lived or died Christ was the beginning and end of the story. To Paul, living his life was valuable only in so much as he could serve Christ in ministry. Paul's goal was to be used by God in whatever He willed and however He led. Paul experienced joy in the midst of his imprisonment because he knew his situation was not dire. Knowing that God intended it for him and that through it he had been able to further the gospel to people whom he would had never met otherwise.

Paul gave us the conditions by which this goal can be accomplished: ". . . whether by life or by death."[4] We've all heard the saying that the only things that are certain in life are death and taxes. Technology has helped us to postpone death but not eliminate it. We can hope for tax relief, but as long as we live under government officials, we will have taxes. Needless to say, we cannot do much about either. Paul recognized that the logical conclusion of his imprisonment might be death. And as he considered the definite possibility of his life coming to a violent end, the apostle was able to recognize God's hand even in death. Dying held no fear for Paul. For a religious person to be willing to die for his or her cause is not extraordinary. Consider the Islam pilots who flew the American planes into the Twin Towers did so to honor their god. They are but one example of devotees willing to die for their god. But Paul's desire to die was not to earn a place in heaven or a heavenly reward. It is unlikely that Paul saw his death as delivering him for his earthly troubles. Paul was willing to die a martyr's death that would not only glorify God but would gain him the privilege of being with Christ. Paul had no reason to live except to be for Christ.

Paul wanted Christ to be magnified in his life no matter what the cost. His heartfelt passion was not that Caesar would spare his life but that Christ would be honored. How Paul responded to his suffering or how he faced death would not deter his determination to exalt Christ. Paul knew that he served a God who could control life and death; after all, He had raised Jesus Christ from the grave.

Often, God gives His saints what we might call "dying grace." While Gary's wife, Debbie, was dying of stomach cancer at the youthful age of 43, she reported that God had spoken directly to her, imparting a very personal message. She had never before made a claim like this, but it was clear that God had given her a special peace about her impending death. She told me (John) that she was not afraid to die, and that although she loved her family dearly, she did not even feel any emotional pain when she thought of being separated from us. In the days and weeks leading up to her death, Debbie spent many mornings sitting in a chair with her arms upraised as she listened to Christian music through her earphones. To the family, these reactions were unmistakable signs that God had blessed her during a very difficult time.[5]

Unless the Rapture occurs first, Christians eventually will leave this world through death. Although when and how we go is up to God, the work and person of the risen Jesus Christ ensures our eternal life in heaven. Paul understood this when he radically claimed that dying and being with Christ is much better than living.[6] Moreover, almost as if to make sure we understood what he was saying, Paul added that he even preferred to die and go be with Jesus Christ, since this was far better than earthly living.[7] While such words may sound pious to some, the implications of the statement are profound. Paul was not being trite in his letter to the Philippians. Deep within his soul he realized that death was not something to be feared but was a doorway to come into God's glory. Paul knew that heaven is being in the presence of Christ, and he understood that death was simply a passing into a wonderful new world—to a home prepared for us by Christ Himself.

Paul was totally consumed with living and serving Jesus Christ. He was one with Christ, and even death could not break that union. In this way, Christ was brought into sharp focus in Paul's life. What was true for Paul can also be true

Paul knew that heaven is being in the presence of Christ

for us. Death is the ultimate healing. It is an end to all misery and discomfort, but not the end of living. The Bible promises that we will be glorified with new bodies.[8] God's way of bringing us to heaven, however, may be through the doorway of pain and suffering.

Paul's declaration of magnifying Christ in his life and death was followed with an exhortation; the Philippian should count it a privilege to suffer for Christ. It is unlikely that the Philippian readers were jumping for joy as they read the apostles words exhorting them to remain steadfast in the face of persecution. But Paul knew they could be bold in their faith because to die for Christ was as rewarding as living for Him.

Gary's Waiting Room

Unlike Paul, Gary's waiting room was facing the impending death of his wife, Debbie. When Debbie was dying of stomach cancer, I recalled frequently a discussion between Job and the Lord.

If you ever wondered what it would be like to have a discussion with the God and Creator of the universe, just check out Job's experience. Over the large majority of his story, he had heard much advice along with many accusations from his three friends who talked to him throughout the majority of the Book of Job. He dialogued with them and protested that they were mistaken in their complaints. He would find out later that many of their allegations angered the Lord.

A fourth friend, Elihu, entered the discussion towards the end of the dialogue and offered much sounder advice. Many think that Elihu generally gave godly advice. Elihu reported both that God had a right to be silent if He wanted to do so (34:29; 35:12), and that God was still communicating with humans in many ways (33:14-30). So, while God was not silent, He chose the times, places, and type of interaction.

But Job challenged God a few times, thinking that he should "have his day in court." Perhaps to his surprise, Job apparently got his wish. God appeared to him in some sense, and for several chapters (38-41), God quizzed Job about a plethora of topics, including nature and biology. He even dared Job more than once to solve the problem of good and evil! Imagine being asked your own question!

Job only wanted to know why he was suffering. However, in the end, he never had his question answered. So why was he satisfied (42:1-6)? Through God's questioning, Job realized that he knew enough about God to trust Him in those areas that he didn't know or understand. In other words, what he knew about God was sufficient for him to learn to trust Him when he did not have the answers. After all, not having specific solutions is not the same as there being no answers at all!

While Debbie was sleeping upstairs, I sat on our front porch with a monitor at my side, listening every time she turned over or moaned, frequently running up the stairs to make sure that she was okay. By way of personal application, I wonder how we would respond if we demanded a hearing before God, only to find ourselves dialoguing directly with Him! That would be more than we bargained for! I found myself imagining what it would be like if I were to have a discussion with the Lord. I discovered that I was not angry with God, which I largely attributed to my view of God's gift of free will, but that is a matter for another discussion. Besides, hopefully learning from Job's example, I did not want to plunge in where angels feared to tread! In other words, I knew that God could answer and explain the toughest of my questions in less than a sentence each. So I determined to be polite and proper!

I imagined several conversations with the Lord. After all, I did have some major questions. As I told my closest friends, while I certainly believed that

God was good, at the same time, the worst possible thing I could imagine had come. Debbie was my closest friend on earth and I couldn't envisage losing her. My imagined conversations differed from each other, depending on the lessons that I thought I needed to learn. I also surmised that such a conversation with God would be different for each one of us, depending on our own personal circumstances.

One prominent scenario always went something like this:

"Lord, why is Debbie upstairs in bed, dying? Why stomach cancer? She's only 43 years old! And how am I to take care of our four children and still perform the ministry that you have given me to do?"

"Gary, I only want to ask you one question for now. In terms of your own specific research, what kind of a world is this?"

"Well, Lord, I'm not sure exactly what you're asking for. But from my own research, I would say that this is a world where the Gospel message is true—that your Son died by crucifixion and was raised again from the dead."

"Very good. That's a good place to start. So I raised my Son from the dead, right?"

"Yes, to be sure, Jesus Christ was raised from the dead. But Lord, if you don't mind my asking, how does that apply to Debbie and her battle with terminal cancer? Of course I believe in the resurrection, but my concern right now is for her and my family."

"Let's work through this. I'll repeat my question: did I raise my Son from the dead?"

"Yes you did. However . . . ."

"So we know that my Son was raised from the dead. Why do you think that I did that?"

"But Lord, what about Debbie?"

Taking me gently but firmly by the front of my shirt, the Lord said, "You only have a Ph.D., so I'll speak real slowly here. Did . . . I . . . raise . . . my . . . Son . . . from . . . the . . . dead? You asked me a question. Can we stay on task here?"

"Yes, Lord, you did raise your Son from the dead."

"Why did I do that?"

"I would say that the resurrection clearly indicated and confirmed that Jesus' teachings were true. In other words, what your Son taught makes good sense in light of this event. I cannot imagine that you would have raised a heretic from the dead. This conclusion makes the most sense of your actions."

"And what else does it indicate?"

"It shows that you were in control."

"Am I still in control of the universe?"

"Yes, Lord. It is the same world that it was 2000 years ago when your Son died."

"So do you think that there are reasons to believe that I am God?"

"Absolutely, Lord. To be sure. Yes, I've always . . . ."

"Good. So, you do not know why your family is suffering. Would you say that I know why this is happening?"

"Unquestionably, Sir. Certainly you know."

"Since you know that my Son's message is true, shouldn't that be enough to trust me with things that you don't know about, like Debbie's cancer?"

"Well, I think that follows . . . ."

"And would knowing why she suffered make it any easier for you? Or would knowing why she's sick change the disease?"

"No, it wouldn't. But, Lord, if you'll permit me to say so, this doesn't sound very satisfying."

"It's not satisfying because you are thinking and telling yourself things that are directly contrary to my Word. Your thoughts oppose the truth that I have presented here, too. You tell yourself things like it is unjust, or too painful for you to bear, that things will never get better, or that you just must know the reasons for it, and so on. Each time you say or even think these things, you cause yourself and others much pain. But these comments are untrue, and you clearly don't have to know the reasons for your suffering in order to be healed. You know plenty about my purposes in order to trust that there are real answers, even if you do not presently know what they are."

"Then what should I be saying to others and to myself?"

"Let these truths that we have discussed here seep into and burrow down into your deepest thoughts. When you are bothered, review these truths and take them to heart. Practice this during those tough times. Don't get sidetracked by other issues, no matter how painful they seem. Refuse to carry your heavy burden. Don't allow yourself to say things like you simply must have all the answers to everything. Trust me. After all, I raised my Son from the dead to indicate that there really are satisfying answers to these issues. Though you cannot learn these reasons now, you can learn to lean on Me."

Later I began to practice these truths so that they were my first line of defense against my emotional pain. And the healing did indeed progress. In further studies, I grew quite impressed with Hebrews 5:8, where we are told, rather incredibly, that even though Jesus was God's own Son, He still had to suffer in order to learn obedience to God! And then there was Hebrews 2:10, which states that Jesus was perfected by his suffering! No matter how many times I read these texts, they were simply stunning. This led to another set of insights regarding the nature of suffering.

"Lord, I am still suffering tremendously after the death of my wife and best friend. Do you have any further salve for my pain?"

"Gary, have you considered that even my own Son learned obedience through his suffering?"

"Yes, Lord, I have recently been meditating on this. Still, I can scarcely comprehend it."

"So I ask you: unlike my Son, are you able to learn obedience without suffering? Or perhaps you actually deserve to suffer less than he suffered?"

"I have never considered this angle. And certainly, Lord, I have never thought of myself in these terms."

"Or do you learn more quickly than my Son, or do you not need to be perfected by suffering, as he was?"

"No, I don't say or think these things, Lord. I guess I simply prefer not to suffer, especially so badly!"

"I know it is very difficult and painful, my son, but suffering is necessary in life. There are many reasons for it, as well. It is the result of creatures freely making poor choices. It is the flipside of natural benefits, as heat both warms and kills. And as we have just discussed, suffering causes us to learn and grow, as nothing else does, even in the case of my only begotten Son. Indeed, suffering is an insistent tutor."

"I see this now. These are very deep truths. I surely need to internalize them."

"In the meantime, don't think that you are alone in this. Or don't tell yourself that no one suffered much in biblical times. Internalize these truths. Practice them. They will change your thinking. Until you can answer these questions about my Son's suffering, expect it and allow yourself to grow. It is one of the chief highways to victory."

"I will certainly try, my Lord."

Both Paul and Gary lingered in God's waiting room and both came to understand that God is magnified even in the face of death. It reminds us of the story of William Nagenda, an African evangelist, who clearly understood the hope of heaven. He said, "My life is like a ball bouncing on the floor. Sometimes the devil gives me a blow downwards, but at the deepest spot Jesus is there, and He gives me a blow upwards so that I come up higher than I was before. One day the devil will give William a blow downwards so strong that he will go all the way to the valley of the shadow of death. There Jesus will give William a blow upwards so strong that he will come into heaven. The devil will say, 'Where is William? I don't see him anymore!'"

Some may see death as a step backward. In fact, our human tendency is to pray that a loved one will live. But Paul reminds us that suffering may actually be God's way of bringing a Christian home to heaven. He wants us to understand that death is not a step backward but a step upward. This fact may be hard to accept, but God's ways are not our ways, nor are His thoughts our thoughts.[9] Truly, God's purposes are greater than our own concerns and needs.

SECTION 4:

Will I Ever Get Over This?

Nancy had never really known the freedom for which she desperately longed. As a child, she was imprisoned by poverty and hunger. Physical and sexual abuse complicated the confusing years of adolescence. As a young adult, desperation for love and security resulted in a pregnancy which prompted a hasty marriage. The marriage survived on stubbornness and determination, as well as a healthy dose of God's mercy, and produced three children. The early years of marriage were overshadowed by the duties of parenting little ones. As her girls grew to school age and Nancy found time to catch her breath, the quiet emptiness of the house on school days allowed her to hear the voices of the past that had been suppressed by the busy family. In those quiet hours, sadness turned to sorrow, regret became self-condemnation and depression sank into despair. The culmination of a multitude of troubles, this chasm was deeper and darker than any she had endured before. Was there a way out of or through this bottomless pit?

Chapter 14

HOLDING ON: THE BEDROCK OF OUR ATTITUDE

It was girls' night out and boys' night at home for the Thomas family. My son, Stephen, wanted to spend the last part of our evening playing the well-known game Candy Land. Perhaps you remember that game from your childhood or from playing it with your own children. The object is to move your gingerbread man along the twisting colored road until you finally arrive at the finish. On your turn, you draw a card, which usually has either one or two colored squares on it. You then move your gingerbread man that number of colored spaces on the path. The deck also contains various cards that correspond to pictures on the board. If you draw a picture card, you either move forward or backward to the space corresponding to the picture.

Since it was close to Stephen's bedtime, I realized we would have to make this a quick game. What I had forgotten was how long it takes to play Candy Land. I jumped off to a swift lead but soon drew a picture card that returned me to an early square on the board. As Stephen neared the finish line, he too drew a card that forced him far back on the trail. And so the game went on. Every time one of us neared the finish, a card would be drawn that extended play. I was beginning to think that we would still be playing when Stephen was in college.

This brings me to my confession. In order to finish the game and get my son to bed, I secretly removed all the cards that required moving backward on the board. (I admit that I cheated. But it was for my son's own good – and my own sanity.) Finally, with those obstacles out of the way, Stephen was able to reach the finish, proudly winning the game.

Suffering is much like that board game. In fact, that game can cause great suffering, but that is a story for another time. We want our lives to be fun, enjoyable, and comfortable. Unfortunately, pain and agony often surface, causing us to face the fact that life is hard. Our deepest desire is to rid ourselves of the obstacles that block our path. Just when we think we are about to "make it," we are forced back into pain as if to start all over again.

Sometimes we give up just before relief is to come. Florence Chadwick had been the first female to swim the English Channel in both directions. At the age of 34, she determined to be the first woman to swim twenty-two miles in the chilly ocean waters between Catalina Island and Palo Verde on the California shore. In 1952 Florence set out on her journey in weather conditions that would have deterred many. She swam through foggy weather and choppy seas for over fifteen hours. The cold water and fatigue caused her muscles to cramp. With each stroke her resolve weakened. Riding in a boat alongside, her mother urged her not to give up. But Florence was losing heart. She couldn't see where she was going because of the fog; in addition, the several boats that accompanied her also obscured her view of the finish line. The conditions were so adverse and her body so exhausted that Florence begged to be taken from the water. Finally, when she could go no further and stopped swimming, aids lifted her out of the water and into the boat. As they paddled toward land the fog began to clear and they discovered that Florence had quit less than a half mile from the shore. "All I could see was the fog," she later explained at a news conference. "I think if I could have seen the shore, I would have made it."

We can learn a lot about overcoming suffering from the story of Florence Chadwick. Holding on during periods of adversity requires that we face the challenges along the way and find the stamina that is necessary to endure the entire trial. As such, suffering requires us to work through weariness of soul and body, to find the strength to go further. Helen Keller noted that the struggles of life teach us that although the world is full of suffering, it is also full of the overcoming of it.

Athletes know that there are times when they will hit the wall. Exhaustion, demoralization, and eventually hopelessness plague the resolve of virtually every one at some point. We hate pain and we hate to hurt. But, no matter how much we want to avoid discomfort, there is simply no way around it. The only way out of it is to go through it. Our bent toward pride causes us to want lives that are free of suffering—to become absolute overcomers. A careful reading of the Bible, however, shows that God is much less concerned with us living in a place of peace than He is with us living in peace. It is possible to find shalom, peace in the midst of our suffering.

God wants us to grow from our suffering. When we attempt to avoid suffering, we risk missing God's purpose for the pain. Christians should not suffer in the same way as those who have no hope. Our passion should not be to feel better but to know God better—no matter what hardships we experience.

Friedrich Nietzsche once said, "He who has a *why* to live can bear almost any *how*."[1] As Christians we have a reason to live, a basis for meaning in life. For the Christian, Jesus Christ is the pivotal truth and motivation in life. Yet we must wrestle with the problem of having to move through the pain in a way that honors and capitalizes upon the work God is seeking to accomplish in our lives. The challenge is not if we will get through our valleys, but how.

God promises us His strength, grace, and presence in the midst of our trials and tribulations. He promises us that He is orchestrating a masterpiece in our lives. It is up to us to submit to His will, to allow Him to use us in any way that He deems appropriate. There is a precious pearl within the dark chamber of every calamity, providing we have the courage to seek it out.

This chapter will help you learn to allow God to work out His purposes in your life by holding on. Our desire is not to provide you with easy answers that can be used as a "fix" for suffering. We cannot approach our suffering as we do the common cold: administering relief medicines as fast as possible in order to feel better. A virus has to run its course and so must suffering. However, whereas viruses offer no hope for moving us toward wholeness, suffering is the vehicle by which God moves us toward completeness.

Why is it so Hard to Hold on?

Have you ever wondered why some people respond to trauma with resiliency and others become hopeless and helpless? Why is it that events take such control over our lives, even when our Christian beliefs encourage us to trust God? The answer to those questions is found in the bedrock of human nature: our attitude.

I remember getting a secret decoder ring in a box of cereal as a child. On the back of the box was a map that was unintelligible without the ring. But by using the secret decoder ring, I was able to navigate through the map and find the hidden treasure chest (a prize that made the purchase of the cereal worthwhile).

In the same way, we all have an internal decoder ring that we use to navigate the journey of life and make sense of everything. In essence, this internal ring dictates our perception and understanding of life. This ring is our attitude. An attitude could be described as a relatively consistent way of thinking, feeling, and behaving toward an object, person, group, or idea. Our attitudes involve our personal theories about ourselves, the external world, and the interaction between the two. Because we interpret many of our experiences through our attitudes, our responses have little to do with the actual situations. In other words, suffering is in the eye of the beholder.

For example, when we label an event "catastrophic," we are revealing our attitudes and the way we perceive the situation. I once provided counseling to a group of employees who were being downsized. Two of them merit attention. Both men were forty-five years old, married, with two children; each had one child in college. Both employees had been with the company about twenty-three years, and on the day the layoffs occurred, both men were shocked to learn that their jobs were being eliminated. Each of these employees had a stellar employment history, was well-regarded, and had assumed he would not be on "the list." I met with each of them following their termination meetings. At that time, both were still in shock, but that's where the similarities between these two men ended. One man believed that God would take care of him and his family, and that somehow they would come through stronger than ever. The other man could not move beyond the shock of what had happened to him. He spent most of our time together listing other employees who should have been terminated but were not. He railed against the manager and the company. He feared that he and his family would not be able to survive financially. He lamented having to tell his daughter that she couldn't stay in college and that his son would have to quit martial arts before earning his black belt. Our entire session was dark, bleak, and unproductive.

I met several times with each man as part of their separation packages. After several months, the first man obtained a job with another large firm. Though it required a move, his compensation and benefits were equitable. He expressed gratitude at the way God had used the worst loss of his life to bring his family closer and strengthen his faith. The second man was unwilling to look for a job outside the company. He continued to query other divisions, believing that the company owed him and would give him a job somewhere. Month after month he grew more depressed. Eventually his wife left him, and shortly thereafter he committed suicide. One event, yet they had two completely different perceptions of the event, and two radically divergent responses. Attitude is everything.

The main ingredient in our attitudes is beliefs. What we think and how we think are integral in determining the way we suffer. It's easy to rely too much on human perception, logic, and emotion rather than on God's Word—the basis of truth.[2] If our thinking is congruent with Scripture, however, we will be more able to work through the pain and allow God's purposes to be realized in our lives. If our thinking is false, we will have difficulty responding to trials in a way that will help us learn and grow from them.

Unfortunately, we have all bought into various myths regarding suffering. These unbiblical views have the potential to derail us from spiritual gain and even cause greater pain. Because false information breeds spiritual and emotional turmoil, it is critical that we begin to examine our beliefs regarding suffering. Emotional and spiritual health will elude us until we examine our beliefs, identify the fallacious ones, and replace them with God's truth. Such notions and myths must be eliminated if we are going to successfully trust God through our trials and hardships.

Myth #1: Spiritual People Do Not Suffer

Of all the myths about suffering, the idea that all suffering is sin-related is perhaps the cruelest, since it heaps guilt and shame upon an already-wounded soul. This myth takes on many forms. One links suffering to a lack of faith. Of course, Christ did rebuke His disciples for their lack of faith during the terrifying storm that ensued while they were crossing the Sea of Galilee. Faith does play a role in suffering, but suffering in and of itself does not mean that we are not spiritual or living godly lives. Remember Shadrach, Meshach, and Abednego? Their faith may have gotten them out of the fiery furnace, but it was also what got them thrown into the furnace in the first place.[3]

A second form of this myth says that those who suffer or feel pain are sinning. Job's friends who attempted to "assist" him with his adversity evidenced this belief. Sometimes such thinkers assume that God abandons those who lack commitment to Christ. In response to this myth, the sufferer believes that he or she did something wrong to justify the pain. This perceived infraction could be either sin or poor judgment. The sufferer believes that he or she is responsible for the peril even in the absence of evidence that any violation has been committed. Subsequently, the sufferer feels a sense of guilt and a deep sense of shame.

But it is possible to diligently read the Bible and still not come to know Christ

It is true that suffering may result from someone's sin, mistake, or fault, but this is not always the case. Jesus Himself felt pain and experienced feelings of abandonment. He was the Suffering Servant, and because He suffered without sin, we know that we, too, can suffer without sinning. Just as God never forsook His Son, we know He has not forsaken us either.[4]

The truth of God's Word is that the rain falls on the just and unjust.[5] We cannot manipulate God into indulging our self-serving craving for control. If Christians were spared pain and suffering when it falls on others, Christianity would be degraded to nothing more than an insurance policy. The ultimate end of Christianity is transformed lives, not stress-free followers.

Myth #2: Reading the Bible Solves Every Problem

In some Christian circles, the Bible has been elevated so much that it is considered even more important than having a close relationship with God. In other circles, parishioners are indoctrinated with the belief that intimacy with God is synonymous with Bible reading.

Certainly, reading the Bible is critical to spiritual development. God's Word provides us with the spiritual nourishment we need, not just when we're in the valley of affliction but also when we're on the mountaintop. Discipline in reading and studying God's Word helps us build our spiritual and emotional immune systems. It insulates the mind and strengthens the soul so that we can ward off despair in times of adversity. In fact, it is during periods of suffering that what we have learned from our Bible reading, church attendance, and spiritual teaching are ultimately revealed. Clearly it's impossible to have a close relationship with God without reading the Bible and praying. But it is possible to diligently read the Bible and still not come to know Christ.[6] In the same way, simply reading the Bible does not mean you'll have all you need to address the entire emotional and spiritual side of suffering.

Let's say that you love the game of tennis. You could read numerous books about it and even read the Tennis Association's rule book, but it's not the same as playing the game. Though you need to know the rules to accurately play the game, the game is bigger than the rules. The same can be said about God's Word and our spiritual lives. God's Word provides us with what we need in order to live the Christian life and deal with suffering. But the Christian life and recovering from emotional and spiritual pain require more from us than just reading.

Reading the Bible is a necessary element of the Christian life. It teaches us about God and leads us in our walk of faith. But we are not just to read God's Word; we must also obey it.[7] Reading the Bible is not the same as submission, obedience, faith, and intimacy with the Lord.

By all means, spend time daily with God through Scripture reading and study. But also use other available means such as prayer, meditation, and talking with a Christian friend to work through your pain and struggles.

Myth #3: You Can Handle it Alone

Rugged individualism and the pioneer spirit have long characterized our culture. We have been taught to be self-sufficient. This is particularly true of men. Asking for help is too often seen as a sign of weakness.

John Donne, the famous English poet, once said that "no man is an island, entire of itself."[8] Unfortunately, even Christians buy into self-sufficient thinking, especially when they hurt. Perhaps out of fear or pride, some people are reluctant to open up, choosing instead to privately battle their way through the pain. Others are hurt and disillusioned about the sincerity of other Christians' desire to help. Sadly, many wounded people push others away or do not reach out for help when they need the caring community of God's people most.

Former missionary Elisabeth Elliot once wrote, "Not many of us are much good at being Christian all by ourselves—we're supposed to be a flock or a body. We've got to have help . . .somebody to lift us up when we're down."[9] Because we are all part of the body of Christ, unified together, it is impossible to do anything or experience anything that does not affect the rest of the body.

Research plainly shows that sufferers who have sound social support get through tough times far better than those who go through painful situations alone.[10] In fact, the German army typically divided families in concentration camps as a way of worsening prisoner morale. Those in charge knew that isolation actually intensifies suffering.

Even if it were possible to get through a struggle alone, why put yourself through that added stress? We have already seen how suffering provides an opportunity to illuminate the value of the body of Christ. Suffering gives the church an opportunity to show, not only the world, but other believers as well, that we are Christians by the way we love and the way we mourn.[11]

If you are suffering today, one way to break free from the grip of despair is to share your pain with others and learn from someone who has been there.

Myth #4: God Owes Us

Some people operate on the "heaven's reward" concept, believing that if they do the right thing, God will grant them their desires. To support their logic, some quote Proverbs 3:5-6: "Trust in the LORD with all your heart, and lean not on your own understanding; in all your ways acknowledge Him, and He shall direct your paths." Simply stated: trust God and He will give you what you want.

I once counseled a hurting man named Max who believed that since God hated divorce, his ex-wife would come back to him. In fact, not only did he expect that she would come back, but that God was obligated to restore their marriage because He could not contradict His Word. Max didn't want a divorce, and since he felt he was "doing the right thing," he believed God would reward him with his ex-wife's affection.

Max saw himself as a victim, but he failed to consider the facts. He minimized the years of physical abuse he had inflicted on his wife—abuse so severe that it had resulted in several hospitalizations. He argued that his actions were often provoked, though he did admit that sometimes he had allowed the "flesh to reign." Max said, "I am no longer controlled by the flesh. She should know that." He did not accept free will, believing that God could and would return his wife to him even if she didn't want to be there. No amount of counsel or Scripture seemed to budge this man from his adamant reasoning. Unfortunately, he left counseling bitter at God, his ex-wife, and me. To my knowledge, he has little to do with church or God today.

Just as God reminded Job that the Creator of the world owed him nothing, neither is God indebted to us.[12] God does not owe us smooth sailing. He is not a servant who dutifully carries out our bidding, a genie who pops up to grant our capricious wishes, or an indulgent parent who complies with our selfish demands and desires. In fact, just the opposite is true. If we got what we truly deserved, we would be eternally separated from Him.

Consider the kind of world we would have if God did everything we demanded. In that world, God would be nothing more than a tool for our self-interest. Remember, Adam and Eve's disobedience was in part related to their desire to "be like God."[13]

We need to be thankful that God has sent His Son to provide an avenue that we may spend eternity with Him. He has not abandoned us but has provided us with a Comforter, the Holy Spirit.[14] The abundant life Jesus promised is not about landing a guest spot on Lifestyles of the Rich and Famous. Rather, it is a promise that we will truly know what life is. The word translated life is the Greek word zoe, which means quality of life in a spiritual sense. The abundant life has purpose, meaning, and direction, and when we live it, we are filled with joy and peace because of the indwelling Holy Spirit. No matter how the course of our lives change, we can still exhibit contentment.[15] That is authentic, abundant life.

Myth #5: Pain and Suffering are of no Value

Our culture indoctrinates us to the belief that we should never suffer. Pain medicines, air-conditioning, smooth-riding automobiles, and even euthanasia are all designed to help us avoid discomfort and pain. This idea that suffering is of little value has permeated theology as well.

Some people believe that pain and suffering are simply the results of a broken, sinful world, and therefore they provide no positive benefit to our lives. According to this way of thinking, we must simply endure and try to find relief in whatever way possible. Our only hope is found in heaven, away from such misery.

Maintaining our focus on eternity is certainly a significant way to deal with the groaning of this world and our earthly bodies. But God has not left us without hope in this world. For Christians, this earthly life is actually the beginning of heaven. After all, the abundant life and eternal life begin at salvation. Therefore, we should be living in expectant anticipation of eternity with Christ, living for others, and laying up treasure in heaven.

Aristotle once said that we couldn't learn without pain. God uses this world and our life experiences to teach us a wide array of lessons, and suffering is without a doubt one means by which God achieves the very things we deeply long for.

Former baseball player Roy Campanella tells of his stay at the Institute of Physical Medicine and Rehabilitation. As one of the first African American ballplayers, he was a survivor and thriver who faced difficult challenges. Now Roy was trying to beat the greatest foe of his life: living in a wheelchair. He was discouraged and depressed by the loss of his career and mobility, and he struggled to find any hope in the future. Blinded by his own self-pity, Roy rolled his wheelchair each day down the hallway past a bronze plaque riveted to the wall. It wasn't until he had been at the institute for many months, however, that Roy finally stopped to read the plaque. What he read transformed him. Written by an unknown Confederate soldier, "A Creed for Those Who Suffered" said this:

> *I asked God for strength, that I might achieve.*
> *I was made weak, that I might learn humbly to obey.*
> *I asked for health, that I might do great things.*
> *I was given infirmity, that I might do better things.*
> *I asked for riches, that I might be happy.*
> *I was given poverty, that I might be wise.*
> *I asked for power, that I might have the praise of men.*
> *I was given weakness, that I might feel the need of God.*
> *I asked for all things, that I might enjoy life.*

I was given life, that I might enjoy all things.
I got nothing I asked for—but everything I had hoped for.
Almost despite myself, my unspoken prayers were answered.
I am, among men, most richly blessed![16]

Campy, as he was known, read that plaque over and over again. He claimed that after reading it, a powerful glow began to warm him from the inside out. The experience was so real that he had to hold tightly to the arms of his wheelchair. Following his release from the hospital, Campanella became more famous for the thirty-six years he spent in a wheelchair than he had been as a professional baseball catcher. Vince Scully said that Campy looked at life like a catcher: "He was forever cheering up, pepping up, and counseling people." He saw the value of his disability in his ability to help others who had experienced similar ordeals."[17]

MYTH #6: The God of Love Would Not Allow us to Suffer

This is one of the most prevalent beliefs about suffering. But of this myth, C. S. Lewis wrote:

The problem of reconciling human suffering with the existence of a God who loves, is only insoluble so long as we attach a trivial meaning to the word "love," and look on things as if man were the centre of them. . . . God does not exist for the sake of man. Man does not exist for his own sake. . . . Because He is what He is, His love must, in the nature of things, be impeded and repelled by certain stains in our present character, and because He already loves us He must labour to make us lovable.[18]

As human beings, we tend to view all of life from our own self-serving vantage point. God, however, operates on a different level altogether. As we have seen, God uses suffering for a variety of purposes, and all suffering has value and merit in the life of the believer. It is out of God's love that He seeks to use suffering to improve us; the fact that we so passionately seek comfortable, stress-free lives is an indication that we still do not understand this concept. God's love does not lie in His extinction of suffering. Rather God's love is evident in that

He embraced suffering in order to identify with us. His goal is not to abolish suffering, but to channel it in order to develop the sufferer.

Corrie ten Boom shared her struggle with believing in a God of love while experiencing the horrific conditions of concentration-camp life.

> *"I remember one occasion when I was very discouraged there. Everything around us was dark, and there was darkness in my heart.*
>
> *I remember telling Betsie that I thought God had forgotten us. "No, Corrie," said Betsie. "He has not forgotten us. Remember His Word: 'For as the heavens are high above the earth, so great is his steadfast love toward those who fear him.' There is an ocean of God's love available. . . . There is plenty for everyone."[19]*

When we hold to such beliefs the possibility of holding on through difficult adversity is virtually impossible. We need to understand how beliefs work and build our lives on a sound belief system. Let's examine the role of our belief system more in-depth.

The Bedrock of Our Attitudes

The bedrock of our attitudes is a network of beliefs that we unwittingly build for ourselves. Some of these beliefs are global and abstract, while others are more narrow and concrete. The belief that you are a good tennis player is more specific and less global than the belief that you are a good athlete. But the belief that you are a good athlete is less global and narrower than the belief that you are a competent person. The most significant and pervasive beliefs are those that are more abstract and general. While you may rethink the belief that you are a good tennis player, losing several matches in a row will not necessarily cause you to believe that you are incompetent. You can believe that you are a competent person, even in the face of evidence that your tennis game is abominable. This is because other beliefs comprise your attitude about your competence.

Though beliefs are the foundation of emotions and behavior, they are so embedded within us that we seldom consciously think about them. When challenged, however, people are usually adamant in their resolve to maintain a particular belief, even in the face of contrary evidence. It is this strong bias to preserve what we believe that allows us to make sense of a complex and chaotic world.

From very early on, we observe how the world operates, and we make conclusions about what we see. These conclusions then become part of the lens through which we continue to perceive the world and make further generalizations. We live our lives as if those conclusions were both well-founded and binding, continually reinforcing them through our interpretations of new experiences and observations of others. Although our conclusions may not be biblical, healthy, or accurate, we resist modifying them. We seek to interpret all of our experiences in such a way that our fundamental beliefs are essentially unaffected.

A person's beliefs about what sort of world this is, how he or she should be treated, what to expect from life, and who God is will predominantly determine that person's reaction to adversity. Based upon years of clinical experience, I have identified three key beliefs that make up most people's attitudes and determine our reactions to adversity.[20] These beliefs are:

1. I deserve ease and comfort in life.
2. I deserve a predictable world.
3. I deserve a fair world.

You may assume that these beliefs do not apply to you, but do not quickly dismiss them. Our beliefs are emotionally laden assumptions that operate instinctively, mostly outside our awareness. What you actually believe may be quite different than what you think you believe. Since adversity does not create our attitudes as much as it reveals our attitudes, the best way to know what you truly believe is to examine your reaction to affliction.

I Deserve Ease and Comfort

Since the Garden of Eden, humanity's goal has been to derive as much satisfaction from life as possible. Our sin drives us to pursue the good life and to find fulfillment for our deepest needs apart from Christ. Sigmund Freud spoke of the "pleasure principle" as our primary motivation; namely, to maximize pleasures and avoid pain. Obviously, there have been many times throughout history when a person's exclusive purpose has been survival. But when our basic needs for survival are met, a passion for indulgence is not far behind.

As Americans, we are told that we have been endowed with certain inalienable rights, among which is the pursuit of happiness. Homes, jobs, money, family, friends, sex, health, and social status are supposed to provide us with that fulfillment and happiness. When any of these things are threatened or taken away, we typically react with fear and discomfort.

We have created a world in which we savor comfort and immediate gratification: think microwave ovens and fast food drive-thrus; ATM machines for on-the-spot cash; one-hour dry cleaning for prompt laundry service. We love our remote controls and automatic appliances. While the Son of Man had no place to lay His head, we complain if we don't get a king-sized bed at a hotel.

You might ask what is wrong with these things. In and of themselves, they are not wrong. They provide entertainment and convenience after a long workday. They are humanity's attempt to make a fallen world orderly and comfortable. It seems, however, that comfort has become one of the most sought-after idols of our times. Rather than being pilgrims on a journey through a foreign land, we have become settlers. Instead of feeling out of place in this sin-laden world, we have become accustomed to the thorns and thistles that mark what once was paradise.

The problem is usually not the source of comfort but our passionate pursuit of it. There is nothing inherently wrong with creature comforts. The problem occurs when we have an attitude toward life that demands comfort. When that happens, our self-serving nature compels us to manipulate life to get what we want.[21] We persistently seek and sustain those things that provide the greatest sense of comfort. Hence, we unwittingly make contentment and happiness idols. Yet no matter how hard we try, we are rarely satisfied and seek to fill the void through materialism, alcohol and other drugs, pornography, and violence—all self-designed strategies to numb a chronic heartache. Confession, repentance, and trusting in God typically are not seen as the most effective way to handle problems. In fact, our earnest demands for comfort usually compel us to find ways to elude the undesirable consequences of our actions. Lying, abortion, and divorce are but a few ways to escape the pain and suffering that result from poor choices.

When confronted with the painful reality that life is adverse, we typically assume God is not good. In other words, God is good if I am comfortable and happy.

In one of C.S. Lewis' better-known works, Lewis tackles the problem of pain. He describes the typical view of the nature of God when he writes, "If God were good, He would wish to make His creatures perfectly happy, and if God were almighty, He would be able to do what He wished. But the creatures are not happy. Therefore God lacks either goodness, or power, or both."[22]

The Bible says that in due time God will make His people happy and make things the way He desires them to be.[23] For most of us, however, that seems a long way off, and when life is not what we desire, we often react with intense emotion. Job poignantly captured this idea when he moaned, "I was at ease, but He [God] has shattered me; He also has taken me by my neck, and shaken me to pieces; He has set me up for His target, His archers surround me. He pierces my heart and does not pity; He pours out my gall on the ground. He breaks me with wound upon wound; He runs at me like a warrior."[24] Imagine that testimony coming from the pulpit.

I once counseled a kind Christian woman who lived her life in a noteworthy fashion. She was persistent in serving the Lord, had a caring shoulder for others, and seemed to be the model wife and mother. Her world was rocked to the core, however, when her husband of twenty-seven years informed her that he was leaving her for a younger woman.

"How can I possibly compete with a twenty-two-year-old?" she asked, weeping almost uncontrollably as she poured out her painful story. In a later counseling session, this woman's hostility began to emerge, not just at her husband but at God as well. "I thought if I did everything I was supposed to do, God would take care of me. I don't know what else He wants from me. Christian service has been my life, and this is my reward? When I get to heaven, God is going to owe me an apology for the way that He has treated me!" This woman may not have realized it, but she had a deep-seated commitment to comfort. It wasn't until she experienced the real press of life that the true nature of her heart was revealed.

Another woman told me that God was responsible for the fact that she and her husband had never been able to have children. Pulling promises from Scripture, she lashed out at God for allowing "everyone else" to raise children and to "enjoy the good things of life," while she never could. Finding a soul mate in Hannah—the mother of Samuel the prophet—she tried to pray similarly, but without the results for which she had hoped.[25] To her way of thinking, God was responsible for all of these problems and at least owed her an explanation. I knew she would never find peace until she faced and corrected the many misbeliefs that she had regarding the Lord, His promises, and her situation.

Today Christian books and videos, support groups, and seminars on a wide array of topics meet real needs with biblically sound counsel. Sadly, however, some of these programs actually promote further self-indulgence. We have become victims to be healed rather than sinners to be sanctified. We believe in solutions that are simple and easy, whether they're "eight steps" or "ten ways" or "a simple plan." We have even turned the Bible into a self-help book, using its words of inspiration to help us feel better about ourselves. Holiness, sanctification, and self-denial have been replaced with healing our wounds, personal growth, and improving our self-esteem. Rather than being the central theme of life's drama, God seems to be nothing more than the curtain puller.

In essence, we've replaced serving and glorifying the Lord with seeking the good life. We live to make life as comfortable and convenient as possible. It is this self-consuming nature that makes understanding God's purposes in suffering unreasonable.

Contrast this response with that of Corrie ten Boom, another Christian servant who also traveled a difficult road. This famed survivor of Ravensbrück, the dreadful concentration camp located just north of Berlin, knew much about adversity. Corrie suffered from hunger, sleep deprivation, appalling living conditions, brutality, and the loss of personal possessions. She lived under the constant threat of extermination. Though she had moments of doubt, these circumstances actually fortified her belief in the goodness of God. Years after her release, she perceptively wrote, "Often I have heard people say, 'How good God is. We prayed that it would not rain for our church picnic, and look at this lovely weather!' Yes, God is good when He sends good weather. But God was also good when He allowed my sister Betsie to starve to death before my eyes in the German concentration camp."[26]

Perhaps drawing from the words of Jesus, the apostle Peter instructed us not to think that life would be problem free; in fact, he said we should rejoice because problems let us partake of Christ's sufferings.[27] Common sense nudges us toward the fact that the world is ill equipped to provide constant comfort. Consider the opening sentence of M. Scott Peck's best-selling and controversial book, The Road Less Traveled: "Life is difficult. . . ."[28] Comedian Jerry Seinfeld once said that perhaps the road less traveled is less traveled for a good reason. He was right, since our natural drive for pleasure leads us to choose the easier route.

When it comes to living, most of us prefer a riverboat ride to a roller coaster. Our self-centered drive for comfort wants a smooth, steady ride. But as long as we assume that life must be comfortable, we will never come to accept trials and adversity as normal, especially those hardships that we deem to be undeserved. When people think they've been dealt a bad hand, they often attempt to make that hand work. Rather than depending upon God, they rely on their own power and strategies to maximize pleasure and reduce pain. If unsuccessful, they fold, throw up their hands in despair, and wonder, Where is God?

I Deserve a Predictable World

God created our world with natural laws to provide order. For instance, I know that a ball dropped from a roof will fall toward the ground. Physical realities such as gravity make it easy to predict outcomes and therefore control circumstances. In science, events are intelligible if they fit accepted physical laws. Likewise, events in everyday life are comprehensible if they fit accepted social laws. Because we know that the world operates according to certain physical laws, we similarly assume that nonphysical realities are also predictable. We believe that people and events should make just as much sense as the natural world.

The belief that the world must be predictable is based on the assumption that misfortune is not arbitrary and that events are mostly positive in outcome. Of course, we know of misery and oppression in the world, but we innately distinguish between the world in general and the world in which we live. The people and events that touch us constitute our world, and it is these people and events that shape our attitudes.

Our fundamental belief in order and predictability deals not only with why events happen in our world but, more specifically, why these events happen to particular people. We seek to understand the distribution of good and bad, and in the service of order and predictability, assume a cause-and-effect relationship between people and what they experience. The assumption is that we can directly control what happens to us through our own behaviors. Thus, we believe that if we behave in an appropriate, precautionary way, we will be protected from negative events. Similarly, if we engage in appropriate positive behavior, good things will happen. Because effort, exertion, practice, and planning generally affect outcomes that we can control, we often believe we can control chance outcomes as well.

This attitude leads us to believe that if we train our children right, they will not fall away from God; if we are good workers, we will not lose our jobs; and if we take care of our health, we will not get sick. Certainly such behaviors may decrease the likelihood of the negative outcomes, but they will not reduce the probability to zero. Good parents have rebellious children, good workers do get laid off, and generally healthy people can have heart attacks.

It is our embellished belief in control that contributes to our blaming victims for their tribulations. Research on trauma victims has shown that people naturally look for an explanation for negative events. In one study, two groups of people were given different scenarios of a woman leaving work and going home. In one scenario, the woman arrived home without incident. When the participants were asked if the woman did anything that posed a risk to her safety, they were unable to name anything. The second group read the same scenario, but this time the woman was attacked before entering her home. When these participants were asked the same question about the woman's cautiousness, they reported several things that she could have done or not done to prevent the assault. In order to protect the illusion that our world is predictable and thus controllable, we are strongly motivated to place blame. If we do not or cannot blame someone, suffering becomes more frightening because it's random and unpredictable and we have no hope of controlling life.

Ben, a man who prided himself on his work, had devised a strategy to succeed.

As a child, Ben learned a strong work ethic from his parents. He worked his way through one of the best business schools in the country. Upon his graduation, he went to work for a large, successful company. For the next twenty years, Ben put in long hours. His prudent business mind helped to profit his company. If I do the right thing, I will reap the right result, he thought.

His belief about a predictable world was shattered, however, with one phone call from his boss. Later, he sat in my office, stunned by the fact that he had been laid off. It simply didn't make sense.

"I have done all the right things," Ben lamented, "How could they do this to me? What did I do wrong?" The truth was that the only thing Ben had done wrong was to believe that doing the right thing would always produce the right result—in this case, that he would be rewarded with long-term employment. Ben's belief set him up for great disillusionment.

Psychologists talk about the "illusion of invulnerability," our tendency to underestimate the likelihood of negative events and overestimate the likelihood of positive events. We take our own indestructibility for granted and assume the continuity of a safe existence. This naiveté makes the shock of suffering greater because our attitudes do not allow for the occurrence of adverse events in our lives. When a child dies, a large part of the parents' pain stems from the untimeliness of the loss. Parents naturally do not account for the fact that one of their children could die. Recall the story of Dave, Nia, and Nathan Sours from the Introduction. Although Nathan Sours' close encounters with death revealed his physical fragility, Dave and Nia had been reassured when, during every close call, a miracle had occurred. That gave them the illusion that Nathan would always be okay. The unpredictability of an event shatters our illusion that we can control life. When that assumption is challenged, we feel helpless because we no longer know the right thing to do in order to control the outcome.

When our belief in an orderly and predictable world is crushed by a traumatic event, we often conclude that God cannot be trusted. Believing that the God who created perfect order is unreliable, we again attempt to control our own destinies in order to protect ourselves from life's tragedies. In our minds, or more accurately in our hearts, God is trustworthy only to the extent that things go in the way that we expect them.

We have a belief that life is intrinsically fair and that consequently, people's decency, morality, and goodness essentially determine what happens to them. Therefore, we perceive outcomes as either a reward or punishment.

This assumption—that the world must be fair and that we must be treated fairly—leads us to believe that people should get what they deserve and deserve what they get. This attitude enables us to minimize the role of randomness in our lives. If people get what they deserve, then suffering is the appropriate lot of those who are morally corrupt, but not right for decent people.

Think about the response to the verdict in the Casey Anthony trial. Perhaps the words "It isn't fair" or "it isn't right" flowed from your lips or streamed through your mind. Many Americans thought it was not fair that Casey Anthony was found not guilty regarding the murder of her child. A similar response was seen in the O. J. Simpson trial. Some believed he was unjustly being charged while others contended that it was not fair that a "guilty" man be deemed innocent and set free.

Because God is just, we have a sense of justice, which is appropriate when applied to the ways our judicial system operates, grades are earned, employees are paid, and pies are divided. The problem is not our sense of justice but instead our demand for mercy. Well-known researcher and social psychologist Melvin Lerner conducted a series of experiments on justice. In these studies, Dr. Lerner found that people want retribution when they have been wronged but mercy when they are the ones who have done something wrong.[29]

It's often through the lens of this self-centered notion of fairness that we view suffering and pain. Whether you have said it or not, consider this statement: "Good things should happen to good people and bad things should happen to bad people." Such a statement seems to have great merit. After all, that is the way things should be, but they are not.

At a conscious level, we know that our world is not fair and that we will be treated unfairly. Experience and Scripture both dispel the myth that this world is fair or even that it ought to be. The wise and wealthy Solomon bemoaned the emptiness in the world and acknowledged that bad things happen to good people and good things happen to bad people: "In this life, good people are often treated as though they were wicked, and wicked people are often treated as though they were good. This is so meaningless!"[30]

When we assume that our world is fair, our ability to tolerate and accept calamity is dramatically affected. We bristle when we experience unfairness, and we demand fair treatment. When we perceive injustice, we question whether God is truly just. Theologically, we may know that the notion of justice stems from God and that He is the epitome of fairness. Our doubts about God's justice are not rational but emotional.

The True Nature of Suffering

Modern Christianity has become quite comfortable with a theology of instant healing and recovery. We are quick to find passages to support these beliefs, but slow to consider that suffering can also be a tool of God.

At times, hindsight helps us see the good that results from our trials. But when we're tightly clenched in the grip of suffering, hearing that God has a purpose for our pain just adds salt to an already raw wound. The notion that suffering ultimately serves some better purpose seems cruel. Our painful feelings are too strong, making it nearly impossible to accept that idea in spite of what our theology might say. We would rather God simply leave us alone; we are content to forfeit the growth and blessings that might come out of our trials.

Valarie's childhood was devoid of most modern creature comforts.[31] Living in an economically depressed Arkansas county, Valarie's parents had little time to give individual attention to their seven children. Valarie was often left on her own or with a variety of relatives and acquaintances, some of whom sexually abused her. As often happens in such cases, Valarie carried these feelings and memories into adulthood, and in one way or another, almost every aspect of her adult life was overshadowed by them. She actually found purpose, meaning, and fulfillment in developing her role as a victim, and years of counseling helped her to firmly barricade herself within the safety of that position.

But Valarie was depressed, unhappy in her marriage, and ineffective as a parent. Though she expressed a desire to feel better, she seemed unable to move beyond her pain. As a victim of various forms of abuse, she was quick to discuss how unfair life had been to her. After much pressing, Valarie acknowledged that she believed God was unfair. If God was everywhere, how could He watch her be abused and do nothing? In her mind, God owed her. Asking Valarie to consider what God might want to accomplish through her suffering was simply adding insult to injury.

Valarie believed that God should deal fairly with people, particularly with her. She further expected God to always treat her graciously and kindly, as she understood these terms. Her belief that God must treat her well because she was a good person prevented her from seeing things any other way. According to Valarie, if God was operating at all, He was behaving in a way that didn't make sense to her. In fact, God had wronged her.

It is true that Valarie was abused and that her early years lacked nurturing, tenderness, and security. But these events had become the foundation upon which she built her life. In her unconscious commitment to protect her role as victim, she continued to sabotage the attempts of others to guide her to help and healing. Her friends saw her as someone to be cared for, a project rather than a person capable of a mutually supportive friendship.

In reality, being a victim relieved Valarie of accepting responsibility for her choices and actions. By maintaining this role she remained miserable and powerless to do anything else. Unfortunately, Valarie is not unique in her self-devotion. People seek counseling services because something is wrong in their lives that they want fixed. Often their spoken or unspoken goal is for their pain to go away. We all want to feel better, but some people are unwilling to do the difficult and uncomfortable work required to move beyond the pain.

Our inclination to pursue comfort by imposing order and fairness on a naturally random and unfair universe endorses our futile struggles to manipulate life to meet our selfish demands. Therefore, we tend to choose only black or white, right or wrong, good or bad.

Making Sense of Nonsense

Most experts on attitude agree that the more that you know about a person, thing, or idea, the more stable your attitude will be. Likewise, the more strongly you feel about something, the more difficult it will be for someone to convince you to change your view.

Scientists speak about working within the confines of "accepted paradigms," which is nothing more than a framework or reliable theory. By way of paradigms, scientists theorize, test, and make modifications as necessary to their conceptualization of the problem. Unless some new discovery produces a mound of evidence that is so compelling that the old paradigm no longer holds true, scientists continue to incorporate new data into what they already know. This method is one reason that many scientists continue to use the evolution paradigm to explain the origin of the universe in the face of contrary evidence.

Our attitudes are built and reinforced by years of living. Originating in our earliest experiences, our views about the world, God, and ourselves are colored by the caregivers who attended to us, what they taught us, and how they lived before us.

Although our beliefs enable us to live each day, they go further in providing us with a feeling of relative invulnerability. When the great Titanic set sail on its fateful voyage, people believed that the ship was indestructible. Even when it became evident that the boat was sinking, the crew still failed to believe that it was vulnerable. This false illusion of invincibility set up the crew and passengers for tragic results. In like manner, our own illusions of security lead so many sufferers to say, "I can't believe this happened to me!" We know that bad things do happen, but in our guts we believe we are exempt.

Just as scientists process any new information through their accepted theories, we deal with new information by processing it through our own beliefs. Unless the evidence is so overwhelming that we cannot maintain our worldviews, we naturally resist changing what we believe.

Extreme crises profoundly challenge our worldviews and in fact shatter them: our typical framework for looking at the world and making sense of it cannot accommodate the event. The new puzzle piece doesn't fit neatly into our puzzle frame. Nothing seems to be as we once thought. Suddenly, presumed beliefs about others and ourselves are questionable at best or clearly mistaken. The comfort and complacency provided by our attitudes are seen as completely inadequate and painfully untrue. When we are no longer able to stretch our paradigms by distorting the new information so that it fits neatly into our views of life, we must entirely modify our theories of life to make sense of the trauma.

It's important to note that it is not wrong to have a mind-set that sees the world a particular way. All humans have a system for making sense of what they experience. The problem is that when we are confronted with a tragedy, the realization that our paradigms are not equipped to explain things disrupts our lives massively. Jarred out of our complacency, we face an additional problem. Not only have our worldviews been shattered, exposing how vulnerable we really are, but the disintegration of our presumptions has left us without a lens to navigate life.

Chapter 15

LETTING GO OF CONTROL

For God to accomplish His plan, we must turn our suffering over to Him. We must surrender to His will and recognize His lordship.

In this chapter we will examine seven Rs to assist us in placing ourselves and our struggles into God's trustworthy hands. Psalm 143 will be our scriptural foundation as we examine each of these steps.

Release Your Feeling to God

It's natural for negative and painful feelings to emerge when we experience adversity. In order to cope, some try to suppress distressing feelings and keep the hurt at bay. Fearful of opening up to the varying layers of their hurt, they try to rationalize their emotions or distract themselves from them. Perhaps they're afraid that if they allow their hurt to stream forth, they'll unleash a flood of never-ending tears or, even worse, go crazy. The problem with avoiding our feelings, however, is that when we swallow them, we swallow them alive. Feelings that are not dealt with do not go away; instead they become distorted and lie in wait. Like a jack-in-the-box, they have a way of rearing their ugly heads when least expected and ultimately lengthening the sentence of suffering. In fact, latent feelings influence everything we think or do.

Many people find it easier to brace themselves against hurt than to embrace it. Very few have been taught how to handle hurt so that it can lead to a better place. Hence, we've become masters of distracting ourselves from pain, holding it at arm's length.

Admitting our pain is the doorway to healing, but we cannot admit what we do not know. First, we must acknowledge the reality of pain's presence and power. Unless we are willing to face the depth of our pain, we will stay trapped in the pit of despair.

Let's look at two important aspects of releasing our feelings to God:

Get Real!

Many advertising campaigns use the phrase "Get real!" But those simple words can be pretty difficult to apply to ourselves.

One of the greatest things about the psalms is that they reflect a naked, honest heart before God. In the opening verses of Psalm 143, the writer bears his soul:

> *Hear my prayer, O Lord, Give ear to my supplications! In Your faithfulness answer me, and in Your righteousness. Do not enter into judgment with Your servant, for in Your sight no one living is righteous. . . . Therefore my spirit is overwhelmed within me; my heart within me is distressed. Psalm 143:1-2, 4*

The psalmist genuinely relates to God with all the passion that is within him. He does not approach God piously or pretentiously; instead, he candidly speaks what is in his heart, knowing that because God is faithful and righteous, He will answer him.

But suffering has a way of drawing out our deep-seated core beliefs and revealing that our hearts aren't always focused toward God. Even though Job did not sin in his initial response to his affliction, he clearly felt overwhelming despair.[1] In the pit of anguish, Job even accused God of trying to destroy him, of being unjust, of oppression, and of killing hope.[2] Because he believed that God had been unfair, Job felt he had a right to complain.[3] Evidently, Job believed that he could reason with God.[4] In defending himself against his friend's accusations, Job was brutally honest. He was real about what he felt and thought.

Suffering often produces more than just despair; those in pain experience the full range of emotions. The prophet Jeremiah understood this when he authentically poured his heart out to God: "I have suffered much because God was angry"; "I am the only one He punishes over and over again without ever stopping"; "Even when I shouted and prayed for help, He refused to listen"; "God has turned my life sour."[5] Jeremiah was experiencing despair, anguish, rejection, and helplessness. And he wasn't the first to feel this way.

The shepherd David sang songs that would put most country and western songs to shame. He groaned and cried all night because of his grief and brokenness.[6] The Psalms are filled with these raw expressions of anguish, depression, trouble, fatigue, and isolation. Like Job, the writers accuse God of abandoning them—of causing their hopelessness and pain.[7]

Some people advocate that sufferers should simply "grin and bear it," but that idea is contrary to Scripture. This type of thinking actually encourages us to derive strength solely from ourselves. But as we've already seen, biblical authors didn't do this. They expressed their hearts honestly to the Lord and sought their strength from Him.

Dealing with suffering requires getting real with our thoughts and feelings, and getting honest with God about the truth of our pain. Let's face it: we cannot conceal anything from God so we might as well be honest with Him—even if it means sharing the fact that He is the one we're most angry with. Many Christians have a problem admitting they are angry with God. Afraid that God might send a bolt of lightning or something worse, they conceal their feelings of anger. But nowhere in the Bible do we see God zapping someone for being honest.

Even the Psalms express anger toward God. In one passage, He is indicted for selling Israel to heathen nations and making no profit on the deal.[8] In another, He is accused of mistreating the psalmist by removing him from his friends and causing them to hate him.[9]

Yes, it is true that none of us has the right to be angry with God. The point is not that we need to get angry with Him, but that we do get angry with God. We often blame Him for hard times, and since He already knows what is on our hearts, we might as well admit and express our true feelings.

Being real with God is actually an act of trust. A prudent person does not usually reveal his or her deepest thoughts and feelings to someone who is untrustworthy. When we choose to open up to someone about how we feel, we are implying that the person is able to handle our most ugly and intense feelings—especially if those feelings are directed toward that person. Likewise, when we open up our hearts to God, we are showing our trust in Him.

Let us be clear again about the issue of telling God what is on our minds. It is possible to cross a line; being honest with God is not a license to say anything we want. God acknowledged Job's integrity when He noted that Job did not sin or blame Him in his suffering.[10] Remember, while it is normal and natural to feel anger when we are hurting, it is not God's will for us to stay there.

As we discussed earlier, one of the main reasons we become angry with God is because He is not conforming to our plans. We demand that He make life comfortable, easy, predictable, and orderly for us. According to God, however, the only time we can demand our way and negotiate with Him is when we are able to tilt the world on its axis and keep it spinning at just the right speed.[11]

Our willingness to struggle with God must be open and genuine. If we choose to be dishonest, we will only distance ourselves from Him. Marriages grow distant and cold when marital partners believe they are unable to speak honestly and forthrightly with one another. In counseling, husbands have told me that they cannot tell their wives certain things because it will upset them. In other words, they assume that their wives can't handle the news. For that reason, I think the marital vows ought to include something about trusting the other partner enough to always tell the truth.

In the same way, we must trust God with the truth of our feelings—no matter what they are. God is "man" enough to handle it. And when we admit our hurt, anger, frustration, and disappointment, we deepen our ability to trust in God the next time.

David realized that God was able to tolerate heartfelt feelings when he wrote, "For He has not despised or disdained the suffering of the afflicted one; he has not hidden his face from him but has listened to his cry for help."[12] James encouraged us to ask God when we need wisdom because He will not mock, belittle, or shame us when we come to Him.[13] God does not backhand us across our mouths, saying, "Shame on you for saying that or thinking that!" We can come boldly before the throne of grace.[14] So it's time to get real.

Sometimes in the midst of suffering, we have a hard time getting real because we simply don't feel anything. This numbness may be an indication that we have not yet moved beyond the shock stage in the grief process. At other times, however, it may reflect an unwillingness or inability to face the sadness of life. We'd rather psychologically anesthetize the pain. Beneath the surface, however, is often deep-seated anger. By avoiding our true feelings, though, we aren't seeing things as they really are, but as we prefer them to be.

Having a biblically sound view of pain and suffering doesn't mean we won't hurt or that painful feelings will simply evaporate. It does, however, provide a frame of reference for moving beyond the pain. Before we can intellectually resolve our afflictions, we must reckon with our emotions.

Exposing our feelings to the light is critical to avoid being controlled by them. Even Sigmund Freud illustrated the importance of getting things off one's chest when he borrowed the word catharsis from Aristotle.[15] Catharsis comes from the Greek and means "purification." It was used to speak of the discharge of painful memories and emotions. While the term has broad significance to psychotherapy, it underscores the importance of releasing our hurtful feelings to other caring individuals, including our heavenly Father.

The psalmist recognizes the value of opening his heart to God. "I cry out to the LORD with my voice; with my voice to the LORD I make my supplication. I pour out my complaint before Him; I declare before Him my trouble."[16] God can provide us with the ability and the security to face the most awful truths and feelings about ourselves. He can give us the courage to traverse the unexplored ground of our pain so we can heal and grow. We may not know what lies ahead, but God can help us avoid turning back and retreating to the familiarity of our pain.

Understand the Truth About Feelings

It is important to remember in facing our feelings that they, too, were affected by the Fall. Of course, not every feeling or thought is sinful. Our feelings, however, are not amoral; they have the potential to take us in directions either toward or away from God. For this reason we have to guard against our tendency to wallow in self-pity.

Jesus protected Himself from falling into self-pity by heading it off at the pass. At one point Jesus prophesied about His upcoming crucifixion. Alarmed by his Master's words, Peter boldly entreated Christ to avoid crucifixion. Without missing a beat, Jesus rebuked Peter, "Get behind Me, Satan!"[17] Jesus knew how easy it would be to give in to temptation and not go to the Cross. In addition to the pain of dying this way, Jesus would bear the sin of the world. But anything that interfered with the Cross or salvation was of Satan. In essence, Jesus was associating self-pity with the devil.

Review the Nature of Your Suffering

Regardless of the cause of the pain, adversity generally creates suffering. Before we can respond to the pain, however, we must understand the cause, since that will dictate what we must do.

Examine Why you are Suffering

The psalmist realized the need to review why he was suffering. "For the enemy has persecuted my soul; he has crushed my life to the ground; he has made me dwell in darkness, like those who have long been dead."[18] David was suffering at the hands of his enemy, and his pain was the result of the choices and actions of others.

It's important that we come to understand the nature of our suffering if we are going to do something about it. For instance, if suffering is caused by other people, we really have little choice but to accept it. Of course, we should do what we can to deal with those who are harming us, make changes to prevent further harm, or find ways to minimize their efforts. But even then, we might not be successful in stopping them from hurting us further. Sometimes we must simply cope with circumstances in our lives because they are outside our realm of control. In fact, the word cope literally means to "embattle" and suggests war. Obviously, coping is not a simple process. Christ knew victimization but did not allow Himself to be a victim. As we have seen, He didn't run from the Cross but instead faced His realities.

While the psalmist experienced suffering because of others, Jeremiah acknowledged that he and the people of Israel were suffering because of their own actions: "We have transgressed and rebelled; You have not pardoned."[19] There is always a message in suffering. Sometimes it informs us that there is something we need to learn or attend to.

When we bring on our own suffering, we should take the proper steps to correct the situation. Sometimes this requires brokenness and repentance about sin. Sometimes it means acknowledging our wrong choices. Like the children of Israel, we sometimes do what we want, the way we want, when we want without giving God much thought. In dealing with Israel's sin against God and the subsequent punishment, Jeremiah cried out to God, affirming the sin. God promises that He is near to those whose hearts are broken and contrite, and He will forgive our sins.[20]

Suffering strips away the pretense that life is comfortable, orderly, and fair, a delusion that keeps us looking in all the wrong places for satisfaction. The fact that we seek fulfillment apart from God is the major reason we experience sociological problems, psychological maladies, and even physical illnesses. We are bent on looking away from God to find wholeness. Of the many truths we can extract from the Garden of Eden, one is that a life free of suffering will not guarantee that a person will choose God.

Examine Yourself

People respond to mirrors in different ways. Some individuals spend hours examining themselves in a mirror in order to find ways to cover up all the imperfections they perceive. Some take only a causal look, preferring not to see any problems that might need attention. Others try to avoid mirrors altogether. God wants us to inspect ourselves in the mirror of His Word and in light of the suffering we are experiencing. Regardless of the reason we are suffering, God wants us to uncover areas in our lives that are not completely given over to Him. He wants us to acknowledge our imperfections. It is not evident, based on Scripture, that Job did anything to bring about his suffering. Yet God used Job's pain to expose the arrogance of his heart. In the same way, we need to use the painful circumstances of our lives to deepen our spiritual walks. We need to become more consumed with our unholiness than we are with our discomfort and pain. As we respond to suffering by examining our hearts, we will find unholiness. And as we face our unholiness, we will grow as Christians. Over the course of our lifetimes, we should find that as we examine our souls, we see more and more the image of Christ reflected back to us and less and less our own flawed images. Take time to examine yourself to see what you depend upon for satisfaction.

David's sincerity and contemplation bring him to consider the activity of God. "I remember the days of old; I meditate on all Your works; I muse on the work of Your hands."[21] The psalmist reflects on the good things God had done for him; he declares the wonderful works of God. And in the midst of his pain, he ponders the mysterious ways of God.

God seems to thrive on surprises. Just when we think we understand how God acts, He shows us that we were badly mistaken. As long as our microscopes are too narrowly focused, the meaning of our suffering may always remain a mystery. Although we will never understand the ways of the Almighty, there are some things that we can know about Him.

God is Unchanging

Sometimes it's difficult to relate to the way God worked in the lives of various Bible characters. Even if we wholeheartedly believe the Bible, the level of intimacy God had with people like Abraham, Moses, and David seems far removed from the way we experience Him today. But the God who did business with these saints is the same God who works with us now. God does not change.[22] The very person, character, and Word of God are today—and always will be—exactly what they were in biblical times.

God's purposes never change,[23] but our understanding of Him does. Because we are so limited in our capacity to grasp the supernatural, our comprehension of God will unfold as we get to know Him. In the same way that husbands and wives grow in their understanding of one another over the years, so, too, do we grow in our understanding of God. The more life we experience, the more we will be confronted with "new" aspects of God's eternal nature.

God is Untamable

In C. S. Lewis's The Lion, the Witch and the Wardrobe, God is represented in the character of Aslan the lion, who had a tendency to show up unexpectedly. When asked about Aslan, Mr. Beaver's description beautifully captures some aspects of God's nature: "If there's anyone who can appear before Aslan without their knees knocking, they're either braver than most or else just silly."

When Lucy asks, then, whether or not Aslan is safe, Mr. Beaver responds: "Safe? . . . Who said anything about safe? 'Course he isn't safe. But he's good. He's the King, I tell you."[24] The God of the Bible cannot be reduced to a set of principles. He is predictably unpredictable, yet absolutely good.

It's difficult to understand how God can be so unpredictable and yet so good at the same time. It's nearly inconceivable how He can allow so many bad things to happen in this world, yet still be considered good. When we are hurting, that goodness is very hard to grasp.

Nevertheless, the Bible makes it very clear that God is good and good is God. God continually shatters our understanding of Him. After all, a God we can understand is not a God at all.

God is Mysterious

Just as God is unpredictable, He is also mysterious.[25] Our God is an enigma that we will never figure out.

We discussed one of the main questions sufferers ask during times of trouble: "Why me?" If you believe in a world of chance, it makes no difference why something happens. It simply does. If, however, you believe in a powerful and loving God, it makes all the difference. While there may be one or more purposes for our suffering, God's ultimate plan is to change us spiritually.

The Bible seems to imply that God typically waits to use negative circumstances until He has tried other avenues to get our attention first. In the physical world, we usually experience pain immediately—as when we are burned by a hot stove. Imagine if God dealt with us in the same fashion. If we chose to disobey, we would quickly be punished. In such a world, God would be the tamer and we would be His trained animals.

But instead God has given us the ability to choose, and sometimes we don't experience the consequences of wrong choices for years. He may send various messengers or expose us to sermons, music, or other people's situations in order to get our attention. Sometimes it is only when we do not respond to Him that He begins using painful circumstances.

Certainly, when God disciplines us He wants us to understand His purpose. I (John) knew a man who adamantly believed that his chronic illness was from God. He was a former deacon, Sunday school teacher, and regular singer at his church, and his fall from the Lord had been very public. This man believed that his illness was God's hand of discipline for leaving his wife. Whether or not that was true, at least his illness caused him to return to the Lord with a repentant heart. God is not obligated to explain Himself.

As in the case of Job, God may never tell us what the storm means. An elderly acquaintance of my family lost his wife in a car accident after the birth of their second son. He has lived these past forty years never knowing why God "took" his wife. In spite of his loss, however, this man never doubted that God knew what He was doing. The point is that we can still love and trust God without ever knowing why.

As we've already seen, it's human nature to want an explanation and cause-and-effect reason for our pain. We look backward for a connection between some action and our present suffering. This is wise, since some personal sins or poor choices might have been the cause of our problems. Confession and learning from experience are essential in order to move ahead. But the Bible typically points us to the end result of suffering--the future. God wants us to look forward in hope and to seek explanations, not so much for the origins of our troubles, but for what He wants to do through our pain.

Researchers have found that rather than asking, "Why me?" trauma victims are better off asking, "For what end?"[26] And as believers, we must even go beyond that question and ask "Who?"—that is, "Who is behind and in the midst of the trauma?"

Consider the story of a lone shipwreck survivor who was washed up on an uninhabited island. After a while, he managed to build himself a hut in which he placed the meager belongings he had salvaged from the wreck. The man prayed for deliverance and anxiously scanned the horizon each day to hail any passing ship. One day upon returning from a hunt, he was horrified to find his hut in flames—everything had gone up in smoke. Broken and dejected, the man slumped next to a tree by the coast to await death. After sleeping through the night, the man was startled to feel someone touch him. As he looked up, he saw the face of a man. "We saw your smoke signal," said the man, the captain of a passing ship. "We came to see if you needed help."[27]

If our lives are in God's hands, all things truly do work together for good.[28] As if creating a complex tapestry, richly embroidered with innumerable intersecting threads, God weaves the contours of human experience into a masterpiece of His design. The late Mother Teresa insightfully captured the creative talents of God when she said, "We are pencils in the hands of a loving God."[29] She truly lived out that belief. Just as a piece of yarn cannot comprehend the plan of the weaver, so we, too, are equally ignorant of our mysterious artisan, God.

Sharon, one of my clients, told me that she needed to forgive God for taking her husband of over twenty years. At first, I wanted to tell her that God does nothing wrong, so she didn't need to forgive Him. Yet Sharon blamed God, and she concluded that in order to heal, she needed to let God off the hook. I realized that Sharon did not need to forgive God in order to release Him from the guilt of wrongdoing, but to release herself from holding God responsible.

God can turn His power on like a faucet wherever and whenever He wishes. We may sense how much we need His comfort, power, and guidance, yet our attempts to compel Him by prayers, confessions, and zeal only reveal that God cannot be manipulated. He will be silent when He chooses to be, and He will be active according to His own purposes. Faith in God glorifies Him as He reveals Himself in and through our circumstances.

When God rocks our world, we are forced to pick up the shattered pieces of our core beliefs. No longer is anything the way it used to be, including our views of God. But it is only as we struggle to see God in a new light that we can once again draw close to Him and move through our pain.

Reaffirm Your Desire to Know God

David released his feelings of sorrow to God, reviewed why he was suffering in order to deal with the problem, and recognized that God had many ways of accomplishing His plan. Now he needed to reaffirm his desire to know God: "I spread out my hands to You; my soul longs for You like a thirsty land."[30]

It is impossible to fully trust anyone we do not know deeply. We will never come to the place where we can depend upon God to get us through adversity unless we take the time to get to know who God really is and what He is truly like. Clearly, David felt this passion for God: a passion to know God in a deeper and more profound way. But this passion emanated from God's goodness.

The wonderful weeping prophet Jeremiah voiced a similar longing: "Deep in my heart I say, 'The LORD is all I need; I can depend on him.'"[31] This prophet knew persecution and suffering. Like Job, he came to know that in spite of his adversity, God was vital to his life, completely good, and dependable. While it is true we can be so heavenly minded that we are no earthly good, the greater problem is often that we're so earthly minded that we are no heavenly good. We must seek God as if we were looking for a priceless antique in a dark attic filled with junk. We know He is there, but sometimes it seems impossible to find Him. There is too much clutter to get through. At times we might spot Him buried under the disarray of our lives, but sadly, He still seems out of reach.

Paul told the Philippians that he had willingly lost all things "that I may know Him and the power of His resurrection . . ."[32] Such words reveal the passion of the apostle's heart and encourage us to get to know God in a deeper way. But Paul did not stop with that sentiment. He continued, ". . . and the fellowship of His sufferings, being conformed to His death." If we were ordering from this menu, we would request the knowledge of God à la carte. Sometimes, however, the only way we can know God and understand the power of His resurrection is through suffering.

Just as an author's biography helps readers better understand his or her point of view as they read, our knowledge of God will help us to accept His creative purposes as they unfold in the story of our lives. The more time we spend with God and the more we worship Him, the better we will be able to grasp His benevolence.

Do You Really Know God?

As we saw in the section on recognizing the ways God works, we are limited in our understanding of God. Part of the problem is that we think we know God, but the notions of God that we embrace are typically not accurate. Often, we don't even embrace the God who is portrayed in the Bible.

As a counselor in training, I was fascinated by C. S. Lewis's brief narrative A Grief Observed, which gives an account of a committed Christian and scholar agonizing over something he could not control. A bachelor until midlife, Lewis found great fulfillment in his marriage. After four years of marriage, Lewis's wife, Joy, died of cancer. As a means of coping with his loss, Lewis turned to his gift of writing to express his heartache. In A Grief Observed, Lewis candidly expressed his fears and doubts. Seeking comfort in God, Lewis felt the door being slammed in his face and double bolted from the inside. Early on, he wrote with searing honesty of his personal journey: "Not that I am . . . in much danger of ceasing to believe in God. The real danger is of coming to believe such dreadful things about Him. The conclusion I dread is not, 'So there's no God after all,' but, 'So this is what God's really like. Deceive yourself no longer.'"[33]

Suffering tends to test and change our views of God, challenging our earthly notions of who God is and what He is like. We can't understand why God would seem to contradict His own nature. Like Lewis, we struggle to grasp God's role in suffering and pain. Job realized that God could not be at odds with Himself, and therefore resolved the apparent contradiction by realizing that the problem was between his idea of God and God as He really is.

Early in the book of Job, God seemed hostile and unjust. Yet in his misery Job recognized that there was another side of God—that He forgave sin, that He did not neglect His creation, and that He was and is a witness in heaven, an advocate on high, a pledge for all those who are scorned.[34] Through his ordeal, Job sensed that in spite of his despair, his Redeemer lived and would at last stand on the earth.[35] In fact, it was not until he arrived at this declaration about his Redeemer that Job wanted someone to take a pen and write his story. It is not the depth of our pain that ought to stop the presses, but the realization that we have a Redeemer.

Suffering transforms our head knowledge of God into an experiential knowledge. The decisive break with the old ideas of God did not come easily for Job. It took immense suffering for Job to radically shift his notions of God.

I know that You can do everything, and that no purpose of Yours can be withheld from You. You asked, "Who is this who hides counsel without knowledge?" Therefore I have uttered what I did not understand, things too wonderful for me, which I did not know.[36]

Job came to understand that knowing about God and truly knowing God are not one and the same. Upon coming to grips with the sovereignty of God, Job's response was one of repentance: "Therefore I abhor myself, and repent in dust and ashes."[37]

Helmut Thielicke, an influential theologian from Hamburg, Germany, pointed out that a fabric viewed through a magnifying glass is clear in the middle and blurred at the edges. But in spite of how it appears, we know the edges are clear because of what we see in the middle. Life, he says, is like a fabric. Many edges are blurred; many events and circumstances we do not understand. But they are to be interpreted by the clarity we see in the center—the Cross of Christ. We are not left to guess about the goodness of God from isolated bits of data. He has clearly revealed His character and dramatically demonstrated it to us on the Cross. As Paul wonderfully expressed, "He who did not spare His own Son, but delivered Him up for us all, how shall He not with Him also freely give us all things?"[38] Meditate on who and what Jesus Christ is and what He has done for you through His life, death, and resurrection. If ever you doubt His love, consider the Cross. No other symbol better signifies love, let alone hope!

We must rid ourselves of myths about God, such as "God helps those who help themselves." Our minds must be saturated with the truths of God that are found in His Word if we are going to survive perilous times. A Christian who was also a recovering alcoholic attended an Alcoholics Anonymous meeting where the topic was surrendering to a higher power. After listening to a lot of discussion about this higher power, the man said that he did not believe in a loving God. His father had been a stern, abusive parent who told him that God would punish him if he disobeyed. This young man learned that God was not someone to approach but someone to be avoided, or at least appeased. A gentleman from the meeting said, "If that was my God I would fire Him." At first, the Christian was put off by that notion, but then the gentleman went on, "Since you need a God, why not try mine?" It was then that the man realized that his "god" was not the God of the Bible.

Children are often very anxious and fearful of doing something wrong. All too often, parents use the threat of God and punishment to control childish behavior. This fear of displeasing God then magnifies our growing sense of guilt and shame. There are some truths in these statements (i.e., God does punish, and it is possible to displease Him), but some of us only see and hold to this lopsided, half-truth view. These distorted images of God then shape our views of Him. When that happens, we must fire the god we've created in our image: the god who abandons us, holds grudges, is not approachable, has no mercy or grace, plays games with our lives, and belittles us at every turn. These unbiblical concepts must be replaced with the whole of Scripture on the nature of God, which includes His enduring love for us.

Sometimes, as C. S. Lewis wrote, our god isn't evil, but neither is he strong or powerful. That god is more like a benevolent grandfather than a father.[39] Fathers want to enjoy a relationship with their children but primarily seek to raise healthy, mature, and well-balanced people. Grandfathers, on the other hand, tend to overlook their grandchildren's faults and avoid interfering in their lives. But the God portrayed in the Bible is not a sentimental, beard-stroking grandfather in the sky. Make sure that the God you get to know is the God of the Bible.

God, who is merciful, patient, and long-suffering, loves us so deeply that He is willing to put up with us.[40] Because God is good and wise, He can make anything we encounter work out for our good, at least in the end.[41] His plans are to help us rather than harm us.[42] Finally, because He is faithful, changeless, and dependable, He has promised never to leave or forsake us.[43]

Even the names of God speak to His wondrous nature. He is Jehovah-Jireh, the God who provides all our needs and supplies relief.[44] He is Jehovah-Rophi, the miraculous healer.[45] One of the most revered of divine titles to Jews and Christians alike is Jehovah-Shalom, the Lord who is peace.[46] He is also Jehovah-Ra-ah, meaning "the Lord the Shepherd," which speaks to His guiding, providing, and protecting His followers.[47] Finally, He is Jehovah El Shaddai, the Almighty God who gives strength and satisfies His people.[48]

Even as you read these words, Jesus is making intercession for you at the right hand of the Father, and the Holy Spirit is indwelling you, sealing you, and providing you comfort.[49]

All of the promises in the Bible are based upon the character of the Promiser, God Himself. He is rich in promises, and they are as sure as His unchanging nature, backed by His faithfulness. This is the God we all need to come to know.

Reassess Your Dependency and Trust in God

Someone has said that "adversity is a means of introducing a man to his real self." While there is truth in that statement, it is incomplete. Adversity also reveals the genuine nature of an individual's faith and dependency in God. God's hope is that adversity will give us a deeper and richer view of Himself.

The psalmist cried out, "Answer me speedily, O LORD; My spirit fails! Do not hide Your face from me, lest I be like those who go down into the pit."[50] David realized he needed God because he could not meet his own needs. It is as if he said, "God, if you don't answer me, I will die!"

He knew that he had not been fully dependent upon God but turned to God as a last resort. It is interesting that when we suffer, most of us eventually arrive at God's doorstep. In the end, the "why" questions always bring us back to God.

What is My Real God?

The greatest wrestling match in a time of suffering occurs when we consider our relationship with God. While we cannot control our circumstances or God's purposes, we can control our trust and dependence in and on Him.

Trust is a relational term. When someone does not fully trust another person, there is an inherent relational deficit. Trust is based on the strength of the relationship. It will not grow or flourish unless tested and ultimately worked through. This idea of trust is the same when it comes to our relationship with God. Consider your response when a significant tragedy befalls you, something you believe you don't deserve. If you believe God should have intervened, that He should have done something to prevent you from experiencing such an awful ordeal, you probably do not trust the character of God. Do you believe that God is still good and gracious to you even when you suffer?

When we're in pain, we tend to look to anything tangible to give us hope. I

(John) remember reading a story about a man condemned to solitary confinement in a pitch-black cell. After hours of boredom and isolation in his dark chamber, he progressively became more and more panicky. Knowing he would not survive his punishment long if his emotions spun out of control, the man sought to solace himself. He realized that he had a marble in his pocket, so he began to occupy himself by repeatedly throwing the marble, his only companion, against the wall. The ill-fated man spent hours listening to his marble bounce and roll along the cold stone floor. Then he would grope in the darkness to find it. In a strange way, this activity gave him comfort and purpose during his confinement. One day the prisoner threw his marble into the air as he always did, but this time it failed to come down. He was naturally disturbed about its disappearance. He combed the cell looking for his marble, but he never could find it. The more he looked, the more panicky he became. Broken by the strange disappearance of his only source of comfort, the prisoner became uncontrollable, pulled out his hair, and died. When the prison officials came in to remove the body, one of the guards noticed something caught in a huge spider's web in a corner of the cell. "Now look at that! How did a marble get up there?"[51]

We so readily place our trust in things that cannot be relied upon. Some depend upon their education or bank accounts. Others rely on their independence or ability to make things happen. But none of these things will prove themselves 100 percent reliable. They are temporal, finite, and limited. Yet God is eternal, infinite, and dependable beyond our definition and imaginations, and He asks us to place our trust in Him. Sadly, we struggle to comply.

The great patriarchs of the Old Testament put their confidence in things they couldn't see.[52] Why then do we struggle so much to relinquish our destinies into God's hands? Charles Haddon Spurgeon is credited with saying, "When you can't trace God's hand, trust His heart."[53] Trust requires us to live with our unanswered questions.

How Can I Trust God?

Before we can place our dependency on God, we must reconcile two questions: First, do we truly believe that God is totally committed to our welfare? If that is true, then do we believe that He is good and right in doing whatever He deems necessary to accomplish His will?

God's goodness doesn't change. The God who raised Jesus from the dead so that we can know eternal life did so because He is good and gracious. This same God, who has the power over death, is still good today even when we hurt.

I knew a couple who was having a difficult time with their toddler. In spite of a well-executed bedtime routine, the child refused to sleep by himself. The frustrated parents would then put the screaming youngster in bed with them in order to get some sleep themselves. With another child on the way, these parents knew something had to change. After spending time loving and comforting their child before bedtime, the parents realized they had to let him cry, and not allow him to get into their bed. It took all their strength to listen to their youngster scream from his crib and not rush in to rescue him. Yet for their son's own good and development, the parents painfully endured his tears and ignored their hearts' desire to ease his pain. Obviously, their son did not understand why they weren't responding, but they rested in the fact that it was best to do nothing. Because these parents were committed to the long-term welfare of their son, they had to leave him alone in his bedroom. The same is true with God. It may seem that He is hiding, but His purpose is to grow us. While we might not fully understand why He would allow our pain and misery to continue, we can rest assured that it will be best for us in the long run.

If we are going to trust God, we must not put our faith and dependence in understanding. While it is appropriate and acceptable to pray that God will give us understanding, God wants us to place knowing Him, believing Him, and accepting His plans as our priority and passion. He never expects us to fully understand His ways. Even if God did give us His rationale, we probably wouldn't really accept His answer as justification for our suffering anyway.

We need to trust Him with the innocence of a child. You may explain to a child all the reasons he must be immunized, but when the doctor gets ready to give the shot, none of those reasons matter. And what does the child do when the needle strikes? He screams for his mommy. Comfort comes, not in knowing the reasons, but in knowing the Comforter.

I have an acquaintance who lost his spouse about four years ago. While in her forties with three young children, she was diagnosed with a rare form of cancer. She endured almost a year of painful treatment to no avail. Even though it has been four years since her death, my friend still does not know why God allowed her to die such a painful death while their children were so young and vulnerable to her loss. He says, "God gives and God takes away. God didn't have to send His Son to die for me or raise Him from the dead so that my wife and I could enjoy eternal life. God was not obligated to explain Himself then, and He is not obligated to explain Himself now." There is not much more that needs to be said. With that attitude, it is not surprising that a look of hope radiates from this man's face whenever I see him.

Relinguish Your Destiny Into God's Trustworthy Hands

As a student in college, I traveled with a group to Haiti to help build some schools and to conduct Bible studies and concerts. One of the meetings was high in the mountains, so we rode donkeys to get there. As we traveled along the windy trails, at many points along the way we were literally riding next to a cliff. Our instructor told us to sit balanced on the donkey, even though our minds were telling us to lean in toward the mountain. The guide tried to reassure us that donkeys are sure-footed animals and that they do not slip. As I looked down over the edge, I thought, Yeah, but they are also dumb. Nevertheless, if we were going to be safe, I knew we had to trust that the donkeys were sure. Obviously, the donkey, dumb or not, survived the trip. But it was difficult to place trust in that animal!

The psalmist David did not desire to place his life at the feet of a donkey but in the hands of a loving God. "Cause me to hear Your loving-kindness in the morning, for in You do I trust; Cause me to know the way in which I should walk, for I lift up my soul to You."[54] David knew he had struggled in the past, but now he was ready to place his trust in God and affirm the Lord's goodness.

Similarly, the prophet Jeremiah wrote a letter to a group of early exiles in Babylon seeking to encourage them with a message from God: "For I know the thoughts that I think toward you, says the LORD, thoughts of peace and not of evil, to give you a future and a hope."[55] If you are suffering, this is a great verse to memorize. It speaks volumes about God's enterprise. In the Hebrew, the word for "thoughts" means "plans." God has a plan for us; we can trust that it is a good plan because it is designed to give us a future and hope.

When my wife and I were married, I brought her to my one-bedroom apartment in Orlando, Florida. As we neared the apartment complex, I lovingly told her that while I had made many preparations to our new home, it was hers to do with as she wanted. We arrived, unloaded the last of our possessions, and settled in for the night. The next morning I kissed my bride good-bye and wished her a pleasant day as I left for work. When I came home that evening, I was shocked to find that my wife had rearranged everything in the apartment. I had to look at the number on the door to make sure I was in the right place!

My wife gave me a huge kiss and enthusiastically told me that she had fun making my apartment our apartment. But I was hurt that she had made so many changes, and I told her so. In fact, I criticized most everything she did (yes, the honeymoon was definitely over!). While you may think little of me for treating my wife poorly, consider how we typically respond to the way God arranges our lives. If you are a Christian, you made a willful decision to turn your life over to the Lord. You gave Him permission to do with you whatever He pleased. You probably even sing "I Surrender All" on Sundays. When, however, God does with you what He pleases, do you find yourself complaining rather than surrendering? It is so much easier to talk and sing about surrender than it is to exhibit it when God stomps on our comfort.

One of the great paradoxes of the Christian faith is that we are never completely free until we have become totally dependent. When we want answers, God offers Himself as the answer to our pain. And until we are willing to accept that, and only that, we are not yet totally dependent.

Genuine trust is independent of understanding. This was true for Daniel's three friends, who affirmed their confidence that God could save them from the furnace. Of course, they did not have the foggiest idea how God would do it, but these three ordinary men were able to face their ordeal with extraordinary composure because they placed their faith in an extraordinary God.[56] While they may not have entirely understood the awesome power of their God, they knew enough to know that they could rest in His care. The apostle John wrote, "For whatever is born of God overcomes the world. And this is the victory that has overcome the world—our faith."[57]

Through Christ all enemies are defeated; the victory is ours, we need only to appropriate it. Of course, that's the hard part. We appropriate faith when we accept it, believe it, and act upon it. Many biblical characters resisted following God's will (e.g., Abraham, Jonah, Samson) only to later regret their decisions. That is why God encourages us not to rely on our own understanding, but in every situation to depend on Him.[58] Put another way, we are to resist following our own plans. Being dependent on God means being willing to accept what He has promised, even when we cannot always explain what He has said. We accept life's mysteries and suffering because God knows them and we know Him. Of course, this does not mean that we are to resign ourselves to our situation. In fact, in the next chapter we'll talk about developing a plan of recovery. The point here is that we are to put our trust in God above our own plans. Because God is the First and the Last, the Everlasting to the Everlasting, we need not fear.[59] It is okay to seek answers, but when none are forthcoming, we must trust. That is why faith is so foundational, not just to salvation, but to day-to-day living.

There is a popular story of a man who went mountain climbing. As he made his way over the rough mountain terrain, his rope gave way and he began to fall. Barely holding on, the panicky climber cried out, "Is anybody there?" Suddenly and miraculously a voice from heaven bellowed, "I am the Lord Your God. I am here and I will rescue you from this mountain. But for Me to help, you must trust Me to save you. Let go of your rope and I will catch you. Just release your grip and my powerful hands will be under you to carry you safely to the ground." After what seemed a long time of silence, the climber yelled, "Is anyone else out there?"

Are you able to say, "When my life seems to break loose, I will trust God no matter how difficult it becomes?" Remember, no matter what circumstances you face, God has promised never to abandon you.[60] Job came to the realization that life has meaning and purpose no matter what is lost here on earth. Our meaning and purpose are always secure because they are not rooted in what we have but in who we are in Christ.

Five Tips for Trusting God

For most of us, trust is not something that comes easily. The following five steps can be helpful when learning to trust God and relinquish our lives into His hands.

1. Get to know God. This is the most important step to developing and nurturing a trusting relationship. We examined the importance of getting to know God in the last section. While we may acknowledge the importance of knowing God intimately, many obstacles stand in our way. One obstacle is caused by our experiences. Knowing God can be very difficult for people who have come from dysfunctional backgrounds where they experienced emotional, mental, physical or sexual abuse, abandonment, and/ or rejection. While transferring human experiences with our parents onto other authority figures is normal, it need not destine us to repeating negative patterns with every person in authority. Likening God to our parents is normal, but it can have devastating consequences. No parent measures up to the attributes and character of God. Therefore, every child must move from earthly expressions of love, mercy, and grace to what those attributes are like as they emanate from God. Because of their backgrounds, this step is harder for some. Their inability to grasp who God is blocks their fellowship with God and their ability to trust Him with the control of their lives. If trust is a problem for you, you may need to seek professional Christian counseling to help you work through this obstacle.

2. Accept what happens as God's way of helping you to grow. He does not needlessly allow us to go through painful experiences. God's goal is always to produce some greater work in our lives. Accomplishing His purpose was so important that God even took the lives of Job's children, as well as allowing Job and his wife to go through emotional and mental torment. It does not seem fair that God might choose to hurt a person as a way of helping someone else. But God seeks conformity to His image, not comfort. He wills faithfulness, not fairness, and holiness over happiness. Therefore, learn to ask, "For what end?" rather than "Why?" Remember that knowing the "Who" will make all the difference in the world.

3. Focus on your response to the problem rather than the cause of it.

Jesus declared that "in the world you will have tribulation; but be of good cheer, I have overcome the world."[61] We can make an idol of our ability to reason and figure things out. Therefore, surrender the need to know everything. Certainly examine your life for any reason that might explain the why. If your teeth fall out, for example, it might be helpful to know it's because you failed to brush them.

4. Focus on God's presence. When we're hurting, our first inclination often is to run from God. But the truth is, there is no greater prescription for suffering than the presence of the Lord. So immerse yourself in Him and rest in these words:

"When you pass through the waters, I will be with you; and when you pass through the rivers, they will not sweep over you. When you walk through the fire, you will not be burned; the flames will not set you ablaze. For I am the LORD, your God, the Holy One of Israel, your Savior."[62] "So do not fear, for I am with you; do not be dismayed, for I am your God. I will strengthen you and help you; I will uphold you with my righteous right hand."[63] "And those who know Your name will put their trust in You; for You, LORD, have not forsaken those who seek You."[64]

5. Make a willful decision to trust the Lord. You may find it difficult to allow God to be fully in charge of your life, but if the alternative is misery, God's authority might be easier to accept. The key is to make the decision, commit to that decision, and trust the outcome to God.

Curt Richter, a psychobiologist from Johns Hopkins, became interested in the consequences of stress after watching so many people give up and die when overwhelmed by pressure.[65] Although stress is often purely psychological, Richter realized that it often caused the patient's body as well as his or her mind to collapse. So he began a series of rather dramatic—and even unkind— experiments to measure the physiological consequences of various highly threatening situations. In one particular study, Richter placed a rat into a large tub filled with water. Since rats are usually great swimmers, it was not surprising that the little fellow stayed afloat by paddling for over eighty hours before succumbing to exhaustion and going under. If the water was too cold or too hot, the rat would give up after less than thirty hours. If a research assistant handled the rats roughly before putting them into the water or blew a jet of air into the animal's face while it was swimming, the rats became exhausted even more quickly. Therefore, Richter found that the more stressful the situation, the greater the rat's suffering. Interestingly, Richter discovered that if he pulled the drowning rat out of the water and let it rest on a table for several minutes, the animal could make a remarkable recovery. Once the rat rested and gathered its wits, it seemed to realize that it could, in fact, survive the traumatic situation. If Richter tossed it back into the water, the rat would swim again for many hours. It seems that hope truly does spring eternal, but apparently only if one has been given a reason to hope.

As Christians, we have every reason to hope because our hope is not based upon happenstance or ourselves. It is based on the Creator of the universe. Therefore, we can confidently trust God with our worries, anxieties, questions, problems, and crises.

Paul Tournier said that the Christian life is sometimes like a trapeze act. You can swing on the bar, exercising and building muscles all you want. But if you want to excel, you have to let go and reach for the next bar—even when there's nothing beneath you. As they say in Alcoholics Anonymous, "Let go and let God!"

Rejoice in How God May Use Your Suffering

While preparing his patient for ear surgery, a physician was explaining the various procedures and associated risks. In trying to calm his anxious patient's fears, he said, "I may hurt you, but I won't injure you." Likewise, our Great Physician speaks the same truth to us. He recognizes that, when used by His skilled hand, pain and suffering provide great benefit. As Friedrich Nietzsche said, "That which does not kill me, makes me stronger."[66]

David understood this. Regardless of his emotional state, he desired to follow after God, knowing that the result would be good. "Teach me to do Your will, for You are my God; Your Spirit is good. Lead me in the land of uprightness. Revive me, O LORD, for Your name's sake! For Your righteousness' sake bring my soul out of trouble. In Your mercy cut off my enemies, and destroy all those who afflict my soul; for I am Your servant."[67] The good things God is doing that we cannot see are far greater than the circumstances we can see. While God may not seem to respond to our every cry, He promises to use trouble and calamity for our good if we allow Him.

Corrie ten Boom wrote, "Praise lifts your eyes from the battle to the victory, for Christ is already Victor in your heart that you might have His victory in your life."[68] There is nothing remarkable about praise when life is going smoothly. But when we are able to worship God in the midst of a storm, that is truly extraordinary.

Some people, including Christians, live with chronic unhappiness and feelings of inferiority. These believers incorrectly assume that unless their self-esteem improves, they are doomed to a life of misery. But solving self-esteem problems is not the answer to having hope and peace. It is possible to have inner joy even with low self-esteem because true peace and joy come from knowing and believing in God's goodness.

Paul put it this way, "Rejoice in the Lord always. Again I will say, rejoice!"[69] At the root of the Greek word for rejoice is the Greek word grace. We can rejoice in suffering because of the grace bestowed upon us through Jesus Christ. Joy is not a response that can be mustered by one's own efforts.

In essence, suffering speaks to the future. But discovering meaning in our sufferings will not necessarily change us. After we have discovered meaning in and through our sufferings, we need to develop a vision for what we can become as a result of that suffering.

Before you strive to rid yourself of pain, take the time to look for the meaning God has in it. Once you understand the significance, you can then take action to achieve the vision God has for you, a vision about what might be and what you can become. Then with the power of the Holy Spirit, you can take steps to achieve that vision. And it doesn't stop there. As you take new actions, you generate new meaning. And so the cycle goes.

God seeks to use broken hearts to draw people to Himself, to deepen fellowship with Him. Perhaps that is why James told us to be joyful when we suffer, and the writer of Hebrews cautioned us not to "despise" the chastening of the Lord.[70] While this counsel deals with discipline, it is applicable to any kind of suffering. Suffering is an opportunity to grow and to know God in richer ways; such transformation would never be possible apart from pain.

People who have experienced and survived difficult ordeals often report that they are truly different people afterward. They have a newfound appreciation of life and a sense of gratitude. I once spoke with a physician who suffered a massive heart attack while in his midthirties. He reported how much more sensitive he became to his patients' complaints and pains. When we come to understand, as Job did, that God can do anything, we are able to experience God in a different way. Just as a brook would lose its song if God removed all the rocks, so we would lose our ability to experience and demonstrate the power and majesty of God if He removed all the stones of suffering in our lives.

A couple of nights ago, my (John) sleep was interrupted by a terrible sound. It was a buzzing noise, and though I couldn't pinpoint the source of the sound in my sleepy state, I knew it was annoying. I soon realized it was the clock, which I quickly turned off so that I could roll over to get more rest. Unfortunately, my day got off to a later start than I had planned. As unpleasant as that alarm was, it was a signal that I needed to get up. It didn't matter how comfortable I was in that warm bed, I needed to rise to the occasion. Pain in our lives is a lot like that alarm clock. Sometimes we work so hard to rid ourselves of the pain that we miss the message and the opportunity to become better people.

When suffering hardships, our focus is on the solution, but the strength we gain in finding the solution and working our way through it is equally important. Perhaps this is what the prophet Isaiah had in mind when he said that God would "give them beauty for ashes,"[71] or as the Contemporary English Version says, "give them flowers in place of their sorrow, olive oil in place of tears, and joyous praise in place of broken hearts." Only a supernatural God who is profoundly committed to us is capable of making masterpieces out of misery. As Oswald Chambers wrote, "If through a broken heart God can bring His purposes to pass in the world, then thank Him for breaking your heart."[72]

Chapter 16

MOVING THROUGH WITH PURPOSE

The cocoon of the emperor moth is flask shaped. In order for the perfect insect to appear, it must force its way through the neck of the cocoon after hours of intense struggle. Once, someone witnessed this insect's labor and out of pity snipped the cocoon's confining threads to make the insect's exit easier. Soon the moth emerged, but it had a swollen body and small, shriveled wings. Because this man had eased the moth's struggle, its wings never developed. It spent its brief life crawling instead of flying through the air on strong wings. The man, in his kindness, did not understand that the moth needed the struggle in order to force fluid from its body into the wings so that flight would be possible.[1]

Life change must be purposed and intentional. Like the emperor moth we must strive to grow and be different, or we will become hardened and more comfortable with a world we were not intended to call home. We must resist our self-defeating, automatic responses and consciously and willfully choose better ways to face hardships. These new ways of thinking and behaving are unfamiliar and frightening, but they offer a new life. We must persistently practice the adopted "new reflexes" in order for them to become both familiar and natural. We shape our futures through the decisions we make today, and these choices involve purposing our hearts, changing our perspectives, and preventing undue stress.

Many paths can lead to recovery. As you read this chapter, do not allow yourself to become overwhelmed with the numerous strategies that are recommended. It is not necessary to master each of the "new reflexes" or skills that we will discuss. My daughter is very creative. When she cuts the grass she makes patterns with the mower that can only be described as art. One of my neighbors likes to mow diagonals across his lawn. When I mow, my objective is to finish the job as quickly as possible so I employ the tried and tested box method. No matter which mowing pattern is used, the end result is the same: the grass is cut. Likewise, there is no specific pattern or strategy to respond to suffering. Some strategies will fit you better than others. Simply find and use the tools that you believe will contribute to your own emotional and spiritual maturity.

Purpose Your Heart

A history professor had been teaching his class about the French-English wars. One of his students asked how the English were able to be consistently victorious. The history professor explained that it wasn't because the English had wiser generals, better equipment, bigger armies, or even better-trained soldiers. The English won because they "learned how to hang on one day longer than the French."

In the face of adversity, especially during long-term trials, sometimes even hanging on one day feels beyond our reach. When we are to get through, however, we must purpose our hearts to recover. Purposing involves four things:

1. *Accepting reality*
2. *Deciding to grow from our pain*
3. *Developing the lines of communication with God*
4. *Tapping into a support system*

Accept Reality

During times of suffering, we all want a quick fix, a parachute that will take us back into the land of normalcy. One client told me that he wanted the shortest cut, easiest road, and the no-pain approach to feeling better. He didn't want a process; he wanted to fly right into health. The idea of having to walk through a valley in order to reach the promised land of healing was not only foreign to this gentleman, it was simply unacceptable.

Quick fixes, shortcuts, and no-pain approaches almost never work. In fact, the result of not accepting adversity is actually greater suffering. Carl Jung believed that all psychological problems were the result of avoiding legitimate suffering.[2]

There are several ways people avoid the truth. One is by denying personal responsibility and blaming someone or something for the way we feel. Another is by exaggerating and overstating the situation. By making the problem bigger than life, we continue to justify our "right" to self-pity.

But as long as we point the finger of blame or wallow in self-pity, we are helpless in the face of suffering. For the committed believer, self-pity has no place. If ever one was justified to feel sorry for Himself, it was Jesus. Yet He displayed no self-pity because He knew His mission. Are we, then, to be exempt from such a process?

Ultimately, we must wrestle with the vexing monsters of the valley if we want to reach the promised land. When we accept this reality, we can finally grow. Dealing with hardship requires that we gain awareness of what happened and accept the reality of it. This acceptance is the key because it gets us to stop living in the problem and to start finding the solution. We must get honest with ourselves, give up self-pity, and allow the circumstances to change us rather than attempt to change our circumstances.

Decide to Grow From Your Pain

Dr. Viktor Frankl observed that his fellow holocaust prisoners' attitudes and outlooks on life were the result of a decision, not concentration-camp influences. All of us, even under such formidable circumstances, have the power to decide what shall become of us—mentally and spiritually. In other words, while we may have been victimized, we do not have to remain victims.

The focus of Dr. Frankl's therapy was to reorient his patients' focus away from their circumstances toward meaning. This reorientation required that the person take responsibility for recovery and for faith, and understand that in the larger scheme of life, suffering is valuable. As Christians we know that true meaning comes from a personal relationship with Christ. We must reorient ourselves from the trials we face to God's higher purposes. Consider the words of Dr. Frankl once again: "Man does not behave morally for the sake of having a good conscience but for the sake of a cause to which he commits himself, or for a person he loves, or for the sake of his God."[3] That is why having a reason for living gives us the ability to endure any circumstance. When we begin to view things from God's perspective, we recognize that knowing Him gives us the ability to endure any trial.

We may never know why we suffer in certain circumstances, but we can harvest something from the study of affliction. According to Dr. Frankl, knowing that there can be meaning in suffering totally transforms the situation from a burden to a quest. He wrote, "Once the meaning of suffering had been revealed to us, we refused to minimize or alleviate the camp's tortures by ignoring them or harboring false illusions and entertaining artificial optimism. Suffering had become a task on which we did not want to turn our backs. We had realized its hidden opportunities for achievement."[4] It seems bizarre that these prisoners did not want to run from their suffering. But as we saw in the last chapter, to run from pain is to run from the chance to advance our emotional and spiritual character. Maturity means facing adversity head-on.

When we stop spending energy on avoiding pain, we can direct that energy to bringing something new into being. Accepting our circumstances and committing ourselves to growth offers hope. Realizing that the ordeal serves a larger purpose redeems it. Many victims of suffering report positive changes in themselves as a direct result of their hardships. Some describe themselves as more compassionate, caring, patient, and loving individuals. Other victims realize they have untapped strengths they never knew of before facing trials. All in all, these individuals are better people now, as difficult as their paths have been. As such, suffering builds character. It also builds us spiritually. Suffering helped Job develop a more personal faith. Paul discovered that he could be content in the midst of dire circumstances. Jonah learned lessons about God's character and the consequences of disobedience.

Call to mind difficulties from your past. What did you learn from those experiences? At the time, you may have believed nothing good could come out of such ordeals. But now, years later, are you able to harvest a great deal of learning from each situation? Some people, like Job, see God in a bigger and more personal way. Others, like Joni Eareckson Tada, develop a more real and genuine faith. Some sufferers develop unfeigned patience. Many find that they are able to minister to other people like never before as suffering provides a more heartfelt compassion for their fellow human beings.

To the Christian, suffering is an opportunity that requires us to do more than bear it. We are called to use it. If you purpose your heart, you too can glean a harvest from your pain. Poet and author Robert Louis Stevenson, who contracted pulmonary tuberculosis, shared his philosophy for dealing with the chronic disease: "Life is not so much a matter of holding good cards, but sometimes of playing a poor hand well."[5]

Opportunity speaks to the future, not the present. It envisions possibilities. Remember that the ultimate aims of the Christian life are becoming like Christ and giving glory to God. We will not arrive there overnight, but we can hold on to the fact that we can eventually be more emotionally and spiritually attuned. If we have an injured leg and remain bedridden to avoid any additional pain, our leg muscles will atrophy and contract. But if we exercise too vigorously, we may reinjure the leg even more severely. Instead, we begin by limping—putting just enough weight on the leg to build strength gradually, but not so much as to strain it and prevent healing. As the muscles strengthen, we are able to bear more and more weight. In the same way, emotional healing is a process that requires us to challenge ourselves to move forward toward growth.

Developing the Lines of Communication With God

God said, "Call upon Me in the day of trouble; I will deliver you, and you shall glorify Me."[6] Victorious Christian living requires that we relentlessly communicate with God. Of course, most Christians have some level of communication with God, perhaps praying at meals or reading the Bible from time to time. But such limited communication will not sustain our spiritual lives in the good times, let alone during times of affliction and adversity.

Prayer is the glue that keeps us close to God, and Scripture is the truth that keeps us grounded in Him. Spending time in prayer gives us an opportunity to seek God's plan for us. When we communicate with God, we need to do so with intensity, honesty, and humility. In adversity, we are driven to pray, to cry out to God from the depths of our hearts and to invite His involvement. Bear in mind the promise that God gives us when we fervently seek Him with all of our hearts: we will find Him.[7] If you believe that God is silent or has abandoned you, the answer is to pray with all your might.

It is not just the frequency or fervency that is an issue with prayer. What we pray is most important. When we experience pain and suffering, our tendency is to pray for deliverance, relief, answers—anything that will bring a sense of comfort. Instead, the nature of our prayer lives should be worshipful, praising God. When our prayer lives become characterized by praise, we will rise above our circumstances. A friend of ours has said that when going through a difficult time, he spends 95 percent of his prayer time praising and worshiping God.

As we saw in the previous chapter, we need to release our feelings to God. Prayer allows us to strip away pretense by revealing our passions, hurts, and longings. Since sin blocks fellowship with God, we need to first confess any sin. As we admit our wrongs to the Lord, we will find that His unconditional love forgives us and cleanses us.[8]

Studying God's Word will help us in many areas. For instance, Psalm 119 shows us that Scripture is more than adequate to help us in addressing any concern. According to this passage, God's Word protects us from sin, provides enlightenment, counsels us, comforts us, offers hope, gives wisdom, guides, and provides peace.[9]

Through Bible study we can get further instruction from God. Because the Bible is a lamp, it promises illumination and guidance.[10] It promises rest to the weary and sustenance to the starving.[11] Since the Bible is brimming with God's promises, it is imperative to spend time in daily Bible reading. In the Old Testament, we can find promises made to the great patriarchs, kings, prophets, and the world at large. In the New Testament, the promises are set forth to the church. God's promises are not ambiguous. They are stated in clear, simple terminology that even a child can understand. You cannot feed on the promises of God and remain hopeless and hapless. Among other disciplines, it requires a regular regimen of prayer, worship, Bible reading, solitude, fasting, and meditation to experience reprieves from suffering. God's grace is often experienced only one a day-to-day basis. As we do our part in drawing near to God, His presence and comfort is experienced in a tangible and meaningful way.

Tapping Into a Support System

Social support plays a powerful role in our psychological and spiritual well-being because we were created as interpersonal beings. Other people play key roles, not only in shaping our attitudes, but also in helping us adjust following a tragedy. It has been well established that the way peers respond to the sufferer dramatically affects that person's adjustment. Research has concluded that social support protects people from the potentially adverse effects of stressful events, and even in the absence of stress, social involvement has beneficial effects on people.[12] In fact, research has even demonstrated that a strong support group can lessen the effects of many physical illnesses, including the common cold.[13] Finding and maintaining a positive support system, a group of fellow believers with whom we can share our struggles, is critical. This need is one reason that regular church attendance is so vital. We need the Word of God and the fellowship and encouragement of other Christians.[14]

Sometimes we can benefit even more from being with people who have suffered similar tragedies. Alcoholics Anonymous is based on this idea; sobriety is maintained by helping another alcoholic to stay sober. As a counselor, I (John) have strongly encouraged grieving people to get together regardless of the nature of their losses, so that through their interaction, everyone can heal. I thank God for the growing movement in the church to offer support groups for different kinds of hurting people.

The Bible encourages us to minister to suffering people. Hence, when we are in need, we should allow the body of Christ to work effectively by going to particular godly individuals for wisdom and guidance. Once we have our support systems, we must share our hearts with them. Even Shakespeare recognized the importance of sharing one's hurts: "Give sorrow words. The grief that does not speak whispers the o'er-fraught heart, and bids it break."[15]

Research clearly spells out the benefits of talking.[16] Disclosing our feelings to caring people unloads the weight of the painful emotions associated with a trial. Talking also helps us organize the experience so that we can make sense of it. Initiating a dialogue and beginning to talk about the pain might initially cause an increase in distress, but over the long haul, those who talk fare much better than those who do not.

Some people have a difficult time admitting they need help. This reluctance is typically nothing more than pride and self-reliance. We always need input from others, especially during times of adversity. There is a favorite saying among the addicted recovering community: "You are only as sick as your secrets." Shame and fear prompt people to hide in order to avoid being open and honest with others. But silence only leads to greater sickness. A caring community of support creates feelings of acceptance, reduces the shame and isolation, and provides a healing remedy for recovery.

Opening up to others means letting people know that we hurt, and it's crucial that we find someone to talk to who is capable of giving godly advice. Some of us feel comfortable talking with our ministers; others should seek the counsel of a mature Christian whom they trust.

Chapter 17

CHANGE YOUR PERSPECTIVE

Abraham Maslow once said, "If the only tool you have is a hammer, you tend to see every problem as a nail."[1] We must widen the windows of our minds to see life from varied angles. Our perspectives are not fixed or unchanging. In fact, perspective can change instantaneously, resulting in a new set of thoughts, feelings, and actions. The way we experience life is based upon a convergence of circumstances, perceptions, and interpretations.

A humorous story is told of two boys who were asked to participate in a study. One of the boys was known for his strong, positive attitude, and the other was equally known for his incredibly negative attitude. The pessimistic boy was taken to a large room filled with countless toys and encouraged to do anything he wanted for one hour. The other boy was put in an adjoining room with only a huge pile of dung heaped on the floor. After an hour, the researchers went to the boy in the toy room and found him sitting on the floor amidst the toys.

"What did you do?" the researchers inquired. "Nothing." said the boy. "I was afraid that if I played with anything it might break and I would get in trouble." When the research team arrived at the room filled with dung, they opened the door to find the young lad shoveling his way through it. "What are you doing?" they asked with a puzzled grin. The boy kept on digging and said, "With all this manure, I figured there had to be a pony in here somewhere."

We might laugh at such a silly illustration, but the point is clear: the circumstance itself has little to nothing to do with our attitude.

When we learn to see life, or a particular circumstance, through new "lenses," we are better equipped to deal with pain and suffering. This fresh vision is akin to watching an old horror film on television that you haven't seen in years. The movie, once so frightening on the big screen, seems tamer, even silly on a small screen with the lights on and the suspense taken away. New perspectives offer ways to translate hopelessness into hope, and despair into optimism.

Examine Your Attitude

Two seriously ill men were in the same room of a large city hospital. The room had one small window. As part of his treatment, one of the men was allowed to sit up in bed for one hour. The other man had to spend all his time flat on his back. Every time the first man was propped up for his hour, he passed the time by describing what he could see through the window. He described a park where there was a lake with ducks and swans, a place where children came to sail model boats. The elderly man described young lovers who walked hand in hand through the park. There were flowers and stretches of grass, games of softball, vendors of all kinds, and the most beautiful trees imaginable. Through the trees, the man was able to see a wonderful view of the city skyline. The man on his back listened intently as the man described the picturesque scenery.

One afternoon, frustrated that his roommate had the pleasure of seeing outside while he remained flat on his back, the second man thought, I, too, should have the chance. He felt ashamed, but the more he tried not to think like that, the more he wanted to switch places with the other man.

One night the lonely, envious man sleeplessly stared at the ceiling. Suddenly, the patient by the window awoke, coughing and choking. Because of his negative attitude toward his roommate, the bitter man did not call for help—even when the sound of the other man's breathing stopped. In the morning, the nurse found the man by the window dead.

As soon as it seemed decent, the envious man asked if he could be switched to the bed by the window. The minute he was alone, he painfully and laboriously propped himself up on one elbow to look out the window. To his amazement, all he could see was a blank wall.[2] It was what the first patient could envision with his attitude that created beauty.

Attitude is one of the most underappreciated aspects of life. With the right attitudes, all the hardships in the world cannot make us despondent. With the wrong attitudes, all the help in the world will not make us joyful. Attitude creates a unique reality in the same way a film creates an image on a movie screen. It predisposes us toward specific thoughts, feelings, and behavior. Attitudes are rigid and limiting because we believe our attitudes are reality, and attitudes are self-validating because we see what we want to see. They can just as easily lock us into a perspective of peace and joy as they can a perspective of unrest and despair.

Clearly, attitudes are something within our ability to control. William James, who is called America's first psychologist, held that the greatest discovery was realizing that if we can change our attitudes, we can change our lives.[3] Some people say that in life, we must deal with the hand that we have been given. The issue is not if we will accept our difficulties, but how. No matter how bad the hand we've received, it must be played. We can fold and hope for a better hand next time, or we can accept the hand and recognize that, skillfully played, we can still win.

Viktor Frankl said that the last human freedom is choosing one's attitude. He noted that those who survived the Nazi concentration camps were not those who had better constitutions, but those who had positive attitudes. He wrote, "When a man finds that it is his destiny to suffer, he will have to accept his suffering as his task; his single and unique task.... His unique opportunity lies in the way in which he bears his burden."[4]

Frankl tells of an elderly doctor who remained intensely depressed for two years after the death of his wife, whom he had loved above all else. Dr. Frankl asked the grieving patient what would have happened if he died before his wife. After momentary reflection, the doctor replied that his wife would have suffered even more greatly than he had. Dr. Frankl pointed out that by surviving and mourning her loss, he had spared his wife's suffering. The doctor stood to his feet, shook Frankl's hand, and calmly left the office. Dr. Frankl artfully writes, "In some way, suffering ceases to be suffering at the moment it finds a meaning, such as the meaning of a sacrifice."[5] Abraham embraced this attitude when God asked him to sacrifice his son, Isaac. He understood that he needed to invest his life to serve God's higher purposes, not his own.

Have A Grateful Attitude

One of my friends was diagnosed with a well-known physical disease, but he demonstrated no fear, sadness, or anger. When I asked how he was dealing with the "tragedy" at such a young age, he responded, "This is not a tragedy;

this is a reality."

One of the most significant beliefs that makes up our attitude is gratitude. Think about what life would be like if we considered what we have, rather than what we don't have. An interesting study found that people who kept gratitude journals fared far better than those who wrote down unpleasant experiences or those who simply recorded events. Gratitude-journaling participants were more likely to help others and to be the recipients of kind acts. Also, grateful people felt better about their lives as a whole, had healthier habits, and were more optimistic about the future. Researchers found that these people were grateful regardless of whether circumstances were good or not.[6] A familiar hymn encourages us to "count your blessings, name them one by one; count your blessings, see what God has done." Such an activity has the power to change our attitudes, even in the midst of suffering. We are not instructed to praise God for the circumstances, but in them. Such thinking will eventually eradicate self-pity.

A great way to influence and change our attitude is through music. Most of us do not sing like the professionals, but we can make a joyful noise to the Lord. Praise choruses, hymns, and other popular Christian songs can take us out of self-pity and despair and help us focus on Christ. In short, they can change our attitudes.

Have a Teachable Attitude

An old Taoist parable tells the story of a student who seeks out a gifted master to learn wisdom. Willing to share his ways, the master began to converse with the student over tea. Interestingly, every time the master started to explain a point, the student would abruptly interrupt him. "Oh, I know that," the student would reply, or "No, that is not a problem for me because . . ." After a few such interchanges, the master stopped talking and picked up the teapot. He began pouring tea to fill the student's empty cup. He continued to pour until the cup was overflowing and spilled out. The student hollered, "Stop! The cup is full." With a wise grin, the master replied, "Yes, your cup is full; therefore I cannot teach you anything until you empty it."

The point of the story is clear: to be teachable we must be open to learn. And to be open we must be humble enough to learn from another. The psalmist penned it this way: "The humble He guides in justice, and the humble He teaches His way."[7] Jesus thanked the Father for hiding His ways from the wise, but not from babes. With childlike openness and humility, we can be taught by others.

Parents know that as children develop, they may become less open and humble to learning. It seems that rather than learning a lesson the first time, they continue to do the same wrong things over and over again, perhaps each time hoping that the outcome will be different this time. But their attempts rarely produce a different outcome. Unfortunately, we are the same way with God. It is impossible to teach people who don't think they need to learn anything new. Pride will block God's ability to teach us His truths during times of adversity.

As our divine parent, God constantly reminds us not to forsake Him, to live for Him, and to obey Him. But we continue to miss the point. As we saw in chapter five, we must learn to accept God's discipline and ways. Like any parent, God wants us to be teachable, learning the lesson the first time. The bottom line is this: learning only takes root in fertile ground.

God has a lesson to teach through every circumstance. Just as successful people know that they must continue to learn, successful Christians accept that all of life is a classroom.

Maintain a Sense of Humor

Dr. Frankl called humor "the soul's weapon in the fight for self-preservation."[8] In order to rise above the horrific conditions of the concentration camp, he and other prisoners tried to share at least one amusing story every day.

I used to have a screen saver on my computer that announced, "Fun is not what you do, but how you experience what you do!" We all need to learn to create fun in our lives—even in the midst of affliction. Find things that make you laugh, and adopt an attitude of playfulness. Read cartoons. Do whatever it takes to lighten things up.

I purposely spent time watching The Three Stooges on television when my wife was first diagnosed with cancer. I was not so much trying to avoid the encroaching darkness of the situation as I was looking for a way to keep a positive perspective on life. You don't have to be outrageous; just allow your mind to be open to positive thoughts. Humor is like a shock absorber for the soul; it will not patch the potholes that lie ahead, but it will provide a smoother ride.

Let Heavenly Rewards Motivate You

We all expect to be rewarded when we work. We want to be recognized for a job well done, especially by those who are in authority over us and in a position to provide compensation or promotion. The apostle Paul understood this when he wrote these lines about pursuing a heavenly prize:

> *Not that I have already obtained all this, or have already been made*
> *perfect, but I press on to take hold of that for which Christ Jesus took hold*
> *of me. Brothers, I do not consider myself yet to have taken hold of it. But*
> *one thing I do: Forgetting what is behind and straining toward what is*
> *ahead, I press on toward the goal to win the prize for which God has called*
> *me heavenward in Christ Jesus.*
> *Philippians 3:12-14, NIV*

And in his letter to Timothy, Paul again talks of future reward:

> *Now there is in store for me the crown of righteousness, which the Lord,*
> *the righteous Judge, will award to me on that day—and not only to me,*
> *but also to all who have longed for his appearing.   2 Timothy 4:8, NIV*

As Christians, the size and scope of our heavenly rewards are determined by the quality and quantity of our earthly service to the Lord. And when we are going through hard times, this service is based upon our attitudes.[9] Is our service done out of obligation and habit, or is it an expression of gratitude and faith?

In chapter eight, we saw that God has no problem using rewards as a means of motivating us. The writer of Hebrews said that God rewards those who diligently seek him, and Jesus told us to lay up treasures in heaven.[10] In fact, Hebrews also tells us that Christ looked ahead to the reward that was before Him when He endured the Cross.[11] As excruciatingly painful as the crucifixion would be, the reward that awaited Him was greater.

Yes, we will receive crowns in heaven. But heaven is a reward in and of itself.

Jesus told His disciples that He was going to prepare a place for them, one apparently still under construction. But Jesus assured His followers that when it was finished, He would take them there.[12]

I like to describe heaven as greater than the most wonderful experience you can imagine. It is greater than the feeling that comes when you lower your aching body into a swirling hot tub. It is greater than the most sensuous sex.

Just as expecting parents await the birth of their first child, we should anticipate our entrance into heaven. The reality of heaven's reward should arouse our hearts' deepest hunger, soon to be satisfied with the most extravagant meal. In the midst of suffering, remind yourself of heaven. It is our present comfort and our eternal hope.

The truly ultimate reward, however, is to fellowship with the Godhead for all eternity. Revelation 22:4 says that we shall see His face. The beauty of the Godhead is beyond words and certainly beyond our imaginations. One day we will bathe in the splendor of God's presence. Nothing we can do on this earth earns us the right to enjoy heaven and the presence of God. That is simply the result of God's voluntary goodness for those who have repented of their sins and trusted Jesus as their Savior.

When my children were small, I used to have them grab onto my clothes in crowded places. "Hold on to my clothes," I would tell them, "and I'll get you safely through the crowd. Even if you cannot see me, you will not lose me if you hold on to me." As we experience the difficulties this fallen world has to offer, we can lay hold of the fabric of heaven's promises and not lose our way. The rewards of heaven are a great attitude adjuster when we find ourselves giving way to self-pity and pessimism.

Change Your Emotions

As we discussed in the preceding chapter, our emotions play a major role in both the experience of suffering and in the way we try to cope. As we saw, it is important and critical for sufferers to honestly express their deepest feelings to God as well as to others.

One problem with feelings is that some people do not understand them. Our feelings seem to come out of nowhere, but feelings actually arise out of our deep-seated beliefs. They are a compass that indicates the quality of our thinking. Feelings do not provide information about life or our circumstances, but rather about who we are deep inside. Feelings reveal our insecurities and the intentions of our hearts.

Many counselors say that feelings are amoral; they are neither right nor wrong. But while feelings are a God-given, natural part of our psychological makeup, they also are part of our fallen nature: flawed because we are flawed.

People generally handle feelings in one of two ways. Some indulge their feelings and experience a downward spiral of negativity. They place too much importance on how they feel. Others run from their feelings to distract themselves from their internal pain—so much so that in time they become hardened to it. Like thoughts, feelings grow when we pay attention to them. I like to compare feelings to goldfish: their growth depends on the size of the pond and how much they are fed.

Consider a mirage. Scientists tell us that the angle of the sun, a person's vision, and the slope of the ground can converge and cause someone to see water where none exists. Viewed from the senses, the mirage is real. Viewed from a higher, broader perspective, the mirage is clearly exposed as an illusion. In the same way, feelings can be illusory. Just as sun exposure leads to sunburn, most people believe that adversity leads to emotional turmoil. But Jesus experienced adversity, yet never allowed it to defeat him emotionally. His spiritual perspective acted as an internal sunscreen, protecting Him from the harmful rays of harsh conditions. Emotions are to be our servants, not our masters. When we are emotional, we do not think logically. Consequently, we cannot rely on feelings as indicators of what we need to do. We must work hard to keep our emotional lives in perspective. When our emotions are out of control, we will not be able to work our way through our hardships.

When life is hard, it's natural to experience profound feelings of shock, hurt, sadness, disillusionment, anger, guilt, fear, fatigue, loneliness, emptiness, and helplessness.

In the initial stages of suffering, shock and numbness typically occur, often experienced as denial or a lack of any feelings at all. Shock is a God-given emotion absorber when the magnitude of our emotions is simply too overwhelming. Numbness serves as an internal psychological Novocain. It protects us from being flooded with feelings.

If suffering is due to the actions of another person, we feel hurt and a sense of sadness that might even lead to depression. Sometimes we cry and other times we feel that there are no more tears. Crying is one of God's ways of helping us release the intensity of our pain.

In the midst of difficulty, it's also common to feel disillusioned with the church, God, family, the medical profession, or friends. Eventually, anger may result. Since anger is the root of many psychological problems, it's important that we understand this stage of the process. If the anger is not adequately acknowledged and faced, it can lead to significant problems. Anger may be displaced onto someone or something else. If someone else can be blamed for our pain, then there is a logical reason we hurt and we are not at fault. Thoughts like this rise out of the core beliefs discussed in chapter 10.

When we turn anger on ourselves, we get depressed. Sometimes when anger is directed this way, it is manifested in the form of guilt or self-reproach. We may feel overly responsible, needlessly accepting blame. Guilt and anger have a way of keeping the focus on the problem, not the solution. It is easy to become stuck within these emotions.

Fear, a major culprit in preventing us from achieving inner peace, is perhaps the single common denominator that can make a painful experience feel unbearable. Christians need not feel worry or fear because our security is in Christ. Of course, we often will feel fearful because we are human, but we can use that fear as a cue to turn to God. "Whenever I am afraid, I will trust in You. In God (I will praise His word), in God I have put my trust; I will not fear. What can flesh do to me?"[13] In his fear, David was driven to God, and in His Word he found comfort. Because he trusted the Lord, he had no need to fear man. Corrie ten Boom said, "Worry does not empty tomorrow of its sorrow, but it empties today of its strength. It does not enable us to escape evil. It makes us unfit to face evil when it comes."[14]

Perhaps the gravest feeling one might experience is hopelessness, the greatest predictor of suicide and a major factor in depression. In certain situations, we find ourselves feeling hopeless, as if we are living in a kind of swamp, bogged down in marsh. Left in the lurch with no evident means of escape, it's easy to languish in our dark thoughts. When faith seems lost, our only view of the future is a continuation of the past or present entanglement. Hope is so foundational to the Christian life that without it we are most miserable.[15] For that reason, Satan often works to rob us of our hope. In so doing, he purloins our joy, trust, and peace. For that reason, we must really work on our thinking and develop a solid biblical basis in which we root our hope in Christ rather than circumstance.

The feelings that seem most natural are not always correct. A proper perspective will help us avoid becoming trapped in emotional despair. In John Bunyan's Pilgrim's Progress, the Giant of Despair captured Christian and Hopeful. Locked up in the dungeon of Doubting Castle, with no apparent means of escape, the two pilgrims were disheartened. Soon they were in deep despair. Yet, somehow Christian remembered that he had the Key of Promise in his pocket that would unlock the dungeon door.[16] Though it seemed as if there was no hope of freedom, they had the means to liberate themselves the entire time.

There are many ways to keep your emotions in proper perspective. One exercise that will help you transcend your pain is writing in a journal. Record what you feel and think. If you don't like to write, speak into a tape recorder. The advantage of translating your feelings into the written or recorded word is that you can read or play back what you have expressed and learn more each time the exercise is revisited.

You can also talk about your feelings with a close friend. Consider singing praise songs, even if doing so feels contrived. The best way to maintain a proper perspective in your emotional life is to convert painful and unpleasant emotions to more positive and pleasant ones. You do this by changing your thinking.

Although thinking is part of attitude, it deserves special attention. Thinking is the steering wheel of personality. It is like breathing—we do it continuously from birth to death. Each thought creates a feeling that makes the thought seem real. One school of psychology believes that it is not so much what happens to us, as what happens in us; in other words, what we think has happened to us actually governs what will happen to us. When life looks a certain way to us, we assume that life really is that way. Cognitive psychology, however, reminds us that events or circumstances are mediated by our thinking.

Two general types of thinking characterize people who are suffering. Some think that compared to others, their suffering is not so bad. While you can typically find someone worse off, minimizing your pain may prevent you from dealing with it. This is fine as long as it's not an attempt to deny the reality of the situation. Whether you are run over by a bike or a tractor-trailer, there will be resultant pain and damage.

Others believe that no one could possibly understand how bad their pain is. They see themselves as perpetual victims. Our tendency to evaluate life in absolute extremes can be a great obstacle to dealing with suffering. Instead of viewing life in extremes, we must balance our thinking. We can neither afford to catastrophize our situation, which leads to self-pity, despair, and hopelessness, nor can we ignore it, which prevents us from learning. We must think soberly, looking for God's hand through our pain.

Certainly, it is human and normal to ask "why?" when we experience adversity. But if we keep asking questions when there are no clear answers, we will experience frustration and confusion, possibly even leading to despair. As we saw earlier, no one can know the mind of the Lord.[17] We simply must trust and ask, "For what end and for Whom?" Like Job, we know enough about God to trust Him in those things we do not understand. Such thinking requires a right attitude and a willingness to challenge our thinking. Whenever we notice wrong beliefs coming into play, we can learn to challenge them and begin to replace them with more accurate understandings—ones that may not be as comforting but will certainly prepare us for greater growth.

As I (John) was writing this section, I suffered from a bad cold with flulike symptoms. My doctor told me that I had a virus and though I could take medicine for the symptoms, there was no remedy for the virus itself. After spending a week on the couch, I called the doctor again to review my symptoms. I guess I wanted him to reconsider his diagnosis and give me something to make me better. Once again the doctor kindly reminded me that I had a virus and would need to wait it out. Obviously, this was news I didn't want to hear but needed to accept.

When we are sick, we want a clear diagnosis and an effective treatment regimen to make us feel better. Regrettably, we live in a world full of illnesses with no cures. We do not want problems, and when they come we want them gone. All too often, however, there are no solutions. If we are to overcome misery, we must adjust our expectations of what this world can and will offer. The world is broken and fallen; it offers no guarantees on most things. We will experience pain and suffering, even when we expect ease and comfort. Clearly, while we cannot control our circumstances, we can control our expectations, beliefs, and attitudes.

In writing to the church at Thessalonica, Paul encouraged his readers not to be unsettled by their trials because they were destined for them.[18] In other words, they were to expect trials, hardships, and adversity. We will not be so easily shaken during bad times when we expect and accept them and take the necessary and appropriate actions. Researchers from the University of Chicago and Southern Illinois University studied victims of tornado damage across the country.[19] They studied a phenomenon related to what psychologists call "locus of control." People with an internal locus of control believe that they are in control of their own fate, whereas externalizers believe outside sources control the outcome.[20] The study found that people who lived in the South suffered a higher frequency of tornado-related deaths than Midwesterners and had developed a fatalistic attitude toward disaster: "If it hits, it hits; there's nothing I can do to stop it." In contrast, whenever severe warning was predicted, Midwesterners listened to weather reports, secured loose equipment, and went to a safe place to wait out tornado warnings.

The writer of Proverbs said, "Trust in the Lord with all your heart, and lean not on your own understanding; in all your ways acknowledge Him, and He shall direct your paths."[21] Examining our responses to suffering will help us determine if we are leaning on the Lord or on our own understanding. If we are leaning entirely on the Lord, we will not panic and demand answers of God. This response does not mean we exercise blind faith. Rather, it implies that we willingly rest in God's reliable character. In short, leaning on God means we will not be insisting that He owes us an explanation.

God's timetable is so different from ours. During a difficult time in my life, a friend wrote the following verse on a note of encouragement: "But when the fullness of the time had come, God sent forth His Son, born of a woman, born under the law."[22] I looked at that note in amazement. What does that have to do with anything? I wondered. Later, I came to realize the depth of truth in those words. After settling in Egypt, the people of Israel had waited four hundred years for God to speak, but God was in no hurry. You would think that by this point in Jewish history, the Israelites would have become accustomed to God's timetable. In fact, they were in bondage approximately 430 years before God sent Moses to deliver them (and He had to develop Moses for forty years before he was ready to tackle that job!). My friend used Galatians 4:4 simply to remind me that God has a timetable to accomplish things in my life. My job was to be patient and wait for God to act. Interestingly, one of my favorite Bible verses in college was Philippians 1:6: "Being confident of this very thing, that He who has begun a good work in you will complete it until the day of Jesus Christ." God will not fail us, though it might seem otherwise at times.

Assess your expectations and make sure that they are realistic and biblical. Expect God to deliver on His promises in His time, no more and no less.

Have a Proper Perspective on Your Life

There are two requirements for having and maintaining a proper life perspective.

1. *We must stay focused on today and live in the present moment.*
2. *We must keep our minds on eternity.*

While these statements may sound like a contradiction, they are actually two sides of the same coin.

When I was suddenly hit by the pain of the kidney stone I mentioned in an earlier chapter, the only thing I could think about was getting rid of the pain as soon as possible. I wanted it to go away; I wanted instant relief. I prayed for the Rapture, death, or instant healing. I would have done anything to ease the constant intensity of that pain. While in the emergency room, I thought that I would never see the doctor and get the necessary painkiller. It took everything I could muster to focus on the immediate moment and wait.

So it is with other kinds of suffering. Our driving goal is to get things back to normal. But the truth is that things will never be back to normal. With each passing day, good or bad, life is forever changed. Broken bones mend and infections dissipate, but soul scars may never completely heal.

As days of suffering turn to months and months become years, our resolve to stand strong weakens. When the future seems bleak, we begin to lose hope and wonder if we will even be able to make it through the day. God, however, remains our timeless refuge. When we are wondering whether the pain will ever cease, the eternal God is already in the future seeing the outcome.

I have a friend who loves to climb mountains. He has told me there is nothing like working his way up a mountain to experience both the feeling of accomplishment and the view from its summit. While the top of the mountain is the goal, my friend appreciates all the vistas along the way. He can look up, keeping his goal firmly in view, and look down to recognize his progress. Such a balanced view allows him to rest, look around, and admire the view from wherever he is at that moment. Unlike climbing a physical mountain, the climb we make in this life never ends at the pinnacle; we simply continue to climb upward every day. Along the way, however, we can all learn to appreciate the journey.

Therefore, we need to avoid becoming consumed with time. A wonderful phrase often found in the Bible is, "And it came to pass . . ." Truly, everything will eventually come to pass, maybe not in this life but certainly in heaven. Our best option is to focus only on today, and if necessary, only on the moment. With God's help, we can handle today, so we shouldn't worry about tomorrow. As we trust God for the grace and strength to make it through this day or moment, we'll be able to deal with whatever suffering comes our way. The apostle Paul had this truth in mind when he said that we should not lose heart because our inner man is being renewed day after day.[23]

Focus on Eternity

Heaven has relevance for our lives today, and it has special significance in addressing our hardships. Paul was obviously well versed in suffering. He wrote:

> *Therefore we do not lose heart. Even though our outward man is perishing, yet the inward man is being renewed day by day. For our light affliction, which is but for a moment, is working for us a far more exceeding and eternal weight of glory, while we do not look at the things which are seen, but at the things which are not seen. For the things which are seen are temporary, but the things which are not seen are eternal.*
> *2 Corinthians 4:16-19*

We won't give up our self-focused demand for ease, predictability, and fairness until we have an equally compelling yearning. For the Christian, that yearning is to know God and to look toward the hope of heaven.

Heaven is not just something to look forward to, but something that can be experienced today. We are told to live life in light of eternity and set our minds on the things that are above. This hope was the mark of the Old Testament heroes of faith. Though heaven had not been realized, they had a definite view toward their future lives. In fact, we are told that they longed for the better country that God had prepared for them.[24] As we saw in chapter nine, we are only in the waiting line of heaven. We are not to see ourselves as earthly dwellers but as pilgrims. And as the psalmist penned, "So teach us to number our days, that we may gain a heart of wisdom."[25]

God has placed eternity in our hearts, and this focus gives us hope and peace. One of Satan's best weapons against the Christian is to rob us of our eternal purpose. But by maintaining an eternal vision, we can keep Satan from using a calamity to engulf us in a sense of hopelessness. Just as a Thanksgiving feast makes us salivate, so God's extravagant table should be something we eagerly anticipate. I call this having a "Christmas morning" view of eternity: we do not know all that God has planned for us, but we do know it will be fantastic.

Eternity gives us more than just the hope that we will one day no longer suffer. It also gives us something that we can be assured of, something to embrace in our trials today. As we focus on the heavenly city, we gain a sense of renewal and refreshment in our spirits—in spite of our outer hurts, aches, and problems. What hope! What comfort! The best is yet to come!

Prevent Undue Stress

During times of suffering, people are often tempted to make major life decisions or take on additional responsibilities. But times of adversity are, more than ever, occasions when we need to limit our activities. These are times when it is best to be still and know that He is God.[26]

Given our emotional state during times of suffering, we are not in the best position to make rational decisions. Unless your situation demands certain immediate changes or it's clear God is attempting to use your adversity to get you to make major life changes, it's usually best to wait until you have been through the suffering to make any significant decisions.

When your life has been turned upside down, you need to take whatever energy is left and channel it in constructive ways. In the movie Apollo 13, the astronauts are in danger of lacking sufficient power to return to earth. In order to conserve as much amperage as possible, the engineers tell the astronauts to shut down their power until they can devise a plan. To help them find a solution, the engineers contact one of the astronauts who had been prohibited from the flight due to illness. Together they fervently work in a simulator to determine a procedure that would allow the astronauts to power up all the necessary reentry equipment with the limited amperage.

In times of crisis, we also are in danger of lacking enough energy to survive. Like the men in Apollo 13, we need to conserve sufficient energy to accomplish the things that must be accomplished. All day, every day, we make choices. Ultimately, we choose to do the things we value, but all too often, our values go awry, and therefore our choices do not serve our best interests. It is hard to prioritize, but now more than ever, we must channel our energies where they will serve us best. Taking care of what God has given us is good stewardship, so it is important to attend to our own needs—physical, emotional, mental, social, and spiritual—during times of difficulty. Often people feel overwhelmed when going through a crisis, and in order to survive the ordeal, they have to step away from dealing with daily life for a time. One woman I counseled felt so overwhelmed at everything she had to do that I encouraged her to list things she did not need to do. I told her every time she looked at the list, she could say, "Hey, there is something I don't need to do!" This comical, but realistic, perspective helped my client feel more in charge of her life.

Attending to yourself physically includes good nutrition, exercise, and hygiene. You may not have an appetite or you may crave unhealthy food. It is necessary, however, to give your body proper fuel. You probably won't feel like getting off the sofa and taking a brisk walk, but do it anyway. Research has clearly shown that exercise will affect your brain chemistry in a way that will help you recover faster.[27]

As we've already seen, growing spiritually means spending time with God in order to know Him in a deeper way. And growing socially involves avoiding isolation. Get with God's people, open up, and be honest.

Redeem Your Pain

Spiritual growth has limited impact unless we take what we've received from God and use it to help others. Think of how many people have been encouraged by the life of Job. Had you told Job during the days of his ordeal that countless people throughout history would receive comfort and hope from his trials, it probably would have offered him little relief. After the ordeal, however, Job probably found great comfort in the thought that, through his pain, he could help others.

A major help in recovering from suffering is to be able to redeem the experience. We can redeem suffering by growing through it and giving it meaning in our lives. Many Vietnam veterans redeemed their war experiences by adopting Vietnamese children, providing assistance to fellow veterans who were struggling with the emotional aftermath of the war, or lobbying for war-related causes. In Old Testament days, the people of Israel often built stone markers to symbolize the significance of a particular event in their journey.

In chapter seven, we read about Belinda, the young woman who was abused by her youth pastor. Today, Belinda would tell you that reaching out to others in need was a major factor in her recovery. She was able to redeem her years of sexual abuse and begin to glorify God through ministry. Belinda is living out Paul's challenge to comfort those with the comfort she has received from God.

Open Yourself to Others

Sometimes when we're suffering, the people around us are not positive or supportive. Often, we decide it's easier to simply act cheerful and optimistic than to open up and be real. We fear being truly known because we fear being criticized or rejected. Putting on a happy mask protects our raw wounds, the places where we are most vulnerable to negative responses, the places where we need encouragement and reassurance the most. We want to be known and accepted for everything we are experiencing, but we fear the thought of being rejected. So we build fortresses of protection. But this dilemma between being real and hidden is in itself traumatic for someone who is already suffering. We often vacillate between expressing our true feelings and putting on a mask to hide the pain, and this ambivalence makes it even more difficult for those who do care and desire to be supportive. They simply do not know when or how to approach us.

Ultimately, hidden suffering makes us feel even more isolated and alone. This is one of Satan's best tools against the wounded believer. And as we've already seen, isolation actually intensifies suffering because there is no outlet for the pain. In studies of various crises, social support has consistently been associated with better adjustment.[28] It was not necessary that the helpers had been through similar experiences, as long as they demonstrated empathetic concern and support for the sufferer. This is offering a "ministry of presence" to those who are hurting, in order to bear the burden that they cannot bear alone.

Chapter 18

REACHING OUT TO HELP OTHERS

There is a saying that is commonly heard in Alcoholics Anonymous: "You have to give it away to get it."[1] This motto has relevance to problems other than alcoholism. By helping others we are constantly reminded who we are, where we came from, and what we could become again.

The point of reaching out is not to avoid your own pain, but to take the inner turmoil you have experienced and connect it with someone else's struggle. Psychologists have found that getting clients to see themselves as helpers and givers, rather than takers and receivers, produces healing.

The word compassion comes from the Latin com, meaning "together," and pati, meaning "to suffer." Compassion is defined as "sorrow for the sufferings or trouble of another, accompanied by the urge to help." However much we may have suffered, we can find meaning in it by transforming pain into compassion. There is great satisfaction and benefit in bringing order into lives beset by pain and turmoil. Helping hurting people see how God's grace is sufficient speaks to your own unresolved questions and issues.

God has commanded us to provide care for struggling souls. "Brethren, if a man is overtaken in any trespass, you who are spiritual restore such a one in a spirit of gentleness, considering yourself lest you also be tempted. Bear one another's burdens, and so fulfill the law of Christ. . . . For each one shall bear his own load."[2] "To restore" is to "mend, to furnish completely" or to "set a bone."[3] Since it is used here in the present tense, the healing and mending of others who are hurting is to be an ongoing process. But in order to help, we need to know what we are to mend. At first glance, this passage seems to present a conflict by urging us to bear other people's burdens while telling each of us to take care of our own. But in encouraging us to take care of our own burden, the Greek term phortion actually means knapsack and refers to the daily load that someone carries. The burden that we are to bear for others refers to boulders (baros), or problems that seem crushing and heavy. These words are also used to speak of the future state of Christians as an "eternal weight of glory."[4] We are not to take on the responsibilities of others, but we are to help those who are stricken with a grievous, weighty load.

In the last chapter we talked about the danger of overtaxing ourselves. Sometimes helping other people can cause us to take on too much responsibility, believing we are responsible for fixing their problems. But we are not the Redeemer or Savior; that job is filled. If one or more people are becoming overly dependent upon you, refer them to a pastor or professional Christian counselor. It is okay to let them know that you are still vulnerable yourself and simply not able to provide all the adequate support necessary to carry them through their own ordeal.

How Could I Possibly Help?

People who have pain of their own often find it difficult to reach out to others. They simply lack the initiative, energy, or knowledge of how to meaningfully touch someone else's pain. But even if you are hurting yourself, sharing God's comfort with someone else will not only help that person, it will help you as well.

You might be someone who has never gone through a significant time of suffering. You might be reading this book to learn what you can do to help a close friend or family member. This section will help you in knowing what to say and do to provide beneficial help.

1. *Give the Wonded Individual the Ministry of Your Presence*

> There is nothing more important than being with someone who is hurting. It is a ministry of your presence. Doing so gives you the essence of being Christ incarnate for the sufferer. As the Holy Spirit comes alongside of us, so too can we come alongside of others. Simply taking the time to be with someone who is hurting does wonders. Job's friends spent seven days sitting with him on an ash heap in silence. In fact, their helpfulness ceased when they opened their mouths. We could learn much from this. We do not have to know exactly what to say. Just

being there can provide a tremendous lift. In being with someone who is suffering, it is helpful to also use appropriate touch. When people are hurting, they are vulnerable, and an appropriate touch can convey a physical presence.

When I (John) visited with my friend Dave Sours in the hospital following the death of his son, Nathan, there were no words that could have had any meaningful impact at that time. When I saw Dave, we hugged long and hard. Throughout our encounters, I often just put my arm around Dave's shoulder, and I could tell my compassionate touch was important to him.

2. *The Best Help That Anyone Can Render in a Time of Crisis is an Empathetic Listening Ear.*

 In the course of several years, the Joe Bayly family lost three of their children. In his book The View from a Hearse, Bayly shared his experience of being helped by two different individuals. "I was sitting there torn by grief. Someone came and talked of God's dealings, of why it happened, of hope beyond the grave. He talked constantly. He said things I knew were true. I was unmoved, except to wish he'd go away. He finally did. Another came and sat beside me. He didn't talk. He didn't ask me leading questions. He just sat beside me for an hour and more, listened when I said something, answered briefly, prayed simply, and left. I was moved. I was comforted. I hated to see him go."[5] By listening, we enter into the suffering of our loved ones. Research shows that sufferers rank listening as the gift that is most meaningful during times of difficulty.[6] Do not worry if you don't know what to say. There is no need to give advice, offer trite Christian slogans, or quote Scripture. Simply listen. Sometimes sufferers do not want you to talk at all. True and attentive listening is hard work. It means allowing the hurting person to express himself or herself in whatever way needed. People who are hurting often have a need to tell others what it is like and what has happened to them. Your listening ear helps your loved ones to sort through and face their feelings.

3. *Be Aware of Your Attitude as you Attempt to Help Another Person.*

Often when people have gone through a great deal of suffering, they
will either approach others with a sense of superiority ("Look what I
have been through!" or "That's nothing compared with what happened
to me!") or inferiority ("Given what I feel, I can offer you very little").
Whether you are currently in the midst of a trial or down the road of
recovery, it is fine to share your experience whenever it is appropriate,
but remember that your objective is not to elicit sympathy for yourself.
Now is the time for you to give, not receive. This principle is beautifully
illustrated in the hours preceding Christ's death. As the guests were
arriving at the Last Supper, Jesus was preparing a basin of water to wash
His disciples' feet. As Jesus moved around the room humbly washing
the dust from their feet, He said, "If you know these things, blessed are
you if you do them."[7] In reaching out to sufferers, you need to maintain
your focus on them and their problems. Therefore, be brief in what
you share. Do not minimize what the other person may be feeling by
swapping war stories. Be compassionate and attempt to understand.

4. *Adopt an Attitude of Love and Acceptance Toward the Hurting.*

Because we have a need to explain the whys of life, we sometimes
speculate as to whether a person brought a problem on himself or
herself. If we decide the person is responsible for his or her own pain,
we think, feel, and act differently toward that person than if we view
him or her as an innocent victim. Research shows that innocent victims
are often wrongly blamed for playing a contributing role in their own
victimization. Put simply, if something bad happens to someone, we
wonder what the person might have done wrong. Like Job's friends,
we jump to conclusions without having all the facts. But just as Jesus
accepted the woman at the well, the woman caught in adultery, and
everyone else He encountered, we must display grace and acceptance. By
demonstrating unfailing love to those who are hurting, we earn the right
to eventually advise and challenge them.

5. *Accept What has Happened to the Individual and the Way That the Person is Responding to the Trial.*

Even if you experienced a similar problem, your experience is different. Perhaps you were quicker to acknowledge the goodness of God. Perhaps this person is feeling things and doing things that you would never have imagined. Remember, it takes time to heal. When someone is hurting, it is not the time to be judgmental. You are not the authority on that person's responses. God accepts and hears the cries of our hearts. Bite your tongue and acknowledge the living hell that the person may be experiencing. In one study of cancer patients, 87 percent reported that they tried to cope by keeping their thoughts and feelings to themselves to avoid bothering or upsetting loved ones.[8] But people need to be able to share their thoughts and feelings without being criticized or minimized and without worrying how the other person will handle what they have to say.

6. *Whenever it is Expected or Appreciated, You Can Still Seek to Instill Hope.*

The hope might come from how you made it through your own experience. It might come from your attitude toward your situation, or it might arise from the bond that occurs between you and the sufferer. Ultimately, hope comes from the Lord, and you can help direct that person toward Him. No matter how it is communicated or felt, this hope is critical to recovery.

7. *Pray*

Do not simply say, "I will pray for you." Rather, ask specifically how you can pray. Take time to pray with the hurting person right then if possible. When I was going through a difficult time, a friend asked me how he could best pray. After my vague response, he simply put his arm around me and prayed for me at that moment. I felt so touched by the sincerity and genuineness of my friend.

8. *Be Practical in Your Help.*

Typically, well-meaning individuals tell those who are hurting to call if they need anything. But we all know that call is rarely made. It's better to anticipate what the person might need, and if you are not able to take care of the need, arrange for someone else to do it. When my father died, I returned home from the funeral to find my grass cut, weeds pulled, and hedges clipped. I cried when I learned that a neighbor whom I didn't even know had done such a wonderful thing for me.

9. *Stay in Contact with the Individual by Making Phone Calls and Sending E-Mail Messages or Cards Throughout the Ordeal, as Well as Over the Next Year or so.*

One family who experienced the death of their son said that after the funeral no one from the church, including the minister, ever spoke to them again about their loss. The hurt was still evident on their faces five years later. If the person is having a difficult time coping, you might recommend that the person talk with a minister or competent Christian counselor. If you received help from that person, share your experience. While some people are reluctant to see professional counselors, even Christian counselors, they will talk to a minister. It the person doesn't have a minister, refer him or her to yours. You might even go with the person if he or she is afraid of talking to a stranger.

As you move through your own recovery, helping others will become a more natural part of your life. The trauma to your soul will be redeemed from the hands of the evil one and be used to further the Kingdom of God.

Our motivation in life should not be to pursue our own comfort and happiness, but to love and serve both God and man. Yes, sometimes in the heat of the fiery furnace we need someone with cold water and a fire extinguisher to assist us. But when the flames have died down, we need to reach out to others who are in need of help.

We began our journey of examining questions sufferers ask by remembering the words that Jesus uttered from the cross. Although Jesus spoke seven times, we focused on the most disturbing of them all: "My God, my God, why have you forsaken me?"

Though those words are of deep mystery, they tell us more than the fact that Jesus felt abandoned by God. Those words express the enormous pressure on Christ's soul by the burden of a world's sins. It demonstrates the length to which He was willing to go in order to be our substitute. Centuries before Christ's birth the prophet Isaiah penned that God would crush His Son (the Messiah) and cause Him to suffer; the iniquity of every human being was laid upon Jesus Christ (53:10, 14). Christians tend to sterilize sin and rank the badness of a particular sin according to our liking. Sins like abortion, homosexuality, and criminal behavior are appalling and lying, criticism, and pride are tolerable. In case we ever wonder what God thinks of sin, simply imagine the physical horror of the act of crucifixion and the horror that Christ must have felt in His soul at being abandoned by God; clearly God does not take sin lightly. Christ's words should stir up our soul's hatred of sin, encourage us to accept His gift of salvation, and live in obedience with God's Word.

It is clear that Jesus feels totally abandoned, even by God. For Mark, this is the ultimate expression of losing one's life for the sake of the gospel (8:35). It is full and complete identification with humanity, a final revelation of the depths of human sin, and undeniable evidence that the ways of God are beyond understanding. Yet Mark has given enough allusions to the other half of the story; the reader cannot attribute total despair to the dying Jesus. Jesus himself is confident of a coming resurrection; it will be God's answer to this cry of despair. Jesus has abandoned himself to the will of God; God will do something amazing in our eyes (12:11; on the use of Ps. 22, see TLC, below).[1]

NOTES

Chapter 1: The Why Questions: Why Me? Why This? Why Now?

1. McGoldrick, M., & Walsh, F. (1983). A systematic view of family history and loss. In M. Aronson & D. Wolberg (Eds.), *Group and family therapy* (pp. 252-270). New York, NY: Brunner/Mazel.

Chapter 2: No One is Exempt: Characteristics of Suffering

1. On hunger, see http://library.thinkquest.org/C002291/high/present/stats.htm.
2. On HIV, see http://www.cdc.gov/hiv/topics/surveillance/basic.htm#hivest.
   On children, see http://www.avert.org/worldstats.htm.
3. On natural disasters, see Intergovernmental Panel on Climate Change, *Climate Change 2001: Impacts, Adaptation and Vulnerability*, James McCarthy, Osvaldo Caniziani, Neil Leary, David Dokken, and Kasey White (Eds.), Chapter 8, pp. 451–486 (2001).
4. On mental disorders, see http://www.slideshare.net/teenmentalhealth/global-context-of-mental-health-and-mental-disorders-presentation.
   On suicide, see http://www.onlineschools.org/blog/suicide-stats/.
5. Hosea 7:14
6. I first heard this analogy from my friend and colleague Larry French, and I've found it very helpful in understanding the unnerving effects of suffering.
7. 2 Corinthians 7:10; Isaiah 1:18; 1 John 1:9; James 5:16

Chapter 3: Eleven Truths of Suffering

1. C. S. Lewis, "Peace Proposals for Brother Every and Mr. Bethell," in *Christian Reflections*, ed. Walter Hopper (Grand Rapids, MI: William B. Eerdman Publishing, 1967), 33.
2. Nietzsche, as quoted in Frankl, *Man's Search for Meaning*, 76.
3. Deuteronomy 29:29
4. 1 Corinthians 12:23-28
5. Hebrews 11
6. Romans 8:36, NASB
7. John 11:25-26; 16:33
8. The tradition of martyrdom has entered deep into the Christian consciousness. "Kenneth Scott Latourette, *A History of Christianity*, Volume I: Beginnings to 1500, rev. ed. (Prince Press, 2000), p. 81., Henry Bettenson and Chris Maunder, eds., *Documents of the Christian Church*, 3rd. ed. (Oxford UP, 1999), p. 2., William H.C. Frend, "Persecution in the Early Church." *Christian History*, Issue 27 (Vol. XI, No. 3), p. 7.
9. Viktor E. Frankl, *Man's Search for Meaning*: An Introduction to Logotherapy (Boston: Beacon, 1967), 67.
10. Ten Boom, *Clippings from My Notebook*, 18.
11. Ecclesiastes 2:1-11
12. Lewis, The Problem of Pain, 93.
13. Genesis 3:17-18
14. Ecclesiastes 1:15
15. Romans 8:22
16. Matthew 9:33; 12:22; 17:15-18; Mark 5:15; 9:25
17. Luke 13:11-16
18. John 17:15-17
19. Job 1:12
20. Job 1:0-12
21. Genesis 4:7-8; 37:12-36; 2 Timothy 4:14-16

22. 2 Timothy 3:12; 2 Corinthians 1:7

23. John 13:34-35

24. Galatians 6:7-9

25. Romans 6

26. Philip Yancey, *Where Is God When It Hurts?* (Grand Rapids: Zondervan, 2002), 5.

27. Acts 9:1-6, 22, 26

28. Oswald Chambers, *My Utmost for His Highest* (New York: Dodd, Mead & Company, 1935), 310.

29. Ecclesiastes 11:5

30. Isaiah 55:8-9; 1 Corinthians 2:10-11

31. H. G. Wells, *Mr. Britling Sees It Through* (New York: Macmillian, 1916), 406.

32. John 11:35

33. Galatians 4:4

34. Exodus 3:7

35. Psalm 56:8

36. Hebrews 4:15

37. Isaiah 53:3

38. Hebrews 2:17-18; 4:15; Isaiah 53:2-5

39. Job 38:4-41

40. Taken from a sermon, October 25, 1998, at Wayne Hills Baptist Church in Waynesboro, Virginia. Used with permission.

41. Job 19:25-27

42. Romans 8:6-8; 1 Peter 1:3-9; Revelation 20:12-15; 21:4

43. Matthew 5:11-12; 2 Corinthians 5:1-2, 8; Revelation 7:16-17; 14:12-13; 21:3-4

44. Romans 10:9

45. Jim Hill, "What a Day That Will Be," in *Hymns for the Family of God* (Nashville: Paragon, 1958), 314.

Chapter 4: Learning to Trust God...Despite Pain

1. For a much earlier version of this essay by Habermas, see Terry L. Miethe and Gary R. Habermas, *Why Believe? God Exists!* (Joplin, Mo: College Press, 1993), Chapter 18.

2. For texts covering a wide variety of issues, perspectives, and levels of difficulty, see: J Hick, *Evil and the God of Love* (New York: Harper and Row, 1966); C.S. Lewis, *The Problem of Pain* (New York: Macmillan, 1962); George I. Mavrodes, *Belief in God, Study in the Epistemology of Religion* (Washington, D.C.: University Press America, 1970); Ronald H. Nash, *Faith and Reason: Searching for a Rational Faith* (Grand Rapids: Zondervan, 1988); Alvin Plantinga, *God, Freedom, and Evil* (Grand Rapids: Eerdmans, 1974); Richard Swinburne, "Natural Evil," *American Philosophical Quarterly,* Volume 15 (1978); John S. Feinberg, *The Many Faces of Evil: Theological Systems and the Problems of Evil* (Wheaton, IL: Crossway Books, 2004); Norman L. Geisler, *If God, Why Evil? A New Way to Think about the Problem* (Minneapolis: Bethany House, 2011); William A. Dembski, *The End of Christianity: Finding a Good God in an Evil World* (Nashville, TN: Broadman and Holman Academic, 2009); N. T. Wright, *Evil and the Justice of God* (Downers Grove, IL: InterVarsity Press, 2006); Paul Copan, *Is God a Moral Monster? Making Sense of the Old Testament God* (Grand Rapids: Baker, 2011); Daniel Howard-Snyder, editor, *The Evidential Argument from Evil* (Bloomington, IN: Indiana University Press, 1996); Marilyn McCord Adams and Robert Merrihew Adams, *The Problem of Evil* (New York: Oxford University Press, 1990); David Baggett and Jerry L. Walls, *Good God: The Theistic Foundations of Morality* (Oxford: Oxford University Press, 2011).

3. David Hume, *Dialogues Concerning Natural Religion*, Section X.

4. Sometimes, sensitive people on the same side of the divide even evaluate the issue differently. In my skeptical days, when arguing with Christians, I don't recall ever using this argument against them. I simply thought believers had too many potential ways out

of it.

5. See Habermas, "Atheism and Evil: A Fatal Dilemma," in Miethe and Habermas, Chapter 20.

6. For a list of options, along with theistic responses, see Norman L. Geisler, *Philosophy of Religion* (Grand Rapids: Zondervan, 1974), 311-317. The latest edition of this volume (1988) is co-authored with Winfried Corduan.

7. Majjhima-nikaya 3:248-252; Anguttara-nikaya 3:134. These texts are contained in Sarvepalli Radhakrishnan and Charles A. Moore, Editors, *A Source Book in Indian Philosophy* (Princeton: Princeton University Press, 1957), pp. 274-278.

8. Geisler, *If God, Why Evil?*, p. 12.

9. Geisler, *Philosophy of Religion*, p. 312.

10. Naturalism is a world view that dictates that nature is all there is and therefore there is no supernatural reality. Knowledge is generally thought to be gained by the scientific method. In this volume, we will be unable to provide a treatment of world views and their critiques.

11. Albert Camus, *The Plague*, translated by S. Gilbert (New York: Random House, 1948).

12. H.J. McCloskey, "*God and Evil*," The Philosophical Quarterly (April, 1960). This essay is also found in Nelson Pike, Editor, God and Evil (Englewood Cliffs: Prentice-Hall, 1964). Geisler evaluates the arguments of both Camus and McCloskey in Philosophy of Religion, Chapter 17.

13. J.L. Mackie, *The Miracle of Theism* (Oxford: The Clarendon Press, 1982).

14. We will consider this subject in the next chapter.

15. The Poverty and Justice Study Bible, Contemporary English Version (N.Y.: American Bible Society, 2008 [notes]) highlights 2,000 verses pertaining to the positive treatment of the poor and oppressed. Many of these passages are relevant to our contemporary situation.

16. One excellent example comes from Paul: "Therefore, as we have opportunity, let us do good to all people, especially to those who belong to the family of believers" (Gal 6:10, NIV).

17. J.L. Mackie, "Evil and Omnipotence," *Mind*, Volume XLIV, Number 1955. This essay is also included in Pike, op. cit.

18. Idealism is another major world view with wide variations, but which generally thinks that reality is chiefly about the mind's ideas, not the material objects around us.

19. Peter A. Bertocci, *An Introduction to the Philosophy of Religion* (N.Y.: Prentice-Hall, 1951), p. 338.

20. Edgar S. Brightman, *A Philosophy of Religion* (N.Y.: Prentice-Hall, 1940), pp. 336-338.

21. Process views emphasize the necessity of change, including the continual transformation of reality. God has both a transcendent and an immanent nature and he grows, develops, and learns.

22. Schubert M. Ogden, *Faith and Freedom: Toward a Theology of Liberation* (Nashville: Abingdon, 1979), pp. 75-82; Schubert M. Ogden, *The Reality of God and Other Essays* (N.Y.: Harper and Row, 1964), Chapter I.

23. For an argument from the resurrection of Jesus to the truth of Christian Theism, see Gary R. Habermas, *The Risen Jesus and Future Hope* (Lanham, MD: Roman and Littlefield, 2003).

24. Many process writings clearly denote some of the lines of demarcation with classical theism, such as: Charles Hartshorne, *Omnipotence and Other Theological Mistakes* (Albany: State University of New York Press, 1984); Delwin Brown, Ralph E. James, and Gene Reeves, Editors, Process Philosophy and Christian Thought (Indianapolis: Bobbs-Merrill, 1971).

25. Brightman, *A Philosophy of Religion*, pp. 336-337.

26. L. Harold DeWolf, *The Religious Revolt Against Reason* (N.Y.: Harper and Brothers, 1949), pp. 172-174; Albert C. Knudson, *The Doctrine of Redemption* (New York: Abingdon-Cokesbury Press, 1933), pp. 206-212. For an introductory discussion of the debate among

idealistic philosophers and theologians as to whether God is finite, including many of the details here, see Warren Young, *A Christian Approach to Philosophy* (Grand Rapid: Baker, 1957), pp. 166-173.

27. Some of these critiques are at least worth considering. DeWolf and Knudson complain that finitist concepts too willingly compromise the nature of God's character and are too anthropomorphic. Further, creation readily evidences the vast extent of God's power (Knudson, pp. 208-209; DeWolf, pp. 172-174; cf. Geisler, *Philosophy of Religion* p. 313). Another fruitful criticism might emerge from questioning the finitistic approach to evil (Knudson, pp. 184-185). For a very perceptive exposition and critique of the more extreme options found in process thought, see Norman L. Geisler, "Process Theology" in *Tensions in Contemporaty Theology*, Second Edition, edited by Stanley N. Gundry and Alan F. Johnson (Grand Rapids: Baker, 1976), pp. 237-284.

28. For a defense of Reformed theology in general, see Robert A. Peterson and Michael D. Williams, *Why I am not an Arminian* (Downers Grove, IL: InterVarsity, 2004). For a rejoinder, see Jerry L. Walls and Joseph R. Dongell, *Why I am not a Calvinist* (Downers Grove, IL: InterVarsity, 2004). Baggett and Walls (Chapter 4) treat the subject from the perspective of ethics.

Chapter 5: Why Does God Allow Suffering?

1. A much older version of this essay by Habermas can be found in Miethe and Habermas, *Why Believe? God Exists!*, Chapter 19.

2. Some philosophers, like Geisler, add a third: metaphysical evil. We will not deal here with this subject. See Geisler, *Philosophy of Religion*, Chapter 15.

3. See Geisler, *Philosophy of Religion*, Chapter 16, for a good discussion of several other scenarios. Geisler treats the subject more recently (2011) in *If God, Why Evil?*, pp. 59-67.

4. Mackie, "Evil and Omnipotence" in Pike, *God and Evil*.

5. Plantinga, *God, Freedom, and Evil*, pp. 48-49.

6. Nash's insightful discussion is found in *Faith and Reason*, pp. 190-194.

7. For a defense of these events, see Gary R. Habermas and Michael R. Licona, *The Case for the Resurrection of Jesus* (Grand Rapids: Kregel, 2004). On the moral implications of such an eternal victory over the problem of evil, see the recent (2011) argument by Baggett and Walls, *Good God*, especially Chapter 10.

8. See Gary R. Habermas, *Why is God Ignoring Me? What to Do When it Feels Like He's Giving You the Silent Treatment* (Carol Stream, IL: Tyndale, 2010), especially Chapters 1-2.

9. David Elton Trueblood, *Philosophy of Religion* (New York: Harper, 1957), p. 248.

10. Trueblood, Philosophy of Religion, p. 253.

11. In this treatment I will follow Nash's outline in *Faith and Reason*, pp. 198-208. However, I will also diverge at several crucial points.

12. Compare Gen 3:1-5, 13-15 with Luke 10:18; 1 John 3:8.

13. Geisler, *Philosophy of Religion,* pp. 392-393; cf. also Geisler, *If God, Why Evil?*, p. 78.

14. Plantinga, God, Freedom, and Evil, pp. 58-59.

15. For example, though he attempts to treat man's vices seriously, referring to them as the "most serious" type of sin, Trueblood still talks about the account of Adam and Eve "according to the legendary story of Genesis" (*Philosophy of Religion*, p. 251).

16. Brian Hebblethwaite, *Evil, Suffering and Religion* (N.Y.: Hawthorne, 1976), p. 73.

17. Hebblethwaite, *Evil, Suffering and Religion*, p. 73.

18. For some of the theists who make these and other responses here, see Michael Peterson, *Evil and the Christian God* (Grand Rapids: Baker, 1992), pp. 115-116; David Basinger, "Evil as Evidence Against God's Existence: Some Clarifications," *Modern Schoolman*, Volume 58 (1980-1981); Nash, *Faith and Reason*, pp. 202-204; Hebblethwaite, *Evil, Suffering and Religion*, pp. 73-74.

19. Hebblethwiate also struggles here (*Evil, Suffering and Religion*, pp. 45-48, 52-53, 70-71,

102), even while allowing that such a response could be to potentially explain the entire problem of evil via the free will defense (p. 70).

20. Plantinga, *God, Freedom, and Evil*, pp. 58-59.
21. Hebblethwaite, *Evil, Suffering and Religion*, p. 75.
22. Antony Flew with Roy Abraham Varghese, *There is a God: How the World's Most Notorious Atheist Changed His Mind* (N.Y.: Harper Collins, 2007), Chapter 5, especially pp. 107-112.
23. See Hick, *Evil and the God of Love*, p. 326.
24. Nash offers a few concise critiques of Hick's view in *Faith and Reason*, p. 205, footnote 27.
25. For a few examples of the well over one dozen times where the believer's resurrection is linked to that of Jesus, see Jn. 14:19; Acts 4:2; 1 Cor. 15:20, 44-57; Phil. 3:21; 1 John 3:2. The resurrection is also the key in some of the advice concerning suffering (2 Cor. 4:14; 1 Pet 1:3).
26. Nash, *Faith and Reason*, p. 199.
27. This is the basis of the entire cognitive revolution in counseling and clinical psychology circles. For just one example, see Chris Thurman, *The Lies We Believe* (Nashville: Thomas Nelson, 1989), especially p. 22, for instance.
28. For a defense of the biblical teaching on the nature of Hell, see Gary R. Habermas and J.P. Moreland, *Beyond Death: Exploring the Evidence for Immortality* (Wheaton, Il: Crossway, 1998), Chapter 11.

Chapter 6: Gratuitous Evil: Is Suffering Purposeful?

1. Geisler, *Philosophy of Religion*, p. 373 (Geisler's emphasis); see also p. 372.
2. Geisler, *Philosophy of Religion*, pp. 396-397.
3. Although Nash rejects this approach, his summary is helpful (*Faith and Reason*, pp. 216-217).
4. Nash, *Faith and Reason*, pp. 216-220. Peterson also defends this position in Evil and the Christian God.
5. Against the counter-suggestion that this position could favor naturalism as well as Christian theism, we would be remiss not to mention that 1) the very conviction of seemingly the vast majority of people is that these dictators exercised their own personal wills, while naturalism tends to judge that there is no such thing as free will whatsoever. 2) Further, it generally seems to be agreed that these dictators' actions were objectively wrong, while naturalism recognizes no ultimate, objective notion of wrongdoing. From this angle, how can naturalists even raise the problem of evil from their own systems, since there is really no objective evil in the world? According to this understanding, evil is something personal that we do not like. But this is hardly an encouraging or comforting notion. 3) Additionally, evidences such as that for the resurrection of Jesus (see note 7 above) strongly favor the Christian option, while naturalism is not established by similar positive arguments. The bottom line is that naturalism leaves much to be desired, philosophically and evidentially, as well as experientially.
6. Classically, the very concept of Hell is that it is marked by separation from God. It is the domain of those who refuse God's graces—general as well as specific.
7. Nash, *Faith and Reason*, p. 219.
8. Plantinga, *God, Freedom, and Evil*, pp. 62-63.

Chapter 7: Refinement by Fire: Drawing Nearer to God Through Trials

1. Michael P. Green, ed., *Illustrations for Biblical Preaching* (Grand Rapids, MI: Baker Book House, 1989), no. 1410.

2. 1 Peter 1:6-9; see also Isaiah 48:10
3. Romans 5:3
4. Ten Boom, *Clippings from My Notebook*, 124.
5. Joni Eareckson Tada is a powerful example of how suffering can better us. You can read her story in her autobiography: *Joni: An Unforgettable Story* (Grand Rapids, MI: Zondervan, 1996).
6. Matthew 8:23-27
7. This is a true story and is used with permission. Some details have been changed, however, in order to provide anonymity.
8. Romans 10:17
9. Hebrews 11:35-38
10. 1 Kings 17:1-24
11. 1 Kings 18:20-40; 19:1-8
12. 2 Corinthians 1:9
13. Hebrews 13:8
14. See http://www.brainyquote.com/quotes/quotes/v/victorhugo152539.html.
15. Romans 5:3-5; 1 Peter 5:10
16. Helen Keller, *The Story of My Life* (New York: Bantam Classics, 1990).
17. See http://www.bestinspiration.com/quotes-1/of/Helen_Keller.htm.
18. 2 Timothy 3:17; Hebrews 2:10; 13:21
19. Howard A. Rusk, *A World to Care For* (New York: Random House, 1972), 281.
20. Acts 4:13
21. Tan, *Encyclopedia of 7700 Illustrations*, no. 6893.
22. From a presentation by Diane Langberg at the American Association of Christian Counselors (AACC) Conference in 1996
23. Hebrews 12:11

Chapter 8: A Tough Maintenence Check: Recentering Your Faith

1. Chambers, *My Utmost for His Highest*, 306.
2. Psalm 6:9; 42:1-2
3. Job 42:5
4. Job 42:1-6
5. Charles H. Spurgeon, *Spurgeon at His Best*, compiled by Tom Carter (Grand Rapids, MI: Baker Books, 1988), 218.
6. Psalm 34:17
7. Exodus 32:11-14
8. Jeremiah 29:11-13
9. Romans 8:26-27
10. 2 Corinthians 12:9
11. Joseph Scriven and Charles Converse, "What a Friend We Have in Jesus," in *Hymns for the Family of God*, ed. Fred Bock (Nashville: Paragon Associates, 1976), 466.
12. Ten Boom, *Clippings from My Notebook,* 25–6.
13. Hebrews 13:8
14. Galatians 4:19

Chapter 9: Demolishing Sin and Reconstructing a Godly Life

1. 1 Corinthians 11:28-34
2. Galatians 6:7-8
3. Numbers 12
4. 2 Samuel 12:15-23
5. Acts 5:1-11
6. Hebrews 12:5-6

7. Walter Bauer, *A Greek-English Lexicon of the New Testament and Other Early Christian Literature*, 2nd ed., rev. by F. W. Gingrich and F. Danker (Chicago: University of Chicago Press, 1979).
8. Acts 22:24
9. Psalm 103:8-10
10. Leviticus 26:14-21
11. Judges 2:7-16
12. Jonah 4:2
13. 1 Samuel 15:22
14. Psalm 119:71
15. Luke 15:18-21
16. Proverbs 20:30
17. Habakkuk 1:5-11
18. Habakkuk 2:20
19. Hebrews 12:6
20. Hebrews 12:10-11
21. 1 Peter 1:16
22. 2 Corinthians 12:1-10
23. Revelation 2:1-7
24. 2 Corinthians 12:9
25. Paul Lee Tan, *Encyclopedia of 7700 Illustrations,* 3rd ed. (Rockville, MD: Assurance Publishers, 1980). No. 6884.

Chapter 10: Collateral Impact: Suffering and the Church

1. Acts 16:25-34.
2. Philippians 1:13.
3. Courtney Anderson, *To the Golden Shore: The Life of Adoniram Judson* (Valley Forge, PA: Judson Press, 1987).
4. We read their story in Daniel 3.
5. Luke 22:42.
6. 2 Timothy 2:8-10.
7. For the second-century account of his death, see "The Martyrdom of S. Polycarp," in *The Apostolic Fathers*, ed. and trans. J. B. Lightfoot and J. R. Harmer (Grand Rapids, MI: Baker Book House, 1992), 101–17.
8. Green, *Illustrations for Biblical Preaching*, 150.
9. 1 Corinthians 12:7-31
10. Romans 12:15; Galatians 6:1-2
11. Acts 2:44
12. Acts 12:5-16
13. Galatians 6:2
14. Proverbs 17:17
15. John 13:35
16. The story of Tom and Maria is based on an interview with Tom Whiteman. Used with permission.
17. 2 Corinthians 1:4
18. 2 Corinthians 1:5
19. 2 Corinthians 1:4
20. Letter to Sheldon Vanauken, April 22, 1953; quoted in *Sheldon Vanauken, A Severe Mercy* (New York: HarperCollins, 1977), 134.
21. From a sermon, October 27, 1998, at Wayne Hills Baptist Church, Waynesboro, Virginia. Used with permission.
22. 2 Corinthians 1:6

Chapter 11: In His Person: Put on the God-Colord Glasses

1. Job 38–39; 40:4-5
2. Job 42:1-3
3. Job 16:6-22
4. Jeremiah 32:17
5. Jeremiah 32:27
6. Corrie ten Boom, *The Hiding Place* (Grand Rapids, MI: Chosen Books, 1971), 63.
7. Ibid ., 217.

Chapter 12: In the Gift: Does Suffering Have Rewards?

1. Job 1:21
2. Job 42:10
3. From the movie Star Trek: The Wrath of Khan. See http://www.imdb.com/title/tt0084726/quotes.
4. Ecclesiastes 7:8
5. Lewis, *The Problem of Pain*, 144.
6. James 1:12
7. Bauer, *A Greek-English Lexicon of the New Testament and Other Early Christian Literature.*
8. 2 Corinthians 4:17-18
9. Frankl, *Man's Search for Meaning*, 74.
10. Gary Habermas and J. P. Moreland, *Beyond Death: Exploring the Evidence for Immortality* (Eugene, OR: Wipf and Stock, 2003), chapter 15.
11. Acts 7:54-56
12. This story is based on an illustration in D. L. Moody, *Anecdotes and Illustrations of D. L. Moody* (Chicago: Rhodes and McClure, 1881), 132.

Chapter 13: Life is the Waiting Room

1. Philippians 1:20-23
2. Romans 12:1
3. Luke 9:23
4. Philippians 1:20
5. Debbie's story is told in Gary R. Habermas, *Forever Loved: A Personal Account of Grief and Resurrection* (Joplin, Mo: College Press, 1997).
6. Philippians 1:21
7. Philippians 1:23
8. Romans 8:30; 2 Corinthians 5:2, 4
9. Isaiah 55:8-9

Chapter 14: Holding On: The Bedrock of Our Attitude

1. Nietzsche, as quoted in Frankl, *Man's Search for Meaning*, 76.
2. 2 Timothy 3:16-17
3. Daniel 3:19-30
4. Isaiah 53; Matthew 26:36-46
5. Matthew 5:45; see also Luke 13:1-5 and John 9:1-3 for additional examples.
6. John 5:39-40
7. James 1:22-25

8. From his work: Meditation XVII. Find this quote at: www.brainyquote.com/quotes/authors/j/john_donne.html.
9. Elisabeth Elliot, *The Mark of a Man* (Grand Rapids, MI: Fleming H. Revell, 1981).
10. Many studies confirm the value of a caring social support. The reader is offered the following examples: C. A. Dunkel-Schetter, "Social Support and Cancer: Findings Based on Patient Interviews and Their Implications," *Journal of Social Issues* 40 (1984): 77–98; S. Cohen et al., "Social Ties and Susceptibility to the Common Cold," *Journal of the American Medical Association* 277, no. 24 (June 5, 1997): 1940–44; J. D. Lindy, M. C. Grace, and B. L. Green, "Survivors: Outreach to a Reluctant Population," *American Journal of Orthopsychiatry* 51 (1981): 468–78; Robert Putnam, *Bowling Alone: The Collapse and Revival of American Community* (New York: Simon & Schuster, 2000); D. Myers, "The Funds, Friends, and Faith of Happy People," *American Psychologist* 55, no. 1 (2000): 56–67.
11. Romans 12:15
12. Job 38:21
13. Genesis 3:4-5
14. John 14:16-18
15. Philippians 4:11-13
16. Jack Canfield and Mark Victor Hansen, eds., *Chicken Soup for the Soul* (Deerfield Beach, FL: Health Communications, 1993), 263.
17. *Encyclopedia of World Biography* (Farmington Hills, MI: Thomson Gale, 2005).
18. Lewis, *The Problem of Pain*, 47–8.
19. Ten Boom, *Clippings from My Notebook*, 56.
20. You may find similar ideas from the following sources: Ronnie Janoff-Bulman, *Shattered Assumptions: Towards a New Psychology of Trauma* (New York: Free Press, 1992); Melvin Lerner, "The Desire for Justice and Reactions to Victims: Social Psychological Studies of Some Antecedents and Consequences," in *Altruism and Helping Behavior*, eds. J. Maculay and L. Berkowitz (New York: Academic Press, 1970); C. Parks, "What Becomes of Redundant World Models? A Contribution to the Study of Adaptation to Change," *British Journal of Medical Psychology* 48 (1975): 131–37.
21. Psalm 14:3; 51:5; 58:3; Romans 3:23-24; 7:20-21
22. C. S. Lewis, *The Problem of Pain* (New York: Macmillan, 1967), 26.
23. Romans 8:21
24. Job 16:12-14
25. 1 Samuel 1:4-28
26. Corrie ten Boom, *Clippings from My Notebook* (Minneapolis: World Wide Publications, 1982), 56.
27. 1 Peter 4:12-13
28. M. Scott Peck, *The Road Less Traveled* (New York: Phoenix Press, 1985), 15. Throughout this manuscript we are not attempting to critique Scott Peck's controversial work and theories but to pull from his work concepts that are relevant to our points.
29. Melvin Lerner, "The Desire for Justice and Reactions to Victims"; M. J. Lerner and G. Matthews, "Reactions to the Suffering of Others under Conditions of Indirect Responsibility," *Journal of Personality and Social Psychology* 5 (1967): 319–25; M. J. Lerner and C. Simmons, "Observers' Reaction to the 'Innocent Victims': Compassion or Rejection?" *Journal of Personality and Social Psychology* 4 (1966): 4, 203–10.
30. Ecclesiastes 8:14, NLT
31. Unless otherwise specified, all characters in the stories used in this book are composites of individuals.

Chapter 15: Letting Go of Control

1. Job 1:22; 3:3, 11
2. Job 6:8-9; 10:3, 10, 18, 20-21; 14:19; 19:7

3. Job 7:11; 23:4-5
4. Job 13:3
5. Lamentations 3:1, 3, 8, 15, cev
6. Psalm 6:6-7; 55:4-5
7. Psalm 88:2-4, 8, 14-16, 18
8. Psalm 44:12
9. Psalm 88:8
10. Job 1:22; 2:3, 10
11. Job 38
12. Psalm 22:24, NIV
13. James 1:5
14. Hebrews 4:16
15. Adnan K. Abdulla, *Catharsis in Literature* (Bloomington: Indiana University, 1985).
16. Psalm 142:1-2
17. Matthew 16:23
18. Psalm 143:3
19. Lamentations 3:42
20. Psalm 34:18; Jeremiah 31:34
21. Psalm 143:5
22. Psalm 90:2; 93:2; Isaiah 48:12; 1 Timothy 6:16; Hebrews 13:8; James 1:17
23. 1 Samuel 15:29; Psalm 33:11
24. C. S. Lewis, *The Lion, the Witch and the Wardrobe* (New York: Collier Books, 1956), 75–6.
25. Romans 11:33-34
26. For a sampling of research the reader is directed to the following sources: M. Webb and K. J. Otto Whitmer, "Abuse History, World Assumptions, and Religious Problem Solving," *Journal for the Scientific Study of Religion* 40, no. 3 (September 2001): 445–53; Yvonne Tauber and Elisheva van der Hal, "Transformation of Perception of Trauma by Child Survivors of the Holocaust in Group Therapy," *Journal of Contemporary Psychotherapy* 27, no. 2 (February 1997): 151–71; Sherry A. Falsetti, Patricia A. Resick, and Joanne L. Davis, "Changes in Religious Beliefs following Trauma," *Journal of Traumatic Stress* 16, no. 4 (2003): 391–98; Mark Waysman, Joseph Schwarzwald, and Zahava Solomon, "Hardiness: An Examination of Its Relationship with Positive and Negative Long Term Changes following Trauma," *Journal of Traumatic Stress* 14, no. 3 (2001): 531–48.
27. Illustration can be found on the following Web site: http://www.bible.org/bits/bits-155.htm.
28. Romans 8:28
29. See http://www.geocities.com/Athens/Acropolis/7989/quotes.html#archive.
30. Psalm 143:6
31. Lamentations 3:24, cev
32. Philippians 3:10
33. C. S. Lewis, *A Grief Observed* (San Francisco: HarperCollins, 1989), 18–9.
34. Job 7:10-21; 10:8-22; 16:19; 17:3
35. Job 19:25
36. Job 42:2-3
37. Job 42:6
38. Romans 8:32
39. Lewis, *The Problem of Pain*, 40.
40. Exodus 34:6; Psalm 36:7; 86:15; 103:8; Daniel 9:9; John 3:16; Romans 5:8; 15:5; Ephesians 2:4-5; 1 John 4:16
41. Exodus 34:6; Job 9:4; Psalm 86:5; 100:5; 139:2-4; Isaiah 55:9; Romans 8:28
42. Jeremiah 29:11
43. Psalm 36:5; 40:10; 88:11; 89:1; 92:2; 119:75; Isaiah 25:1; Lamentations 3:23; Hebrews

13:5, 8
44. Genesis 22:14; Philippians 4:19
45. Exodus 15:26; Psalm 41:4; 103:3; Matthew 12:15; Luke 4:18
46. Judges 6:24
47. Psalm 23
48. Genesis 17:1; 28:3; Exodus 6:3
49. John 14:16-17; Ephesians 1:13
50. Psalm 143:7
51. Story found in James Dobson, *When God Doesn't Make Sense* (Carol Stream, IL: Tyndale House, 1993), 45–6.
52. Hebrews 11:13
53. See http://www.worldofquotes.com/topic/Cliches-and-One~Liners/23.
54. Psalm 143:8
55. Jeremiah 29:11
56. Daniel 3:17-18
57. 1 John 5:4
58. Proverbs 3:5-6
59. Revelation 1:17
60. Matthew 28:20
61. John 16:33
62. Isaiah 43:2-3, NIV
63. Isaiah 41:10, NIV
64. Psalm 9:10
65. For more information on these experiments, see Curt P. Richter, "The Total Self-Regulatory Functions in Animals and Human Beings," *Harvey Lecture Series* no. 38 (1942–1943): 63.
66. Nietzsche, as quoted in Frankl, *Man's Search for Meaning*, 82.
67. Psalm 143:10-12
68. Ten Boom, *Clippings from My Notebook*, 51.
69. Philippians 4:4
70. James 1:2-4; Hebrews 12:5
71. Isaiah 61:3
72. Chambers, *My Utmost for His Highest*, 306.

Chapter 16: Moving Through with Purpose

1. Tan, *Encyclopedia of 7700 Illustrations*, no. 6900.
2. Carl Jung, *Psychology and Religion* (New Haven, CT: Yale University Press, 1938).
3. Frankl, *Man's Search for Meaning*, 101–02.
4. Frankl, *Man's Search for Meaning*, 78.
5. Quoted in Charles Wallis, *The Treasure Chest* (San Francisco: Harper & Row, 1983), 120.
6. Psalm 50:15
7. Jeremiah 29:13
8. 1 John 1:8-9; Psalm 32:3-5
9. Psalm 119:11, 18, 45-46, 52, 74, 98-100, 105, 165
10. Psalm 119:105, 130
11. On rest: Deuteronomy 32:2; 2 Samuel 23:2, 4
    On sustenance: Psalm 119:103; 1 Corinthians 3:2
12. On social support: S. Cobb, "Social Support as a Moderator of Life Stress," *Psychosomatic Medicine* 38 (1976): 300–14; S. Cohen and T. A. Wills, "Stress, Social Support, and the Buffering Hypothesis: A Critical Review," *Psychological Bulletin* 98 (1985): 310–57; R. Kessler and J. McLeod, "Social Support and Mental Health in Community Samples," in *Social Support and Health*, eds. S.

Cohen and S. L. Syme (San Diego, CA: Academic Press, 1985), 219–40. On social involvement: S. Cohen et al., "Measuring the Functional Components of Social Support," in *Social Support: Theory, Research, and Applications*, eds. I. A. Sarason and B. Sarason (Martinus Nijhoff, Holland: The Hague, 1985), 73–94; Kenneth Pargament, *The Psychology of Religion and Coping: Theory, Research, Practice* (New York: Guilford Press, 1997). Pargament's book provides wonderful information on coping and the value of social support.

13. Many studies support the role of social relationships in our physical health. An early study known as the Alameda County study followed over 7,000 people for nine years: L. F. Berkman and L. Syme, "Social Networks, Host Resistance, and Mortality: A Nine-Year Follow-Up Study of Alaeda County Residents," *American Journal of Epidemiology* 109 (1979): 186–203; S. Cohen et al., "Social Ties and Susceptibility to the Common Cold," *Journal of the American Medical Association* 277, no. 24 (June 25, 1997): 1940–44; S. Cohen, L. Underwood, and B. H. Gottlieb, eds., *Social Support Measurement and Intervention: A Guide for Health and Social Scientists* (New York: Oxford University Press, 2000); B. N. Uchino, D. Uno, and J. Holt-Lunstad, "Social Support, Physiological Processes, and Health," Current Directions in Psychological Science 9, no. 5 (October 1999): 141–8.

14. Hebrews 10:24-25

15. William Shakespeare, *Macbeth*, Act IV, scene 3.

16. James W. Pennebaker, *Emotion, Disclosure, and Health* (Washington DC: American Psychological Association, 1995); L. F. Clark, "Stress and the Cognitive-Conversational Benefits of Social Interaction," *Journal of Social and Clinical Psychology* 12 (1993): 25–5; J. Hunt, "Sole Survivor: A Case Study to Evaluate the Dual-Process Model of Grief in Multiple Loss," *Illness, Crisis & Loss* 12, no. 4 (2004): 284–98.

Chapter 17: Change Your Perspective

1. See the following Web sites for more information on Maslow: http://www.maslow.com; http://www.answers.com/topic/abraham-maslow.

2. This story is attributed to Gregg Langill and Jon Antallmi, 1985.

3. William James, *The Will to Believe and Other Essays in Popular Philosophy* (New York: Dover Publications. 1956).

4. Frankl, *Man's Search for Meaning*, 78.

5. Ibid., 114–15.

6. R. A. Emmons, and M. E. McCullough, "Counting Blessings versus Burdens: An Experimental Investigation of Gratitude and Subjective Well-Being in Daily Life," *Journal of Personality and Social Psychology* 84, no. 2 (2003): 377–89.

7. Psalm 25:9

8. Frankl, *Man's Search for Meaning*, 42.

9. 2 Timothy 4:5

10. Hebrews 11:6; Matthew 6:20

11. Hebrews 12:2

12. John 14:1-3

13. Psalm 56:3-4

14. Ten Boom, *Clippings from My Notebook*, 33.

15. 1 Corinthians 15:19

16. John Bunyan, *Pilgrim's Progress* (Grand Rapids, MI: Christian Classics Ethereal Library), section 8.

17. Romans 11:34

18. 1 Thessalonians 3:2-3

19. J. Sims and D. Bauman, "The Tornado Threat: Coping Styles of the North and South," *Science* 176 (1972): 1386–92.

20. For more information on locus of control, see J. Rotter, "Generalized Expectancies for

Internal vs. External Control of Reinforcement," *Psychological Monographs* 80, no. 1 (1966): whole no. 609.

21. Proverbs 3:5-6
22. Galatians 4:4
23. 2 Corinthians 4:16
24. Hebrews 11:13, 16
25. Psalm 90:12
26. Psalm 46:10
27. J. A. Blumenthal et al., "Effects of Exercise Training on Older Patients with Major Depression," *Archives of Internal Medicine* 159, no. 19 (October 25, 1999): 2349–56; G. F. Fletcher et al., "Statement on Exercise: Benefits and Recommendations for Physical Activity Programs for All Americans," A Statement for Health Professionals by the Committee on Exercise and Cardiac Rehabilitation of the Council on Clinical Cardiology, *American Heart Association*, Circulation 94 (1996): 857–62; P. Martin, *Sickening Mind: Brain, Behaviour, Immunity and Disease* (New York: HarperCollins, 1995).
28. In actuality, it is the perceived availability of social support that seems to buffer people from the damaging effects of stress. The buffer may come from emotional support such as feeling cared about or not feeling alone, informational support such as giving helpful advice, and instrumental support such as the practical ways by which people demonstrate their support—cooking meals, cutting grass, etc. Many studies support this, including: S. R. Jenkins, "Coping and Social Support among Emergency Dispatchers: Hurricane Andrew," *Journal of Social Behavior and Personality* 12, no. 1 (February 1997): 201–06; M. C. Logsdon, J. C. Birkimer, and A. P. Barbee, "Social Support Providers for Postpartum Women," *Journal of Social Behavior and Personality* 12 (1997): 89–102; P. Callaghan and J. Morrissey, "Social Support and Health: A Review," *Journal of Advanced Nursing*, 18, no. 2 (1993): 203; B. W. J. H. Penninx, et al., "Direct and Buffer Effects of Social Support and Personal Coping Resources in Individuals with Arthritis," *Social Science and Medicine*, 44, no. 3 (1997): 393–402

Chapter 18: Reaching Out to Help Others

1. See http://www.alcoholics-anonymous.org for more information about their services.
2. Galatians 6:1-2, 5
3. Bauer, A Greek-English Lexicon of the New Testament and Other Early Christian Literature.
4. 2 Corinthians 4:17
5. Joe Bayly, *The View from a Hearse* (Elgin, IL: Cook, 1973), 53–6.
6. The value of listening to troubled people's experiences is not even debated by experts in the field of counseling. Examples of such research are: Boris Drozdek, "Follow-Up Study of Concentration Camp Survivors from Bosnia-Herzegovina: Three Years Later," *Journal of Nervous and Mental Diseases* 185, no. 11 (1997): 690–94; J. J. Wright and D. Davis, "The Therapeutic Relationship in Cognitive-Behavioral Therapy: Patient Perceptions and Therapist Responses," *Cognitive and Behavioral Practice* 1, (n.d.): 25-45; M. B. Gibbons, "Listening to the Lived Experience of Loss," *Pediatric Nursing* 19, no. 6 (1993): 597–99; Christine M. Jonas-Simpson, "The Experience of Being Listened To: A Human Becoming Study with Music," *Nursing Science Quarterly* 16, no. 3 (2003): 232–38.
7. John 13:17
8. C. A. Dunkel-Schetter, "Social Support and Cancer: Findings Based on Patient Interviews and Their Implications," *Journal of Social Issues* 40 (1984): 77–98.

ABOUT THE AUTHORS

John C. Thomas

Dr. John C. Thomas is an Associate Professor with the Center for Counseling and Family Studies at Liberty University. In addition, Thomas provides counseling services through Wyndhurst Counseling Center in Lynchburg, Va.

Thomas is a licensed professional counselor (LPC), certified substance abuse counselor (CSAC), and certified employee assistance consultant (CEAP). He has authored articles for many professional publications, conducts marriage enrichment retreats, and speaks on mental health and organizational issues.

He holds a doctorate of philosophy degree in counseling and a graduate certificate in alcohol and drug studies from the University of South Carolina. He received his master's degree in counseling and his bachelor of science from Liberty University. Thomas also holds a doctorate of philosophy degree in organizational psychology from Capella University.

He is an active member of Thomas Road Baptist Church and resides in Lynchburg with his wife, Denise, and their two children, Katie and Stephen.

To schedule booking engagements or learn more about Thomas, please visit www.source1strategies.com

Gary Habermas is the author, co-author or editor of 37 books, 18 on the subject of Jesus' resurrection. Other research areas include religious doubt, personal suffering and near-death experiences. He has contributed more than 60 chapters or articles to other books, plus over 100 articles and reviews for journals and other publications. In recent years, he has been a visiting or adjunct professor at 15 different graduate schools and seminaries in the United States and abroad.

Habermas earned his Ph.D. at Michigan State University and his Master of Arts at the University of Detroit. He is a distinguished research professor and Chair of the Department of Philosophy at Liberty University. He presently teaches in Liberty's Ph.D. program at Liberty Baptist Theological Seminary. Habermas and his wife Eileen have seven children and 11 grandchildren.

www.garyhabermas.com